The POWER of PARTICIPATION

CREATING CONFERENCES THAT DELIVER LEARNING, CONNECTION, ENGAGEMENT, AND ACTION

ADRIAN SEGAR

Conferences That Work
Marlboro, VT 05344-0086
www.conferencesthatwork.com

Copyright © 2015 by Adrian Segar

All rights reserved. No part of this book may be reproduced in any form by any electronic or mechanical means including photocopying, recording or by any information storage and retrieval system without written permission from the author, except by a reviewer, who may quote brief passages in a review.

ISBN 978-1-51155-598-2

Library of Congress Control Number: 2015906052

Library of Congress subject headings:

Congresses and conventions—Handbooks, manuals, etc.

Congresses and conventions—Planning

Meetings—Handbooks, manuals, etc.

Cover design by Wade Snyder

Interior design by Jeff Miller

Contents

About the Author *ix*
Acknowledgments *x*
Foreword *xi*
How to use this book *xiii*

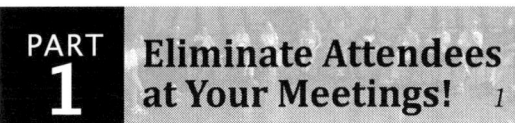

PART 1 — Eliminate Attendees at Your Meetings! *1*

CHAPTER 1
Get on your feet! *3*
A dilemma: Hear or do? *5*

CHAPTER 2
Meetings are a mess—and how they got that way *7*
How technology shapes our system of education *7*
How culture shapes our system of education *10*

CHAPTER 3
Why participation is so important for today's meetings *12*
How adults learn *13*

CHAPTER 4
Active learning *15*
The best way to learn *15*
What is active learning? *16*
How we learn *20*
The learning environment *37*
Learning lessons from physics and programming *41*
Next practices, not best practices *42*
Why we should use active learning at conferences *43*

CHAPTER 5
Connection *45*
How social media (especially Twitter) strengthens my connections in the world of events *46*
The advantages of supporting connection during meeting sessions *47*
Movement and sharing *47*
The classroom as a network *48*
Connecting early and often *48*

iii

Contents

CHAPTER 6
Engagement and community building 50

What is engagement? 50

Measuring event engagement via participant ratings 51

Using outcomes to measure event engagement 52

Should you attempt to measure engagement? 52

From engagement to community 53

What is community? 53

The value of community 54

Communities and associations 54

Building and maintaining community 55

Communities and meetings 56

New kinds of meetings 56

The value of face-to-face meetings in building community 57

Community building, engagement, and participation 58

CHAPTER 7
Action 59

What can we do to get more effective action outcomes from our meetings? 60

CHAPTER 8
Wishes 63

PART 2 — Creating an Environment for Participation 65

CHAPTER 9
Introduction 67

Creating a participatory event environment 68

CHAPTER 10
Badge design 70

CHAPTER 11
Meals 71

CHAPTER 12
The event space 73

Venue layout 74

Physical environment 74

Sound considerations 76

Lighting 77

Room set 77

You don't always get what you set 78

CHAPTER 13
Seating 80

Avoid fixed seating 80

Use comfortable, lightweight chairs 80

Provide just the right number of chairs 81

Seating Matters 82

Provide explicit seating instructions 84

Seating arrangements influence individual and group experience 84

Sit next to someone you don't know 84

When to use tables 85

Rounds 85

CHAPTER 14
Information display 87

Attachment solutions 87

Please let us post! 89

Wall treatment solutions for venues 90

Pens 90

Navigational aids 91

Apps 92

Native and web apps 92

CHAPTER 15
Timing 93

Staying on time 93

Timekeeping for balanced sharing in groups 93

Recommended timekeeping methods 94

How to use FlexTime for group sharing timekeeping 96

CONFERENCE PROCESS

CHAPTER 16
Giving up control *97*
The Myth of Control *98*

CHAPTER 17
Safety *99*
Create an environment in which you can feel OK about making mistakes *100*
The right to not participate *102*
Provide clear instructions *102*
Consider providing explicit ground rules *102*
Conclusion *103*

CHAPTER 18
Ground rules *104*
Explicit versus implicit ground rules *104*
What ground rules should I use? *106*
The Four Freedoms *107*
Confidentiality *108*
Staying on time *108*
Committing to ground rules *109*
Treating participants like adults *109*
Conclusion *109*

CHAPTER 19
Play and fun *110*
Be alert for opportunities for spontaneous play and fun *111*
Laughter *111*
Supply a physical environment that suggests and encourages play and fun *111*
Games *112*
Thoughts about gamification *113*

CHAPTER 20
Facilitation *114*
The task of facilitation *115*
Facilitation as leadership *115*
Process leadership is different from content leadership *116*
Giving directions *116*

Bringing people back on track *117*
Facilitating effective communication *117*
Supporting engagement *118*
The gift of listening *118*

CHAPTER 21
Small group selection *119*
Why you should facilitate small group selection *119*
Goals for small group selection *119*
How large should small groups be? *121*
General considerations when forming groups *122*
Performing group selection *122*

CHAPTER 22
Getting attention *124*
Raising hands *125*
Clap once, clap twice *125*
Distinctive music *125*

CHAPTER 23
Asking questions *126*
Ground rules for questions *126*
Crafting questions *127*
Additional considerations in using questions *127*
When you are asked questions *128*
Meta-questions *128*
Be careful with "Why?" questions *128*
Be comfortable with silence *129*
A (sometimes) magical question *129*
More questions? *129*

CHAPTER 24
White space techniques *130*
Provide more out-of-sessions time *130*
Give attendees explicit permission to miss sessions *131*
Provide longer breaks *131*
Eliminate distracting business and entertainment during meals *132*

Contents

CONFERENCE PROCESS

CHAPTER 25
The conference arc *133*
Openings *133*
Middles *134*
Endings *135*

CHAPTER 26
The conference metaphor *136*
A wedding *136*
A conversation *137*
Saying goodbye *138*
Powerful metaphors *138*

CHAPTER 27
And now for something completely specific *139*

PART 3 — Compendium of Participation Techniques *141*

CHAPTER 28
Participation techniques overview *143*
Introduction *143*
How to use this compendium of techniques *144*
Techniques by goal *146*
Techniques by conference phase *148*
Techniques by group size *149*
Techniques glossary *150*

CHAPTER 29
Techniques for encouraging connection outside conference sessions *153*
Badge It! *153*
Seat Swap *154*

OPENERS

CHAPTER 30
Openers *155*
What are openers for? *156*
Building meaningful connections *156*
Opening techniques . . . and more *156*

CHAPTER 31
The Three Questions *157*
Description *157*
When? *158*
Resources *158*
Why use question cards? *160*
How? *160*

CHAPTER 32
Roundtable *165*
Description *165*
When? *167*
Resources *167*
How? *169*

CHAPTER 33
Human spectrograms *174*
Description *174*
When? *175*
Resources *175*
How? One-dimensional human spectrograms *176*
How? Two-dimensional human spectrograms *181*
How? State-change human spectrograms *182*

CHAPTER 34
The Solution Room *184*
Description *184*
When? *185*
Resources *185*
How? *189*

CHAPTER 35
Post It! *197*
Description *197*
When? *197*
Resources *197*
How? *198*

MIDDLES

CHAPTER 36
Middles *200*

Techniques that facilitate productive small group discussions *200*

Techniques that support effective voting *200*

Techniques that create learning opportunities *201*

CHAPTER 37
Small group discussions *202*

The benefits and pitfalls of small group discussions *202*

The purpose of small group discussions *203*

CHAPTER 38
Pair share *204*

Description *204*
When? *205*
Resources *205*
How? *205*

CHAPTER 39
Guided discussions *208*

Description *208*
When? *209*
Resources *209*
How? *211*

CHAPTER 40
Open Space *214*

Description *214*
Why I don't like unconferences *215*
When? *216*
Resources *216*
How? *217*

CHAPTER 41
World Café *220*

Description *220*
When? *221*
Resources *221*
How? *225*

World Café Lite *229*

CHAPTER 42
Fishbowls *230*

Description *230*
When? *231*
Resources *231*
How? *233*

CHAPTER 43
Affinity grouping *235*

Description *235*
When? *236*
Resources *236*
How? *236*

CHAPTER 44
Participatory voting *241*

Ways to use participatory voting *241*

Low-tech versus high-tech voting solutions *243*

CHAPTER 45
Hand/stand voting *245*

Description *245*
When? *245*
Resources *246*
How? *246*

CHAPTER 46
Roman Voting *247*

Description *247*
When? *247*
Resources *248*
How? *248*

CHAPTER 47
Card voting *249*

Description *249*
When? *250*
Resources *251*
How? *251*

MIDDLES

CHAPTER 48
Table voting *254*
Description *254*
When? *254*
Resources *255*
How? *255*

CHAPTER 49
Dot voting *256*
Description *256*
When? *256*
Resources *257*
How? *259*

CHAPTER 50
Anonymous voting *261*
Description *261*
When? *261*
Resources *262*
How? *262*

CHAPTER 51
Creating learning opportunities *263*

CHAPTER 52
Short form presentations: Pecha Kucha & Ignite *264*
Description *264*
When? *265*
Resources *265*
How? *265*

CHAPTER 53
Case studies and simulations *272*
Description *272*
When? *275*
Resources *276*
How? *276*
A simulation example: Harvest by Dennis Meadows *279*

ENDINGS

CHAPTER 54
Endings—consolidating learning and moving to outcomes *281*

CHAPTER 55
Pro Action Café *282*
Description *282*
When? *282*
Resources *283*
How? *283*

CHAPTER 56
Plus/Delta *285*
Description *285*
When? *287*
Resources *287*
How? *287*

CHAPTER 57
Personal introspective *290*
Description *290*
When? *291*
Resources *291*
How? *292*

CHAPTER 58
Group spective *297*
Description *297*
When? *298*
Resources *298*
How? *298*

APPENDIX 1
Minimum Room Dimensions for Roundtable and Closing Sessions *301*

APPENDIX 2
Personal Introspective Question Card *302*

Notes *303*

About the Author

Adrian Segar is a meeting architect and event facilitator with over thirty years experience, and an energetic champion for participation-rich and participant-led meetings that uncover and satisfy attendee needs for relevant learning, connection, engagement, and community. He is the author of *Conferences That Work: Creating Events That People Love* (2009).

Adrian has been named one of the most innovative people in events by BizBash Magazine, one of MeetingNet's most influential online personalities in meetings and travel, and has been quoted on the front page of the Wall Street Journal. He has presented and facilitated at just about every meetings industry conference, including Meeting Professionals International's World Education Congress; Professional Convention Management Association's Education Conference and Convening Leaders; EIBTM; MPI's Chapter Business Summit; MPI Chapter meetings; HSMAI's MEET, FRESH, GMIC, and NESAE annual conferences; and many association conferences. Adrian writes regularly on event design and related issues on his blog *www.conferencesthatwork.com*. He is the community manager of the Google Plus #eventprofs community, and tweets frequently *@ASegar* on all manner of topics.

Adrian was an independent information technology consultant for 23 years, taught college computer science for 10 years, and co-owned and managed a solar domestic hot water heating systems manufacturing company before that. He has an ancient Ph.D. in experimental high-energy particle physics, lives in Marlboro, Vermont, and Boston, Massachusetts, and loves to sing and dance.

Acknowledgments

I thought writing a second book would be easier than the first.

I was wrong.

Luckily, I had a lot of help. Contributions from the following folks made this work possible.

Thank you Celia for your love and support over the last 40 years, especially the four when this book was written. Thank you Jeannie Courtney and Jerry Weinberg for bringing me to a place where I was ready to do this work. Naomi Karten—I owe you special thanks. You emboldened me at a critical point to write about participative events, and you've been a constant source of encouragement over the years.

Many thanks to Mitchell Beer, Jeremy Birch, Chris Corrigan, Bernie DeKoven, Esther Derby, Dahlia El Gazzar, Eric de Groot, Ruud Janssen, Shawna McKinley, Dennis Meadows, Julie Lineberger, Sue Pelletier, Julius Solaris, Thiagi, Heidi Thorne, and Mike van der Vijver for all manner of benefactions that made this book better.

Since *Conferences That Work* was published in 2009, I've presented hundreds of sessions and workshops in North America and Europe, and consulted with innumerable clients on improving their conference designs. I continue to learn from every experience I'm offered. Thank you everyone who asked me to share what I do, who shared back, and who touched my life in the process.

Small portions of this book are derived from my first book *Conferences That Work: Creating Events That People Love*, and some sections were previously published on my blog *www.conferencesthatwork.com*. Sometimes you say it right the first time.

Foreword

> "If you had to identify, in one word, the reason why the human race has not achieved, and never will achieve, its full potential, that word would be 'meetings.'" —*Dave Barry*

My first book, *Conferences That Work: Creating Events That People Love*, covered the why and how of participant-driven events: conferences and professional meetings that become what the participants want and need them to be. For more than 30 years I've facilitated, presented at, and experienced hundreds of conferences. I've become fascinated by the amazing things that can happen when conference-goers are gently led to step outside the limited traditional conference sessions that we all know so well.

My fascination reflects a wider interest in what happens (and often, sadly, doesn't happen) when people come together at meetings. Meetings are rapidly evolving from what they have been for hundreds of years—places where the few teach the many—toward places where people connect and engage about what they need and want to learn. In addition, we are discovering (some would say rediscovering) how to build genuine grassroots community at our events, a community that can change participants' worlds and, ultimately, the world we all inhabit.

During a quarter of a century as an independent information technology consultant, I worked with hundreds of companies. As my consulting experience grew, I realized that just about all of the client-labeled "technical problems" I was hired to solve were fundamentally people problems. I found myself drawn to learning more about the rich complexity of organizational culture and the function and dysfunction it engenders. This experience has informed my work on conference design—not too surprising when you consider that both organizations and meetings are human-created structures for bringing people together, albeit for different purposes.

Foreword

Once *Conferences That Work: Creating Events That People Love* was published, I thought I had finished writing books. Yet, as word of the book spread and increasing numbers of clients asked me to consult on event design, it became clear that there was a need for a book that concentrated on a finer level of detail: the meeting session itself. Over and over again, clients wanted to know how to improve their sessions—and by extension their events—as measured ultimately by increased attendee satisfaction and retention.

Yes, the *Conferences That Work* meeting format improves conferences immensely by providing structure and support for powerful participant connection and learning. But it does not directly address the design of individual conference sessions: the heart of any conference, whether traditional or participant-driven. Unfortunately, we have all spent far too much time sitting through boring and ineffective sessions listening to uninteresting and poorly presented content.

However, this is not a book about effective public speaking. (For that, I recommend Scott Berkun's book *Confessions of a Public Speaker*.)[1] Rather, this book explains and shows how to improve meeting and session effectiveness by turning passive *attendees* into active *participants*. The techniques I describe can be incorporated by any event organizer, presenter, or session facilitator who wants to maximize the learning, connection, engagement, community building, and consequential action that takes place at her sessions and meetings.

Creating active participants is not hard. But the useful techniques are scattered among a range of practitioners, unfamiliar to most people, and consequently rarely used. This book covers what you need to know in one place.

One final note: This is a mere book; *reading* it is a passive activity, the very antithesis of the book's thesis. If what you read in these pages stays in your head, it will benefit no one. Get on your feet and *do* what you read here when you meet. You and the people you'll meet will reap significant rewards!

How to use this book

This book has three parts.

- Part One covers *why* it's so important to incorporate participant action into every aspect of your event.
- Part Two explains how to go about *creating an environment that supports and encourages participation*.
- Part Three—by far the longest—is about the *how*: a practical compendium of techniques you can use to radically improve your sessions and meetings.

If you're skeptical (or have to convince a skeptical boss) about the need to change sessions and meetings by turning attendees into participants, read Part One.

If you don't have to be convinced of the value of getting attendees actively involved in their learning and connection at your events, feel free to skip Part One and dive right in to Part Two.

I've made Part Two a comprehensive introduction to creating the right event environment, and some of the material there may already be familiar. Skim if you like, but pay careful attention—there's important information sprinkled throughout!

Once you've absorbed the essentials of fashioning a participative event environment, it's time for what you've been waiting for—the techniques themselves.

The nitty-gritty of this book, a rich smorgasbord of techniques that you can adopt to improve every aspect of your meetings, can be found in Part Three. The opening Overview chapter provides you a quick way of finding techniques appropriate for your needs—by goal, conference phase, and group size—and a helpful glossary. The techniques follow, each with its own chapter.

How to use this book

Every technique chapter has the same four-part design:

- A descriptive overview of the technique.
- When to use it.
- Required resources and pre-planning.
- Step-by-step implementation guidance.

Naturally, you'll find all the endnote references at the back of the book.

Last but not least, if you've enjoyed this book please consider any or all (preferably all) of the following:

- Writing a review on Amazon.com.
- Letting others know about this book on your blog or favorite online services.
- Recommending this book to anyone who might find it useful.
- Checking out my website www.conferencesthatwork.com where I blog mightily on all kinds of interesting topics. It's also the place where digital updates to this book will be posted for you to download for free. Email me <adrian@segar.com> and I'll let you know when new updates become available.

Thank you!

PART 1

Eliminate Attendees at Your Meetings!

CHAPTER 1
Get on your feet!

As a teenager in the sixties, I loved to dance. Then something happened; somehow I became self-conscious and didn't dance again until March 29, 2003. I was at a workshop, and if you had told me beforehand that I would dress up in costume and dance solo in front of thirty people to Neil Diamond's "Be" I would have (a) said you were crazy and (b) skipped the workshop. I'm very glad I wasn't warned, because at that workshop I remembered that I love to dance, and I've been dancing ever since.[1]

If I had been *reminded* at the workshop that I liked to dance, I wouldn't have remembered. All the *thinking* in the world about dancing wouldn't have shifted my belief that I didn't really like to dance anymore. As Jeannie Courtney,[2] who runs the workshop, describes it: "We can't *tell* you this. You have to *experience* it."

I had to get on my feet and dance.

You definitely don't have to dance to find this book useful and, hopefully, valuable. But, like every other book, this book can only tell you things. If you read it and don't get on your feet and try things out, well, you might miss out on something important.

In some ways, my experience and your potential experience is the heart of this book. The philosopher Martin Buber said, "all actual life is encounter."[3] *The Power of Participation* is about improving what happens when people come together—at meetings/conferences/events; whatever you choose to call them—via a simple yet radical concept.

Eliminate attendees by turning them into participants.

If you're like me, you've spent far too much of your life stuck in bad meetings. Conferences where most of your time is spent listening to other people talk, and where opportunities to connect with interesting people are limited to a few chance interactions during meals. Events that leave you drained instead of energized. Meetings that are supposed to lead to action but instead accomplish little or nothing except generating confusion and disillusionment.

Why do we meet? Ask a random sample of meeting attendees and you'll find that the two most important reasons are to *learn* and to *connect*. In addition, at some meetings, planning for the future is an important goal. This book will introduce you to numerous powerful techniques that will help you significantly improve the learning, connecting, and planning for action at your events.

We desperately need these techniques because for hundreds of years we've been conditioned and fettered by the education processes used in our schools. We spend the majority of our time in school hearing one person, a teacher, talk, and are led to believe that this is how we are supposed to learn. Consequently, it's not surprising that when we're asked to create a group learning experience for adults, we fall back on the overriding model of teaching demonstrated during our formative years. When you only have a hammer, everything looks like a nail.

I believe that a broadcast-heavy pedagogy is a poor model for providing what we want from our adult meetings: critical learning and appropriate rich connection, together with improved participant engagement, effective community building, and consequential action.

The key to improving learning and connection in our meetings and events is to use process that requires and supports purposeful participant activity. When people are actively involved in their learning they learn more, and retain what they learn longer and more accurately.

Participatory techniques don't have to be complex or protracted. In this book you'll discover, for example, how:

- Every person in a room can engage in active learning—in 2 minutes.
- A group of 300 strangers from all over the world can meet everyone who lives near them—in 5 minutes. Or, in the same amount of time, they can uncover and begin to explore their diversity of opinions on any topic.
- Conference participants can obtain an accurate public understanding and appreciation of their collective multifaceted experience of an event—in 20 minutes.
- Fifty strangers can learn about each other in ways that are maximally useful to each person present—in 90 minutes.

If you aren't including these kinds of experiences in your meetings, your attendees are not receiving the full potential benefits of their time together. Facilitating them isn't rocket science; this book provides the information you need to incorporate them into your events. The hardest barrier to overcome is likely to be your reluctance to try them out for the first time and risk doing something new.

When I got on my feet to dance in public for the first time in 32 years I felt a strange mixture of emotions, best described as *nervous excitement*. I had given up the idea that I had control over what might happen and was all too aware of the scary possibility that I might feel self-conscious or embarrassed. Simultaneously, there was a part of me that was tremendously curious and excited about what I was about to do.

A dilemma: Hear or do?

In July 2011 I led a workshop at Meeting Professionals International's World Education Congress in Orlando. The 150-minute session covered a variety of techniques that foster and support meaningful participation during meetings. Participants spent most of their time using these techniques to learn about and connect with each other and explore questions about their experience at the event and in the session itself.

As the workshop progressed, and I heard from the 46 participants, it became clear that one of them, whom I'll call J, had considerable prior experience with the techniques I was facilitating.

Near the end of the workshop I ran *Plus/Delta* (described in Chapter 56): a technique that provides a fast, public evaluation of a session or entire meeting. The subject of our Plus/Delta was a group evaluation of the workshop itself. During the evaluation, J commented that he had hoped that I would cover more techniques by talking about them rather than having attendees experience them directly. He then contributed a simple and ingenious way to extend Plus/Delta that was new to me.

My heart sank a little. Here was J, an experienced facilitator of participation techniques, proposing that I should spend the workshop *talking* about techniques rather than *facilitating experiences of them*. Could I be going about this wrong?

I moved into the last technique of the workshop, running *fishbowl*: a simple way to facilitate focused discussion with a large group (described in Chapter 42). All participants sit in a large circle of chairs, but only people who enter the "fishbowl," a small circle of chairs at the center, can speak. After a few minutes of comments, J entered the fishbowl.

J said he had read about fishbowls many times before and he understood how they worked, but he had never tried one.

And then, to my surprise and delight, he told us that experiencing the fishbowl had been a revelation to him. He had just directly experienced the power of the technique in a way that significantly enhanced his understanding, which, until that moment he had believed to be sufficient. It was poignant for me to hear J air his new point of view, and I admired his courage in sharing his learning with all of us.

I too have struggled over the years to define the best balance between understanding techniques through description and understanding them through direct experience. J's lightbulb moment fits for me; these days, in workshops, I am content to let attendees learn participation techniques, first through direct experience and then, if necessary, via reflection and discussion.

I hope that this book inspires you to try out these techniques and discover their power to transform and improve the quality and efficacy of time that a group of people spend together.

Postscript

At the end of the workshop, J hung around and we talked while I was packing up equipment before my flight home.

He told me that his fishbowl sharing had unexpectedly reminded him of a session he had once attended, "*One hundred icebreakers in one hundred minutes,*" that consisted of rapid descriptions of a hundred ways to introduce attendees to each other.

His rueful comment?

"I don't remember any of them."

But once the music began, I began to dance and was swept up in the joy of dancing, remembering how important it was to me all those years earlier. Taking that risk started me on a journey that took me from a world of organizing meetings to one of facilitating learning, connection, engagement, community building, and action and brought this book into being.

I hope you are inspired to get on your feet and put into practice what you learn in these pages. Those meeting and conference attendees you turn into participants will not be the only beneficiaries. You will be too.

CHAPTER 2
Meetings are a mess— and how they got that way

> "Things are the way they are because they got that way."
> —*Quip attributed to Kenneth Boulding*

The hundreds-of-years-dominant paradigm for sessions, conferences, and meetings is *broadcast*: most of the time, one person presents and everyone else listens and watches. Why?

I think there are two principal historic reasons: one shaped by technology, the other by culture.

How technology shapes our system of education

Perhaps you're thinking: *Technology? Isn't technology a relatively recent development? How could technology have influenced how we learned hundreds of years ago?*

To answer these questions, let's take a journey back in time. It'll take a while, but stay with me and I'll shine some light on some rarely examined foundations of our current educational paradigm.

Understandably, we tend to think of technology these days as material devices such as cars, printers, and smartphones or, increasingly, as computer programs: software and apps. But this definition of what is and isn't "technology" is far too narrow.

> "Technology is anything that was invented after you were born."
> —*Alan Kay, at a Hong Kong press conference in the late 1980s*

An older reader will immediately recognize a typewriter (my Ph.D. thesis was typed on one) but a child might stare in puzzlement at a 1945 Smith-Corona Sterling. A device found on a table at a yard sale appears to be a piece of rusty sculpture until a Google search reveals it's a 90-year-old cherry stoner. By Alan Kay's definition, anything made after you became aware is technology. *Anything that's really old, we don't even recognize as technology!*

This worldview exists because human beings are incredibly good at adapting to new circumstances. This ability greatly increases our chances of surviving a hostile and treacherous world. But there's a downside. When we start making changes to our environment by making useful things, what was once new becomes part of our everyday existence. In the process, *what was formerly new becomes largely invisible to our senses*, focused as they are on the new and unexpected. As David Weinberger remarks: "Technology sinks below our consciousness like the eye blinks our brain filters out."[4]

So let's adopt a wider definition of technology and see where it takes us. (I've been influenced here by Kevin Kelly, in his thought-provoking book *What Technology Wants*.)[5]

> "Technology is anything made to solve a problem."
> —*Adrian's definition, a paraphrase of Wikipedia's definition of technology*[6]

This definition is useful because it opens our eyes to technology that we've been using for a very long time.

For example, by this definition, *science* is technology! Science is just a way that we've invented to understand the patterns we notice in the world we live in.

Agriculture is also technology: a set of procedures that solves the problem of having enough food by allowing us to produce it more efficiently.

Science and agriculture are old. Writing is older. Writing allows us to communicate asynchronously with each other.

Writing is technology!

And oldest of all—we don't really know how old—*language* is technology. Every culture, every tribe has its own languages, invented to solve the problem of real-time communication between its members.

These technologies are so old that they are invisible to us. They are part of our culture, the human air we breathe. Language, writing, and science are tools outside our conventional, narrow-scope view of technology. We instantiate these tools using invented conventions: sounds, gestures, and symbols. These sounds, gestures, and symbols, however, are secondary features of these ancient technologies. Ultimately, language, writing, and science are primarily about *human process*.

Human process has become the most invisible technology. It is inexorably and continually built into every one of us by our culture, starting the moment we are born. Our culture teaches us throughout our life the signs, sounds, and movements that allow us to communicate with others and cope with the world. We are superbly equipped to learn to speak, write, and think before we have any self-awareness of what we are being taught.

> "We seldom realize, for example that our most private thoughts and emotions are not actually our own. For we think in terms of languages and images which we did not invent, but which were given to us by our society." —*Alan Watts*[7]

We are at best minimally aware of the processes we constantly use to learn and make sense of the world and to connect with others. They are like breathing, largely automatic and unconscious. Yet the old process technology that we adopted for practical purposes long before recorded history continues to shape our lives today.

Before language arose, we had no way to transfer what we learned during our all-too-brief lives to our tribe and following generations. "*These plants are safe to eat.*" "*You can make a sharp spearhead from this rock.*" "*Snakes live in that cave.*" All such learning had to be painfully acquired from scratch by every individual. Language allowed parents and tribal elders to pass on valuable knowledge orally, improving survival and quality of life.

Similarly, the later development of writing made it possible to share, physically transfer, and expand a permanent repository of human knowledge. And the evolution of the process methodology of science enabled us to design experiments about our world, codify the patterns we discovered, and turn them into inventions that transform our lives.

Now let's consider the effect of the historical development of language, writing, and science on education. For almost all of human history, language was our dominant mode of communication and our single most important educational tool. If you wanted to learn something, you had to travel to where someone knew what you needed to learn so they could tell it to you. Eventually schools developed: establishments for improving the efficiency of oral communication of information by bringing many students together so they could learn simultaneously from one teacher.

Language reigned supreme for millennia, thus becoming an invisible technology. Only when writing became established was it finally possible for information to be transmitted asynchronously. By that time, the model of the single teacher and multiple students was buried deep in our collective psyche. To a large extent, the book paradigm mirrored the language process, as most books were written by a single expert and absorbed by a much larger number of readers.[8]

Even science started as an individual enterprise—the early study of "natural philosophy" by Socrates, Aristotle, and others used an oral teacher–students model. Although science today is largely an intensely cooperative enterprise, we still see considerable leftovers of the older invisible technologies in its societal organization: prescribed progressions toward mastery of fields, formal paths to tenure, the format of academic meetings, and so on.

What is the impact of these powerful invisible technologies on our educational archetypes? When our culture has been steeped in technologies such as language, writing, and science for millennia, it becomes very difficult for people to consider learning models other than broadcast, even though other models may be far more appropriate today.

The earliest organized religious schools are a few thousand years old, and the oldest non-religious universities were founded almost a thousand years ago. For centuries, oral learning was the predominant modality in schools. It wasn't until the invention of the printing press in the fifteenth century that a significant number of people could learn independently from books and newspapers, which are, of course, broadcast media. While the invention of inexpensive mass-printing revolutionized society, the old broadcast teaching models were sunk so deeply and invisibly into our culture that they persist to this day. When you are taught by broadcast by teachers who were taught by broadcast it is not surprising that, when you are asked to teach, you employ the same methods.

When we are asked as adults to create a meeting, we are thus naturally primed to choose a broadcast paradigm for the "learning" portions. Even when it is brought to our attention, it is still very difficult for an individual to break away from the years of broadcast process to which he was subjected as a child.

The process we've been using for so long inhibits our ability to consider alternatives, but the quantity of "knowledge" that we currently expect adults to possess also plays a role. And this leads to the second reason why meetings are infused with broadcast methodology.

How culture shapes our system of education

For most of human history, learning was predominantly experiential. Life expectancy was low by modern standards and formal education nonexistent. Even after schools became important institutions, curricula were modest and the numbers educated were few. In the Middle Ages, formal education of children was rare; in the fifteenth century only a small percentage of European children learned to read and write, usually as a prerequisite for acceptance as a guild apprentice.

Up until around a hundred years ago, advanced education was only available for a tiny number of students, and the prerequisites for those entering university were laughable by today's standards. Isaac Newton, for example, received no formal mathematics teaching until he entered Trinity College, Cambridge, in 1661.[9] Algebra wasn't routinely taught even at university until the eighteenth century. In the Victorian era, secondary school students were expected to master the "three R's"—reading, writing and 'rithmetic—plus perhaps a few other topics such as needlework (girls only), geography, and history.

The need for jobs has driven education ever since the birth of apprenticeship programs in the Middle East four millennia ago. Apprenticeship remained the dominant model of education until the advent of the Industrial Revolution, which brought a growing need for workers just-enough capable to handle repetitive work, plus some with specialized new trainable skills such as bookkeeping and shop-work. A period of emphasis on career and technical education ensued. Once formal education became a social and legislative requirement for a majority of children, curricula wars erupted between the conflicting goals of content and pedagogy, and these wars have been with us in some form ever since.

Whatever you think about the relative merits of "traditionalist" and "progressive" approaches to education,[10] the key cultural reason why broadcast methods remain firmly embedded in our children's education is the sheer *quantity* of high-level knowledge that society—for whatever reasons—is determined to cram into young heads during formal education. Foreign languages, advanced mathematics, social studies, health, science, and many other subjects have been added to the spelling, arithmetic, grammar, history, and geography lessons of the past, and the material taught concentrates more on conceptual understanding than memorizing facts. We now require young adults to be exposed to and absorb a staggering diversity and quantity of topics compared to our expectations of the past.

As a result, *there is no way for this added knowledge to be taught experientially in the time available*. It took centuries for some of our brightest minds to formulate the algebra that today we routinely teach to 11-year-olds! While we have probably developed better paths and techniques for sharing this educational content, any increased efficiency in delivery has not kept pace with the massive increase in expected knowledge mastery.

It is this significant cultural imposition that requires us to use primarily broadcast methods to educate our youth. The consequent mistake we make is to assume that the broadcast learning we're all exposed to as children should be extended into adulthood. While receiving specialized adult learning from an expert made sense for human history up until the industrial age, as relevant knowledge increasingly resides in our networks of colleagues and online, we have an urgent need to develop alternative adult learning. Today, most of what we need to learn to do our jobs is based on working informally and creatively with novel problems, and finding solutions that often require just-in-time information from our peers.

Being taught in school, however inefficiently, via lecture about the amazing things humans have created, discovered, and invented indoctrinates us to believe that lecturing is the normal way to learn. That's why we continue to inflict lecturing on conference audiences. It's what we're used to, and sadly we're mostly unfamiliar with alternative and more effective learning modalities that are becoming ever more important in today's world.

This book is my attempt to redress the balance by sharing techniques for adult meetings that reintroduce the experiential, participative learning that dominates our early childhood as we begin to learn to connect with others, navigate our surroundings, speak with those around us, and make sense of our world. We are richly equipped to learn through these modalities and never lose our abilities to do so. In the next chapter we'll explore key benefits we gain by turning attendees into participants.

CHAPTER 3
Why participation is so important for today's meetings

> "You send your child to the schoolmaster, but 'tis the schoolboys who educate him."
> —Ralph Waldo Emerson, "Culture," The Conduct of Life (1860)

At a recent medical appointment, my primary care physician didn't think twice about using the computer he brings to every consultation to check a medication dosage in my presence. Twenty years ago, such activity would have implied that he was deficient in remembering important professional information. Today, this is just standard medical practice. With the rise of computers and online access to information, much of what in the industrial age passed as knowledge is now readily available when and where we need it. Never before have we had just-in-time access to so much collective human knowledge.

This rapid unprecedented change has had a massive impact on the very nature of what is considered a skilled job. Work that does not rely on unique or hard to replicate human attributes is being eliminated via automation or moved to parts of the world with the lowest "cost of doing business." The jobs that remain are increasingly those providing services rather than creating objects.

Until about three decades ago, adults learned most of what they needed to know to do their jobs in the classroom. But the whole nature of "work" has changed dramatically since the last century. Today, it turns out, we learn the majority of what we need to know in order to do our jobs informally: through on-the-job experience and practice, connections with our peers, and self-directed learning.

Research that began in the 1980s at the Center for Creative Leadership (CCL) found that *about 70% of managerial learning comes from the job itself.*[11] Additional research, published by the US Bureau of Labor Statistics in 1998, suggested that *people learn about 70% of their jobs informally* and the 70%

CHAPTER 3: Why participation is so important for today's meetings

figure appeared again in a 2-year study of workers at large companies published by the Education Development Center.[12]

Is classroom learning the delivery system for the majority of the rest of what we need to learn? No. The CCL study referenced above also concluded that about *20% of individual professional development comes from peer learning*: informal coaching, personal networks, and other collaborative and co-operative actions, and the EDC study concludes that approximately *20% of what we need to know is provided by self-directed learning*. This is learning we control ourselves: asking colleagues for help, reading a relevant book or article, searching for answers on the internet, watching online instructional or lecture videos, and so on.

Learning from your peers is also called social learning. Increasingly, we don't have the luxury of being able to wait for scheduled training opportunities in order to respond to new job challenges. Instead, when we need to learn something professionally we tend to consult our peers and professional networks first. This is just-in-time learning in action: We learn what we need to learn when we need it.

Table 3.1[13] summarizes how learning has been transformed from a *transaction* to a *process*.

TABLE 3.1 • *Learning as a transaction compared to learning as a process*

LEARNING AS TRANSACTION	LEARNING AS PROCESS
Knowledge is a "thing" that is transferred from one person to another.	Knowledge is a relationship between the knower and the known; knowledge is "created" through this relationship.
Knowledge is objective and certain.	Knowledge is subjective and provisional.
Knowledge is organized in stable, hierarchical structures that can be treated independently of one another.	Knowledge is organized "ecologically"—disciplines are integrative and interactive.
We learn alone, with our minds, based on our innate abilities.	We learn in social contexts, through mind, body, and emotions.
Learners receive knowledge.	Learners create knowledge.
We learn best passively, by listening and watching.	We learn best by actively doing and managing our own learning.
Our "intelligence" is based on our individual abilities.	Our "intelligence" is based on our networks.

How adults learn

Put together, the above research indicates that *informal* learning—experiential, social, and self-directed—makes up about 90% of the learning modalities that professionals use today. Only 10% of adult learning uses formal classroom or meeting presentation learning formats. This ratio of experiential: peer/self-directed: formal learning is known as the *70:20:10 model*.[14]

PART 1: Eliminate Attendees at Your Meetings!

What are the implications for event and session design?

Ninety percent of the learning modalities adult workers need and use these days are informal—and yet we persist in making the bulk of "education" at most meetings formal presentations by experts!

Instead, *we need to mirror the learning approaches that professionals need and use in their work environments.* Our conferences provide a unique opportunity to tap the peer expertise and experience of participants. Rather than listen to experts using broadcast models that today can be largely replaced by books, recordings, articles, and online resources, we should format sessions to supply and support the experiential and peer-to-peer learning that attendees actually need and use.

Ralph Waldo Emerson realized 150 years ago that our most important learning comes mostly from our peers and ourselves. It's time that our meeting designs reflected this reality. We need to turn formerly passive attendees into active participants who learn from each other via interaction, not broadcast.

But active learning and increased connection aren't the only rewards we reap from turning meeting attendees into participants. Participant engagement and consequent community building are greatly enhanced, and we increase the likelihood that the group or smaller subgroups will develop and carry out effective action outcomes.

In the next four chapters we'll explore more deeply these key benefits of incorporating appropriate participation into our sessions and conferences—*active learning*, *connection*, *engagement and community building*, and *action*.

CHAPTER 4
Active learning

The best way to learn

> "Most learning is not the result of instruction. It is rather the result of unhampered participation in a meaningful setting."
> —Ivan Illich[15]

In January 2002 I learned one of the most important lessons of my life. In just twenty minutes I discovered that a group of total strangers could see through the false self I had projected to others my whole life—a rational, in control, persona—to the emotional human being underneath. Among other things, this insight led to switching my profession to event design, which eventually led to writing this book.

No kind of received learning could have penetrated the deep-seated view I held of myself. Instead I learned this lesson at the start of a three-day workshop in a shabby windowless hotel meeting room, during a simple small group feedback activity in which everyone took turns giving and receiving feedback about the other members. The uncomfortable experience of realizing that people I had just met could see what I was really like forced me to confront the suddenly largely pointless cost of trying to be someone I was not.

To be clear, I am *not* proposing that meetings should focus on personal development (although I'd argue that learning and growing involve personal change, and, if you aren't changed by a meeting in some important way, your time could perhaps have been better spent elsewhere). What I do believe is that *learning through active experience* beats the pants off the "receiving knowledge" learning model that has been drummed into our heads through years of listening to teachers at school.

> "The most important thing any teacher has to learn, not to be learned in any school of education I ever heard of, can be expressed in seven words: Learning is not the product of teaching. Learning is the product of the activity of learners." —*John Holt*[16]

As the home-schooling champion John Holt pointed out in 1984, learning is not a passive process. Yet the principal advertised activity at most meetings is largely passive—sitting and listening to one or more speakers for the majority of each session. Even if we put aside attendees' needs for connection and view conferences solely as a time for learning, all traditional conferences adopt this non-participative model.

An exercise

Try this.

Find a quiet place, sit comfortably, and relax.

Now take a couple of minutes to think of the three most important things you've learned in your life.

(Don't worry. Even if I could, I'm not going to ask you what they are!)

Take your time.

Done? I have two questions for you:

How many of the three most important things you've learned in your life did you learn while interacting with another person or small group?

And how many of them did you learn while sitting in a meeting room or classroom listening to someone talk?

I've run this exercise with many groups.

So far, everyone's answers have been 3 and 0.

Our important learning occurs while interacting with others.

That's *active learning*. Let's explore it in more detail.

What is active learning?

> "I don't think there's any scientist who thinks the way we typically do university courses has anything to do with the best methods for getting people to learn. I think what actually happens at universities, and in our high school system as well, is that we learn how to go to school." —*Alison Gopnik, Professor of Psychology at UC Berkeley*[17]

CHAPTER 4: Active learning

I was talking late one night with my sister Alison at her home in Burlington, Vermont, when her new roommate came in. André, a first-year medical student, had just returned from celebrating his birthday and he was tired.

ANDRÉ: "I have a couple of hours of reading tonight before classes tomorrow."

ALISON: "Why don't you skip the reading tonight?"

ANDRÉ: "I can't. We have team discussion groups on the reading first thing, and I won't be able to participate if I haven't done the reading. That's how they teach us; we read and watch videos for homework and in class we learn together in teams. There's a name for it."

ME: "Flipped classroom?"

ANDRÉ: "Yes! How did you know?"

I told André about my interest in active learning, and how pleased I was to hear how his college education was going to be so much different from mine—three years of interminable lectures, plus two weeklong sets of exams that determined the "class" of my degree.

André's medical school has adopted active learning because it's a better way to educate doctors. As we'll see, it's actually a better way to learn just about anything, and many schools are increasingly incorporating active learning into their everyday teaching practices.

So, what is active learning?

> "Jean Piaget, the Swiss philosopher and psychologist, proposed that learning was a process of constructing—not receiving—new knowledge. The learner could not simply sit back passively, and obtain learning through the manipulations of another person—a 'teacher.' The learner was neither an 'empty vessel' to be filled with knowledge or a 'blank slate' on which knowledge could be inscribed, but a system that learned through its own interaction with its environment.
> What we like best about Piaget's model is the way it makes the learner an active participant in the learning process."
> —*Jerry Weinberg, Experiential Learning: Beginning*[18]

> "... students must do more than just listen: They must read, write, discuss, or be engaged in solving problems. Most important, to be actively involved, students must engage in such higher-order thinking tasks as analysis, synthesis, and evaluation. Within this context, it is proposed that strategy promoting active learning be defined as instructional activities involving students in doing things and thinking about what they are doing."
> —*Charles Bonwell and James Eison, Active Learning: Creating Excitement in the Classroom*[19]

In the broadest sense, active learning occurs every time we *do* something purposeful and, in the process, *think about* what we're doing. Though the term was first used in the 1980s, the increasingly sophisticated tools developed during the Stone Age provide evidence that active learning is millions of years old. Older makers passed on their techniques to future generations by demonstrating how pebbles and flint could be shaped into useful tools and having youngsters practice what they had seen.

More specifically, active learning has four prerequisites:[20]

- Meaningful context (*"We need to make arrowheads to hunt game."*)
- A challenge that evokes thinking (*"You've watched me make one; what did I do first? Then what did I do?"*)
- Opportunities to actively respond to the challenge, rather than just process it internally (*"You've watched me make one; now you try!"*)
- Feedback that reveals the effectiveness of the participant's actions (*"Next time, remove those thin pieces first and you'll end up with a stronger edge."*)

All of these components need to be present for active learning to take place.

Three key kinds of learning

Given their clear importance to our lives and culture, it's surprising that we lump distinctly different activities into the single word *learning*. Perhaps this reflects the reality that learning acquisition is a largely unconscious process, in the same way our casual familiarity with snow leads us to possess far fewer words for it than the Inuit. Whatever the reasons, it's useful to distinguish between three different categories of learning: *factual information acquisition*, *problem solving*, and *building a process toolkit*.

Factual knowledge acquisition involves what it sounds like: learning factual information: multiplication tables, names and typical dosages of medications, foreign language nouns, and the millions of facts that we don't even know that we know until someone asks us. It also includes sensory knowledge: the ability to recognize whether a skin lesion is benign, the sound of Mahler's Second Symphony, the feel of satin, the smell of a skunk, or the taste of rhubarb.

Problem solving calls for a different level of learning. In essence, it requires noticing or discovering relationships between pieces of information and using these associations to infer answers to relevant problems. Problem solving provides useful process that operates on our knowledge.

Building a process toolkit is an even higher form of learning. After all, in many situations—for example, multiplying two 4-digit numbers using paper and pen—problem solving can be done by rote. But *developing* novel process frequently challenges our best minds, sometimes over generations, as illustrated by the growth of scientific understanding over millennia. Whether we construct our own process or appropriate useful process developed by others, building a collection of processes that are relevant to our lives is perhaps the most powerful kind of learning we can perform.

I make these distinctions because any specific instance of learning incorporates a different mixture of each category, and, to complicate things further, the effectiveness of each kind of learning is influenced by disparate factors. (As a result, books about learning tend to contain a bewildering variety and quantity of information about aspects of learning, and the chapter you're reading has been the hardest one to write.)

Let's illustrate with some examples.

Consider training workers to determine whether an applicant is eligible for government benefit—something that could involve many days teaching a large number of complex requirements. Success might be defined as the workers being able to consistently understand, remember, and apply the correct requirements for each applicant. Such learning will concentrate on acquiring relevant factual knowledge plus the capacity to follow a defined process determined by senior administrators. Factors such as retention of key knowledge, maintaining the level of accuracy necessary to make correct decisions, and the ability to recall relevant material over time are clearly important.

Compare this with the mysterious multiyear process by which some graduate students develop from novice researchers into leading practitioners in their field. This involves all three categories of learning: (1) obtaining a wide range of relevant and not-obviously-relevant knowledge, (2) comfort and familiarity with the discipline's existing body of process and problem solving, and (3) developing a toolkit of novel process that can, hopefully, extend the field further. While the government workers need to concentrate on retaining well-defined information, the researchers will likely acquire far more information than ultimately needed to make an advance or breakthrough. Consequently, the graduate students need to learn how to refine—both narrow and broaden—their focus on a wide range of information, constantly making decisions on what they will concentrate and what they will, possibly temporarily, put aside. The capacity to do this well, combined with ability to effectively problem-solve and develop novel process defines successful learning in this situation.

As a final example of the complex ways that learning and learning approaches can be affected by multiple factors, let's take a quick look at some differences between how children and adults typically learn.

Pedagogy and Andragogy

In Chapter 2 I explained how we typically extend into adulthood the pedagogy we're all exposed to as kids. The word *pedagogy* comes from the Greek *paid*, meaning "child" and *ago* meaning "lead." So pedagogy literally means "to lead the child."

The much less familiar term *andragogy*, first coined in the 1830s, has had multiple definitions over the years, but its modern meaning was shaped by Malcolm Knowles in his 1980 book *The Modern Practice of Adult Education: From Pedagogy to Andragogy*,[21] based on the Greek word *aner* with the stem *andra* meaning "man, not boy" (i.e., adult), and *agogus* meaning "leader of." Knowles defined the term as "the art and science of adult learning" and argued that we need to take into account differences between child and adult learners. Specifically, he posited the following changes as individuals mature:

1. Personality moves from dependent to self-directed.
2. Learning focus moves from content acquisition to problem solving.
3. Experience provides a growing resource for their learning activity.

4. Readiness to learn becomes increasingly aligned with their life roles.
5. Motivation to learn is more likely to be generated internally than externally.

My professional life journey illustrates all these transformations. At school I was force-fed a concentrated diet of science and mathematics. Besides making a broad decision to study the sciences rather than the arts, I had very little say in what classes I was expected to take. Since then:

1. My subsequent career path—elementary particle physics research, running a solar manufacturing business, teaching computer science, IT consulting, and, most recently, meeting design—displays a steady movement *from* doing what I was told I was able to do *to* what I chose to pursue for my own reasons.
2. As a physicist, much of my work depended on what I learned at school, university, and academic conferences. As my experience grew, my professional work became increasingly centered on creative problem solving for clients.
3. In academia, I relied chiefly on classroom learning. Over time, my 30+ years experience has become key to my effectiveness as a meeting designer and convener.
4. Discovering that I love bringing people together motivates the work of learning what I need to know to perform my work well.
5. Although financial factors now play a smaller role in determining how much I work, my mission to share what I think is of value drives my desire to learn how to improve my effectiveness and scope.

Take a moment to review your own professional life and see if Knowles's maturation concepts reflect differences in how you learned in school and now learn as an adult.

Of course, just as there isn't a clear boundary between childlike and adult behaviors, there's no clearcut distinction between pedagogy and andragogy. Both terms encompass motivations and contexts for learning, and it's most accurate to view them as endpoints on a spectrum of learning behaviors. Nevertheless, Knowles's five assertions, each positing progression from passivity to action, provide critical insight into why active learning becomes an increasingly important learning modality as we mature.

How we learn

A no-brainer

> "Three brains are tucked inside your head, and parts of their structure took millions of years to design."
> —*John Medina, Brain Rules*[22]

Stop right there. Every book about learning (and there are hundreds in print) contains at least one chapter about the human brain. This one will not. So if you want to learn more about the 3 pound,

23 watt, 85 billion cell, 150 trillion synapse biological marvel we all possess, check out my favorite gentle introductions in the notes section at the end of this book.[23]

Instead I'm going to concentrate on knowledge about active learning that's directly applicable to making conferences and sessions better. Hopefully, a brief discussion of relevant topics including memory, multisensory learning, movement, multitasking, novelty, emotions, and social learning will prove useful without making this chapter any longer than necessary.

We'll begin with *memory*. While we're still far away from definitive, quantitative statements about how memory works and the best ways to learn, we know enough to shed some useful light on this slippery fundamental ability.

Memory

During my lecture-based childhood schooling, I spent years learning British history, Latin, geography, and clever ways to integrate mathematical functions—knowledge which I can barely, if at all, recall today.

Can we be said to have learned something if we don't remember it? Clearly, memory is inextricably bound up with our ability to learn. Without long-term memory we couldn't learn to speak and write; to communicate via a common language. In a fundamental sense, memory allows us to be consciously aware.

And yet, our memories are surely one of the most mysterious things about us. Based on our ability to function in a complex world, by responding (mostly) appropriately to an unpredictable and ever-changing stream of events and circumstances, an outside observer would surely say we seem to *know* a great deal. But on closer examination, what we know turns out to be surprisingly hard to pin down.

We can reel off facts: 10 + 10 = 20; Washington's the capital of the United States; and the Nile is a river in Egypt. Except that context creeps in: 10 + 10 = 100 in binary; the capital of the United States before 1800 was *not* Washington; and, if you're into death metal music, the Nile is a Greenville, South Carolina, band.

Tacit knowledge

Even if we're comfortable with the concept of contextual knowledge, we still have to grapple with the reality that most of our knowledge is *tacit*. One kind of tacit knowledge is that which cannot be easily shared verbally or in writing—as philosopher Michael Polanyi says, ". . . we can know more than we can tell."[24] Simple examples of this kind of tacit knowledge are effortlessly riding a bicycle while being unable to explain how to ride a bicycle, or proficiently typing on a keyboard while being unable to list the order of the letters.

A second aspect of tacit knowledge is that we may not even be aware that we know it. Often, we only become conscious that we know something when triggered by circumstances—when the wallpaper pattern in our childhood bedroom is unexpectedly called to mind by the scent of a musty carpet, or the discovery that we still remember Pythagoras's theorem when our son asks for help with his homework.

A third facet of tacit knowledge is that we all possess unexamined and/or unconscious beliefs, attitudes, and assumptions that limit or distort our ability to understand, question, or respond to events in our lives. Often these unconscious factors remain buried, though sometimes they become exposed. For example, until the workshop experience described at the start of this chapter I believed that my emotions were not a significant influence on my professional life, and consequently remained unaware of how much I enjoyed bringing people together in productive and fulfilling ways. Discovering and embracing my emotional self ultimately motivated me to make a major career change.

The tacit nature of our knowledge makes it hard for us to "unlearn" knowledge that is incorrect or inaccurate. Challenging tacit knowledge is difficult because it's tough to reflect on or process something that you can't communicate, don't know that you know, or don't understand!

The memory life cycle

Most research on memory has been via experiments on our conscious memory—so-called *declarative* memory—and that's what we'll concentrate on in this chapter. Molecular biologist John Medina divides the life cycle of declarative memory into four steps: encoding, storing, forgetting, and retrieving. All of these stages are imperfectly understood; here is a summary of what we know.

Encoding our experience occurs in different parts of our brain. We've known this since at least the nineteenth century, due to observations of the strange effects of rare head injuries on the memories and abilities of various unfortunate individuals. Much of our sensory input is not encoded; think about the difference between *hearing* and *listening*. The way that information is presented can make a big difference in the ease and/or likelihood that it will be encoded. Mnemonics, for example—"Richard of York Gained Battles In Vain" for the order of rainbow colors "Red, Orange, Yellow, Green, Blue, Indigo, Violet"—encode hard to remember information in a distinctive word, phrase, or even music (e.g., the children's "ABC" song that encapsulates the sequence of letters in the English alphabet). In general, the more ways we encode incoming information, the more likely we are to remember it later. For example, when shopping for a new car, I am more likely to remember a sporty blue sedan's price if I notice that it's the same color as my wife's eyes, while costing about the same amount we spent for our last car, but more than what we were planning to spend, though less than the payment we just made for our daughter's college tuition.

Storing our memories seems to occur in the same parts of the brain used to encode them. We possess several kinds of storage mechanisms that comprise *working* memory (formerly known as short-term memory) and others that *consolidate* certain memories into *long-term* memory (which, despite its name, comes with no long-term guarantee of permanence). There's evidence that long-term memory contains everything deliberately committed to memory, though retrieving it is another matter. We know ways to improve the likelihood that working memory will become long-term (see below).

Forgetting what we have learned is generally considered a regrettable occurrence; something that invariably occurs more often as we age. While forgetting your spouse's anniversary or an important

8 a.m. client meeting can indeed lead to unfortunate consequences, forgetting is actually an essential component of learning. As the psychologist William James wrote in 1890, "Selection is the very keel on which our mental ship is built. And in this case of memory its utility is obvious. If we remembered everything, we should on most occasions be as ill off as if we remembered nothing."[25] Forgetting, in other words, allows us to avoid being overwhelmed by the information that assaults our senses every waking moment.

When we successfully *retrieve* a memory, we can be said to have remembered something. You might think that this process, at least, is relatively straightforward—either we remember something or we don't. It turns out that memory is not like storage on a computer hard drive; it's continually being reconstructed. The very act of remembering something alters the relevant stored memory in subtle ways. For example, if we are reminded of someone we last met long ago, we may then be able to retrieve information about that person—a tee-shirt she was wearing, her distinctive laugh—that we had forgotten we knew. The initial memory retrieval strengthens associated long-term memories.

Active learning capitalizes on these complex qualities of declarative memory. How? Read on!

Remembering and forgetting over time

In 1885, the German psychologist Hermann Ebbinghaus published *Memory: A Contribution to Experimental Psychology*,[26] the first experimental investigation of memory. Ebbinghaus experimented on himself, memorizing lists of nonsense syllables to avoid any bias due to previous memories. For this type of memorization, he showed that:

1. Memory is lost over time when no attempts are made to retain it. Ebbinghaus's *forgetting curve*, describing how much is remembered over time, has an exponential shape; that is, memory loss is fastest right after the memorization and slows over time.

2. Memorization improves with repetition. The greatest improvement occurs with the first attempt; each subsequent reception leads to less improvement.

3. When memorizing a sequence of items, we recall the beginning and ending items better than those in the middle of the list.

4. Items that were learned perfectly through repetition and then forgotten (declaratively) over time can be relearned faster on a subsequent occasion.

Each of these findings, known and confirmed for over a century, imply important consequent benefits of active learning compared to passive listening:

1. According to Ebbinghaus, people typically forget about 80% of what they learn in a class after a month.[27] Information imparted solely during lectures is rapidly lost over time because there is no opportunity to reinforce what has been said, while active learning provides an environment in which participants can immediately reinforce what has been shared by rephrasing/responding with their peers. (While some people make notes during lectures and go over them afterwards to improve retention, many do not.)

2. Active learning—through the discussion of short chunks of content or questions—encourages pertinent recapitulation and repetition, thus leading to improved memorization via guided reprocessing of content.

3. Because active learning breaks large chunks of information into smaller pieces, it provides multiple opportunities for processing content, each with its better-memorized beginning and ending.

4. Active learning that supplies multiple time-separated opportunities for memorization will be cumulatively more effective than a single exposure.

Practice testing, distributed practice, and other learning strategies

During our childhood education, we all—often reluctantly—discovered that self-tests or classroom practice tests of what we have been given to learn helped us retain the material. And who among us has not endured an "all-nighter"—cramming for a test in an effort to boost our score the next day? Clearly, repeated attention to specific learning has a positive effect. Given the massive amounts of time we spend attempting to learn things, you'd expect the human race to have figured out the best strategies to get and keep knowledge in our heads.

Not yet. We know some things, but there's still plenty of uncertainty and disagreement on the best ways to learn. Here's what we know so far.

In 2013, psychology professor John Dunlosky[28] published a summary of decades of research on evaluating the effectiveness of 10 commonly used learning strategies:

1. Practice testing: self-testing or taking practice tests on to-be-learned material.
2. Distributed practice: implementing a schedule of practice that spreads out study activities over time.
3. Interleaved practice: implementing a schedule of practice that mixes different kinds of problems, or a schedule of study that mixes different kinds of material, within a single study session.
4. Elaborative interrogation: generating an explanation for why an explicitly stated fact or concept is true.
5. Self-explanation: explaining how new information is related to known information, or explaining steps taken during problem solving.
6. Rereading: restudying text material again after an initial reading.
7. Highlighting and underlining: marking potentially important portions of to-be-learned materials while reading.
8. Summarization: writing summaries (of various lengths) of to-be-learned texts.
9. Keyword mnemonic: using keywords and mental imagery to associate verbal materials.
10. Imagery for text: attempting to form mental images of text materials while reading or listening.

CHAPTER 4: Active learning

He chose these particular strategies because they:

- Can all be used to improve learning in a relatively short amount of class time.
- Are accessible to all students using only low-tech items such as pen and paper.
- Include strategies that students often use even though they are not necessarily recommended.
- Focus on different aspects of learning (e.g., memory, comprehension, or both).

Dunlosky found the first two strategies—*practice testing* and *distributed practice*—to be the most effective because they can help students regardless of age, enhance learning and comprehension of a large range of materials, and boost student achievement.

Over a hundred years ago, Edwina E. Abbott showed[29] that *practice testing* was effective for improving student performance. Having learners receive content and then retrieve answers to test questions improves long-term memory of the material. In addition, practice testing provides feedback on topics that the learner needs to restudy, further improving the strategy's efficacy. Note that practice testing is an active learning strategy, as William James observed: "A curious peculiarity of our memory is that things are impressed better by active than by passive repetition. I mean that in learning—by heart, for example—when we almost know the piece, it pays to wait and recollect by an effort from within, than to look at the book again."

Distributed practice, in which learning activity is spread out over time, is a time-tested method to improve learning. It has been shown to be more effective than *mass practice*, in which a learning activity is repeated immediately.[30] Gradually incorporating new information into the repetitions is the best way to expand on retained knowledge. An example is the common strategy in mathematics education of providing mixed problem sets that require practice on the entire curriculum to date, after introducing each new topic or concept.

One of the problems of interpreting research on learning strategies is that most of it has been performed on children, leading to an important distinction when applied to adult learning. Adults invariably need just-in-time learning, rather than information dumps that may not be relevant for several years, if ever. Adult meetings that support active learning opportunities like peer discussion allow concentrated practice testing and distributed practice of immediately useful material.

Dunlosky rated three more of the above strategies—*interleaved practice*, *elaborative interrogation*, and *self-explanation*—as "promising" but "stopped short of calling them the most effective because we wanted to see additional research about how broadly they improve student learning."

The five remaining strategies listed above "have not fared so well when considered with an eye toward effectiveness." In particular, *rereading*, *highlighting*, and *underlining* are "particularly popular with students" but Dunlosky concludes that there are more effective uses of a student's time.

What I find important in these findings is that *active learning can be used for the five effective strategies described above*, while the less effective strategies are all single-learner activities!

Memory consolidation and reconsolidation

Two thousand years ago, the Roman teacher Quintilian observed: "It is a curious fact, of which the reason is not obvious, that the interval of a single night will greatly increase the strength of the memory."[31]

In my experience, overnights during a conference facilitate processing of experiences from the days' events. I find that the torrent of information shared during the first day of peer conferences seems to acquire shape and form in my mind overnight—the next morning brings clarity to the dominant themes and interests shared by the participants. Although we all appreciate time to consciously process our experience, there is growing evidence that short-term memories are turned into lasting long-term memories during sleep.[32] The effect of sleep on memory is an example of memory *consolidation*: the processes by which working memory becomes long-term memory.

A harder-to-study related phenomenon is memory *reconsolidation*: how we maintain, strengthen, and modify memories already stored in long-term memory. Current research tells us little about how reconsolidation works, while exposing subtle and often unexpected findings. For example, while forgetting generally gets rid of clutter, certain kinds of information, such as poetry and visual imagery, tend to be recalled more clearly in the few days following exposure than during an initial attempt. This unintuitive finding was named *reminiscence* by Philip Ballard a hundred years ago.[33] Another surprising finding is that memory retrieval is improved if it takes place under the same conditions when the memory was formed—tested in an unusual experiment in which people who learned a list of words while floating underwater recalled them better later when they were tested in the same environment than when they were on dry land, and vice versa.[34]

Psychologist Matthew Hugh Erdelyi summarizes these and other peculiar behaviors as follows: "Memory is a heterogeneous, mottled system that both improves and declines over time."[35] It's safe to say that consolidation and reconsolidation research is still in its infancy, a reminder of our current limited understanding of the memory life-cycle.

Multisensory learning

> "Five blind men met a camel. Each one touched another part of the animal. Afterward all of them recognized it as a camel.
> 'How did you know?' someone asked.
> 'It smelled like a camel,' said the five blind men." —*Sparrow*[36]

We are so accustomed to receiving the bulk of what we think of as "knowledge" through our eyes and ears that it's easy to overlook the contributions of our other senses. We still know little about how human touch, smell, taste, and kinesthetic (used here as a blanket term for our proprioceptive and vestibular senses) senses affect learning. But there are some intriguing insights.

Let's start with smell. In a review of over thirty studies of the effect of smell on memory, psychologists Simon Chu and John Downes conclude that "there is at least preliminary evidence that olfactory stimuli can cue autobiographical memories more effectively than cues from other sensory modalities."[37] There's evidence that odors improve retrieval best for emotional and autobiographical memories that are naturally associated with the smell; for example, the recall of movie details is heightened by the smell of popcorn.[38] These findings are heightened by recent research indicating that the human sense of smell can detect more than a trillion different odor combinations (far more than the number of distinguishable colors or tones).[39]

> "I vividly remember Dana, at Summer Music Clinic in Madison, Wis., giving me her five-digit dorm phone number not by just saying it but by taking my hand and push-button-dialing 4-3458 on my palm. That was in 1988 but I will remember it until the day I die." —*Dan Kois*[40]

Yes, touch also facilitates learning. One powerful touch modality is the manipulation of physical objects. A good example is LEGO® SERIOUS PLAY®,[41] a sequence of exercises that get people to "think through their fingers." This tactile, interactive process uses working with Lego® to quickly move small groups of people into creative sharing and collaboration on real-life problems. In addition, even minimal appropriate interactive touch can significantly improve relationships between participants. Standing in a circle holding hands during a brief welcome, or playing a two-person momentary hand touching game like *Grab!*[42] during a break can heighten connections, reducing barriers to learning with others.

Last but not least, the positive potential of physical movement on improving learning is commonly overlooked. We do not understand how body kinesthetics feeds into our learning capabilities, but it's clear—as described in the next section of this chapter—that movement and moderate exercise can have dramatically beneficial effects on our learning and creativity.

Now I've finished focusing on pertinent features of individual senses, it's important to realize that, most of the time, *we learn simultaneously through multiple senses*. Experiments show that when information is delivered through multisensory channels it is recalled more accurately, in more detail, and retained longer than when the same information is delivered in a unisensory manner. Problem solving and the speed of response are also improved. The extra processing required for multisensory information seems to help a learner better integrate the material. Psychologist Richard Mayer has researched multisensory learning for over forty years and offers, among others, the following guidelines for maximizing it:[43]

- People learn better from words and pictures than words alone.
- Minimize explanatory text, as extraneous words—verbal or text—overload working memory.
- Present corresponding words and pictures simultaneously, rather than successively.
- Animation and narration are more effective than animation with accompanying text.
- Avoid extraneous audio (e.g., music in the background).
- Collocate text and graphics appropriately (i.e., place text explanations next to associated graphic features).

These principles are especially relevant to presenters and designers of learning experiences, and can be easily adopted to improve the quality of resulting learning.

Memory and active learning

Our whirlwind tour through the intricacies of memory has barely scratched the surface. Nevertheless, what should now be apparent is how the efficacy of memory is ineluctably entwined with the means we employ to influence it. Hopefully you've noticed repeatedly, as I did while writing this chapter, how the more successful approaches to build useful adult memory all involve active learning. Next we'll take a more expansive look at the relationship between movement and active learning.

Movement improves learning and sharing

My five careers to date—physicist, running a solar manufacturing business, computer science professor, information technology consultant, and, most recently, meeting architect—have not been notable for the degree of physical activity required. In 2012 I began working daily at a treadmill desk, created with the addition of an inexpensive plastic shelf to an existing treadmill in my home.

The results were dramatic. Walking at an easy pace, I quickly discovered an improved ability to concentrate on my work, both on and off the treadmill.[44] Walking and working for 25-minute stretches interspersed with 5-minute breaks for a couple of hours a day created a noticeable increase in the quality, creativity, and quantity of my thinking and writing. I was surprised and pleased by the effects of this simple change in my daily routine: one that has consequently become a permanent component of the way I work.

Research performed at Stanford supports my experience.[45] Marily Oppezzo and Daniel L. Schwartz found that walking improves creativity by an average of 60%. Interestingly, they found that there was no significant difference between the creativity boost provided by walking on a treadmill or outdoors.

We used to hunt mammoths

Until relatively recently, exercise was a significant part of everyday life. Just obtaining enough nourishment required hours of daily manual activity: hunting, growing crops, fetching water. While life for most was brutal and short, a sedentary lifestyle was rare and human bodies—when sufficiently nourished and not injured by a punishing environment—were lean and fit.

Today, many of us spend our days in knowledge work, requiring little or no bodily movement during the workday. Instead, we stare at screens for hours each day, and then return to our homes to watch different screens. When we attend meetings we spend large tracts of time sitting and listening to others. Two-thirds of U.S. adults are obese or overweight, and one in ten suffer from type 2 diabetes.

The benefits of increasing physical activity during events

Although we're not going to eliminate societal fitness problems by decreasing attendees' routine passivity during events, there are compelling reasons to introduce physical activity into our meeting sessions. Psychiatrist John Ratey's book *Spark! The Revolutionary New Science of Exercise and the Brain*[46] makes a persuasive case that exercise improves our ability to learn.

> "In addition to priming our state of mind, exercise influences learning directly, at the cellular level, improving the brain's potential to log in and process new information...."[47]

> "... When we exercise, particularly if the exercise requires complex motor movement, we're also exercising the areas of the brain involved in the full suite of cognitive functions. We're causing the brain to fire signals along the same network of cells, which solidifies their connections."[48]

While a variety of research points to a significant positive relationship between physical activity and cognitive function in children,[49] there has been surprisingly little research on the effect of physical activity on cognitive function in adult humans, though experiments on adult rodents support the benefit of exercise for brain function.[50]

As a result, current research has not yet clarified the level of "exercise" that provides a meaningful boost to learning ability during an event, although the Stanford experiments showed meaningful differences in as little as 5 minutes while walking. However, my observations from over thirty years of running conferences and introducing appropriate physical activity into conference sessions over the last ten years, have convinced me that even moderate, periodic participant movement has a marked effect on energy levels and engagement. Others have reached similar, if more informal, conclusions.

> "The concerts give me energy. It's a physical fact: the way to get energy is to get your blood circulating. If I'm sitting in the house, on the telephone or trying to write letters, and I start feeling no energy, I go out and chop wood or I do something to get my blood running. The modern age may be easy on the muscles, but it's hard on the nervous system. The happiest people are usually those who use their muscles in some way."
> —*Pete Seeger, 1981 interview in The Sun*

It seems reasonable, but remains unproven to date, that body movement provides additional input for memory to represent and retrieve what is learned. Actively responding to information, rather than simply seeing or hearing it, likely creates richer and more numerous memory paths, making it easier to retain and recall what has been learned.

One final potential benefit of movement during meetings is worth noting here. In his book *Contagious*,[51] marketing professor Jonah Berger describes an experiment he performed that found that experimental subjects who jogged in place for a minute were more than twice as likely to share an interesting article they subsequently read with their friends than a group who relaxed in a chair for a minute. He concludes that physiological arousal caused by movement seems to increase the likelihood that people will share with others.

Although research in this area is still in its infancy, current findings indicate that even low to moderate amounts of movement during a conference session may well improve participants' creative and cognitive learning potential and concomitant sharing. And it may even burn a few of those tempting breakfast doughnut calories too!

PART 1: Eliminate Attendees at Your Meetings!

Multitasking

Although we are starting to enhance active learning by taking advantage of the features of memory and movement we've just explored, the news is not all good. A significant quantity of research indicates that our increasingly common predilection for multitasking is interfering with effective learning.

While distractions to learning have always been with us—minds fuzzy from too little sleep, surreptitious note passing in class, daydreaming, and so on—the relatively recent addition of online media and communications has added significant seductive diversions to learners' worlds. A 2010 Kaiser Family Foundation study found that youth media multitasking—the proportion of media time spent using more than one medium concurrently—almost doubled from 1999 (16%) to 2009 (29%), with total media viewing increasing in the same period from 6:19 to 7:38 hours per day, 7 days a week.[52] In addition, almost a third of those surveyed said that when they were doing homework, "most of the time" they were also watching TV, texting, listening to music, or using some other medium. The quantity of public and private information and communication channels has expanded dramatically and our attention is being stretched as we try to maintain awareness of the information that actually matters.

The ease of use and ubiquity of these new interpersonal communication channels has led to a substantial increase in multitasking. In 2013, social neuroscientist Carl Marci used biometric monitoring to compare task-switching between those in their 20s ("Digital Natives") with older workers ("Digital Immigrants"). He found that the Natives switched their attention every couple of minutes, twice the frequency of the Immigrants.[53] Research by psychologist Larry Rosen of middle school, high school, and university student study habits found that in a 15-minute "important study" period, students spent only 65% of their time studying, and that heavy multitasking "had a strongly negative impact on learning."[54]

Sometimes it's possible to reduce multitasking options by making deliberate choices about the learning environment. For example, if lunchtime networking during an event is deemed important, we can decide not to include distracting background music or entertainment. But in general, rather than fight the encroachment of multitasking into learning culture—*"Turn off your cell phones and listen to me!"*—it makes more sense to design a learning environment that provides scheduled times for checking email, texting, and so on, interspersed with short participatory learning stretches that encourage immersion to the exclusion of competing channels. As Rosen puts it:

> "The bottom line is that our students are multitasking and we cannot stop them without placing them in a boring, unmotivating environment. The trick is to develop educational models that allow for appropriate multitasking and that improve learning."
>
> —Larry Rosen, *Rewired: Understanding the iGeneration and the Way They Learn*[55]

Novelty

Limited research suggests that novelty—exposure to new experiences—improves memory.[56] It's proposed that this takes place because when we are exposed to something new it's seen as having potential to reward us. This increases our motivation to explore our environment for prospective rewards, which in turn leads to better learning. Mildly different experiences don't seem to trigger the effect, only truly novel experiences.

If this research is correct, it implies that providing novel learning experiences at meetings—such as innovative formats and unusual physical environments that complement meeting goals—should improve learning. In addition, this research indicates that we may learn better immediately after being exposed to unfamiliar stimuli. Care should be taken, however, that any novel techniques and environment introduced support desired learning rather than distract attention away from it. Beware of novelty and unique experiences becoming ends in themselves.

Stories

During a 2003 workshop dinner, a German software engineer asked my polymath mentor Jerry Weinberg a question. "Well," Jerry answered, "let me tell you a story . . ." For the next 20 minutes he enthralled us with a detective mystery: tracking down why a hundred million dollar software development project for a major bank was running disastrously late. Engrossed in the tale, I was jolted at the denouement—which turned on the uncovering of a key programmer who "smelled so bad that nobody could sit next to him long enough to look at his programs"—when I realized that the entire story beautifully answered Hans's original question.

Years later, I still remember this experience, illustrating how stories can be one of the most powerful and effective ways we learn. We are evolved and socialized to use the stories we hear as a tool for putting facts into a relevant emotional context: to fit the story into our existing experience. There's neuroscience evidence for this—it turns out that when we listen to an effective story, our brain activity mirrors that of the teller![57]

Remember how much of our knowledge is tacit? Storytelling can help you explore your tacit knowledge in two ways:

- By examining honestly the stories you tell others. Ultimately, we are the stories we tell about ourselves (see below). Your own stories illuminate the tacit in you—they craftily bypass your conscious limitations. If you scrutinize your own stories that have emotional resonance, you can learn much about yourself that would otherwise stay hidden.

- By noticing the stories of others that evoke emotions in you. When you respond to someone's story by feeling an emotional response that seems incongruous in some way, there's a good chance you can learn about some aspect of your tacit knowledge from what you have just heard.

Great stories have staying power, and are used every day to get messages across. For example, when I was the treasurer of my local United Way I experienced firsthand the impact of our annual giving campaigns. We knew that people respond better to specific examples of how their money will be used than statistics, so we filled our appeals with stories—*"John & Maria now have an affordable place to live, thanks to your support!"*—rather than *"Giving is up 8% this year!"* Stories are simply more memorable and effective than bare facts—and we can leverage this at our events.

Active learning provides opportunities to both tell and hear relevant stories during sessions and events. Some of the techniques described in Part Three, such as *Roundtables* and *The Solution Room*, give participants structured time to share stories. Presenters can, of course, do the same thing, but peer learning allows participants to tell their own stories, rather than being restricted to a speaker's predetermined plan.

Bollywood director Shekhar Kapur has a popular TED talk entitled "We are the stories we tell ourselves."[58] I prefer a slightly different formulation: "We are the stories we tell *about* ourselves." Our stories are central to who we are and who we become. Our stories, large or small, don't really fully exist until we tell them to others. *In the telling, we learn who we are.* In my experience, while telling ourselves stories has a certain power, telling them to *others* is the core process by which we become who we are. Active learning techniques supply environment, structure, appropriate activities, and permission to discover ourselves by sharing our stories with our peers. This is different from a teacher/lecturer using stories to illustrate what's being taught.

I can't think of a better gift to give participants at a conference.

Emotions

We'd like to think our decisions are rational, but in reality they often aren't. For example, as I mentioned earlier, people give more money to worthwhile causes if they are emotionally engaged when they are asked to give. Similarly, research indicates that *learners who are more emotionally engaged in what they are learning are more likely to learn.*[59]

Social psychologist Jonathan Haidt introduced the oft-cited metaphor that "the mind is divided, like a rider on an elephant, and the rider's job is to serve the elephant. The rider is our conscious reasoning. . . . The elephant is the other 99 percent of mental processes—the ones that occur outside awareness but that actually govern most of our behavior."[60] Similarly, Nobel Prize-winning psychologist Daniel Kahneman divides thinking into two parts—System 1 and System 2—the fast (elephant) and slow (rider) types of thinking in his wonderfully accessible book *Thinking, Fast and Slow*.[61] Our rational mind is, ostensibly, the driver of our behavior, but where we actually end up going is ultimately determined by our emotional elephant.

So, what is useful to know about how emotions affect learning? Here are two useful pointers:

Memory is heightened in emotionally charged situations. I vividly remember driving home with my kids one winter day, noticing my car start to drift as I rounded an icy curve, and wondering in fear whether we would slide off the road. (Luckily, we didn't.) In emotionally charged situations like these, time seems to stand still and we remember much more vividly than usual. While not suggesting that we fill our conferences with potential brushes with disaster, we can heighten recall and learning by including surprises at key learning moments during presentations and events. For example, I use the

Idea Swap (Chapter 50) technique in workshops for participants to anonymously share their most important adult learning experiences, which are often very intimate. The tension of hearing what you have written read aloud by a stranger, together with the dramatic sharing by others, reinforces for participants the key point that momentous learning rarely happens when listening to a lecture.

To be most effective, learning environments should mirror the desired emotional context when learning will be applied. For example, practicing a nerve-wracking large-group presentation in advance will be more effective if you practice it in front of a small live audience rather than to an empty room. This is why fire and emergency drills are usually unannounced, as the subsequent evacuation is emotionally heightened and participants will better recall the procedures if a real emergency occurs. And it's why the heightened emotional contexts of participative exercises, simulations, and role-playing can provide more effective learning experiences.

Social learning and organizational/event culture

When I, as a complete amateur, started creating participant-driven events in 1992, I never dreamed that one day I would be championing these designs to the entire event profession. One of the reasons for my naiveté was that I possessed only a hazy intuition of the transformative power that participation-rich formats offer to those who attend. It took many years for me to understand that the intense connections formed and enthusiastic evaluations shared at these events were not one-off occurrences but rather natural outcomes of the *social learning event culture* fostered by participant-driven and participation-rich designs.

Conferences are places that offer the possibility of introducing people to new ways of learning and connecting; we can take people out of their habitual organization culture and share something new with them. (Chapter 2 explains why, unfortunately, we rarely do this.) Simply providing a well-facilitated social learning experience, like the opening roundtable described in Chapter 32, makes a radical difference. I've learned over the last twenty plus years that ostensibly small changes can radically improve social learning.

A stunning example from the world of college education comes from research by Stanford psychologists Geoff Cohen and Greg Walton, who found that first-year African-American students who heard a short testimonial from an older student that mitigated worries that they might not fit in with European-American students obtained significantly higher grades over the following 3 years than those who did not.[62] That an hour's intervention for a first-year student can raise her grades for the rest of her college education should give you a taste of the potential power of social learning.

We'll explore the power of social learning after confronting . . .

. . . an inconvenient truth

Take a minute to think back on all the conference presentations you've attended.

Done that? OK, how much of what happened there do you remember?

Be honest now. I'm not going to check.

Nearly all the people to whom I've asked this question reply, in effect, "not much." This is depressing news for speakers in general, and for me in particular, as I'm frequently asked to "speak" at conferences.

When I ask about the most memorable presentations, people (after adjusting for the reality that memories fade as time passes) tend to mention *sessions in which there was a lot of interaction with the presenter and/or among the audience*: in other words, sessions in which they weren't passive attendees but *actively participated*.

Take a moment to see whether that's your experience too.

We are social beings

> "Question: How do we know that informal [social] learning works?
> Answer: How did you learn to walk, to talk, to kiss a sweetheart or to be productive in society?"
> —Jay Cross, *Overcoming bipolar thinking*[63]

Or, as psychologist Matthew Lieberman puts it:

> "Our brains are built to practice thinking about the social world and our place in it."
> —Matthew Lieberman, *Social: Why Our Brains Are Wired To Connect*[64]

From birth our brains are wired to default to social thinking when we are not engaged in other activities. By the age of ten, Lieberman tells us, most of us have completed the "10,000 hours" that Malcolm Gladwell claims are necessary[65] for us to become experts in social engagement.

For example, consider how you learned vocabulary as a child. It was primarily through active immersion in an environment in which language was used (typically tens of thousands of words), rather than through vocabulary enrichment lessons at school (typically a few hundred words). In this case, active, interactive learning was far more effective than passive reception of a teacher's lessons. Like learning a living language, social knowledge acquisition requires active interaction with others, not passive reception of information.

While it's common to think of knowledge as something an individual possesses, in reality knowledge is socially constructed with others. (Remember Socrates in ancient Greece, pursuing knowledge through dialogue?) Conversation is a helpful tool. Other people can see our blind spots and share with us what they see. By reflecting and gently challenging the beliefs, attitudes, and assumptions that form our knowledge, they can provide us an opening to, at least, become aware of what was formerly invisible to us.

Social learning and adult work

The 70:20:10 model I introduced earlier tells us that the majority of learning in the workplace today occurs through our individual and peer experiences on the job, not from structured learning. This is one consequence of a massive shift documented by management practices consultant Robert Kelley, who has been asking groups the question *"What percentage of the knowledge you need to do your job is stored in your own mind?"* since 1986. In that year, the average answer was that most people estimated that they had about 75% in their heads.[66] Ten years later, the figure had dropped to 20%, and recent surveys indicate percentages of 10% or less.

This dramatic change implies that *social learning—the learning that occurs through connection, engagement, and conversations with our peers—is rapidly becoming the predominant modality for professional learning.* Workplace transformation consultant Harold Jarche lays out a 10-sentence elevator pitch for how social learning "makes social business work."

1. The increasing complexity of our work is a result of our global interconnectedness.
2. Today, simple work is being automated (e.g. bank tellers).
3. Complicated work (e.g. accounting) is getting outsourced.
4. Complex and creative work is what gives companies unique business advantages.
5. Complex and creative work is difficult to replicate, constantly changes and requires greater tacit knowledge.
6. Tacit knowledge is best developed through conversations and social relationships.
7. Training courses are artifacts of a time when information was scarce and connections were few; that time has passed.
8. Social learning networks enable better and faster knowledge feedback loops.
9. Hierarchies constrain social interactions so traditional management models must change.
10. Learning amongst ourselves is the real work in social businesses and management's role is to support social learning.

—*Harold Jarche, Social learning for business*[67]

Adult professional learning is no longer a one-way transfer of information from experts to learners, but a two-way social process. Knowledge, once locked up in separate mutually exclusive silos, is increasingly perceived as socially constructed, subjective, and fluid. The old locale for acquiring and creating new knowledge—the classroom or conference lecture—is being replaced by the *process* of social learning.

Business process improvement specialist Jay Cross summarizes the trend toward social learning as shown in Table 4.1.

PART 1: Eliminate Attendees at Your Meetings!

TABLE 4.1 • *Social Learning Gets Real*[68]

PAST	FUTURE
Subject matter experts	Subject matter networks
Need to know	Need to share
Curriculum	Competency
Clockwork, predictable	Complexity, surprising
Stocks [of knowledge]	Flow
Clock time	Time-to-accomplishment
Worker-centric	Team-centric

Conferences as a venue for social learning

Conferences provide an ideal environment for social learning. Participative conference sessions are perhaps the purest form of social learning network because we are intentionally brought together to interact face-to-face. And yet most conference sessions, invariably promoted as the heart of every conference, squander this opportunity by clinging to the old presenter-as-broadcaster-of-wisdom model.

From a *learning* perspective, here's why supporting social learning during conference sessions makes a great deal of sense:

- Active participants learn and retain learning better than passive attendees.
- Discussion allows participants to check their understanding and make sense of content.
- Participants meet and learn about each other, rather than sitting next to strangers who remain strangers during a session.
- Participants influence session content and structure toward what they want to learn, which is often different from what a presenter expects.
- Being active during a session increases engagement, creating better learning outcomes.
- Actively participating during a session is invariably much more fun!
- Social learning sessions support *just-in-time* learning, rather than serving up predetermined content that may not be relevant to participants for months or years, if ever.
- Useful knowledge can be co-created by participants working together.

The last two points deserve a little commentary.

Just-in-time learning: Ebbinghaus long ago demonstrated that people forget much of what they are "taught" if they have no inclination or opportunity to reinforce what's important for them to remember. Because social learners can choose what they want to learn when they want to learn it, they are much more likely to retain just-in-time learning because they are motivated to integrate it immediately via discussion and reframing with their peers, instead of trying to recall it when they discover they need it 6 months later.

Knowledge co-creation: Because knowledge is socially constructed, active learning is the best way to leverage the experience and expertise of peers into useful *new* knowledge, leading to improved outcomes. As Jonathan Haidt explains, "... if you put individuals together in the right way, such that some individuals can use their reasoning powers to disconfirm the claims of others, and all individuals feel some common bond or shared fate that allows them to interact civilly, you can create a group that ends up producing good reasoning as an emergent property of the social system."[69]

Group size and social learning

Before we leave our survey of social learning and how we learn, I want to emphasize the importance of *group size*. Unlike lectures, conversations and discussions do not scale. A conversation between two people is different from a discussion among ten people, while functional "discussions" are, at best, of low quality in a single group of a hundred people. For larger groups, competition for resources becomes increasingly important. Similarly, as conversation/discussion groups get larger their individual members increasingly compete for attention. While an equivalent maximum "discussion number" for effective social learning in small groups has not been researched, my experience leads me to propose a maximum in the range of six to eight people.

The learning environment

Your learning is embedded in a context. You are not a well-bounded rational machine; you possess a brain in a body with senses and feelings, constantly interacting with and influenced by your environment. Furthermore, a large contributor to your success in navigating the world is that you will learn *something* under almost *any* circumstances, because you are built to learn from your experiences whatever they might be. Given that your environment has a profound effect on what and how you learn, shaping not only the specific learning but also its amount, quality, and effectiveness, how can we create the best possible conditions for optimal participant learning?

Ask me about learning environments and I recall sitting in a classroom full of ancient wooden desks, hinged lids inscribed with the penknife carvings, initials, and crude drawings of generations of semi-bored schoolboys. A thin film of chalk dust covers everything, and distant trees and blue sky beckon faintly through the windows. The teacher is talking. If it's a subject I like—science, math, or English—I am present, working to pick up the wisdom imparted, motivated by my curiosity about the world and the desire to not appear stupid in front of my classmates. If it's a subject I am not passionate about—foreign languages, history, art, or geography—I do what I need to do to get by.

When asked to think about creating an environment for learning we tend to focus, as I just did, on the physical environment and our motivations for learning. We have a certain amount of control over both of these ingredients. Let's examine them individually.

Our *physical environment* is mostly under the control of whoever's in charge of the learning opportunity. If we are attempting to learn something ourselves, we can pick our body stance (e.g., sitting, lounging, standing at a desk, or walking) and a location (e.g., a coffee shop, the library, our bedroom, or the beach) and an appropriate sensory environment (e.g., listening to music, wearing earplugs, facing a favorite picture, or watching waves roll in). Event organizers can choose venues that offer a physical environment that supports the kind of learning we expect to occur, such as an auditorium for lectures, breakout rooms for workshops and discussions, and social spaces for attendees to informally gather. A desirable physical environment maximizes conditions for learning and minimizes potential distractions.

Our *motivations for learning* are usually less clearly defined. Individual motivations may be extrinsic (*"I need to learn this to keep my job/get a raise"*), intrinsic (e.g., curiosity or pride in mastery), or a mixture of the two (*"I need to learn this so I don't feel stupid around my colleagues"*). When considering motivations for learning at events, a central question arises: *Whose motivations are we taking into account?* Each attendee possesses her own mix of intrinsic and extrinsic motivations for learning, while event organizers, who generally don't have much insight into attendees' motivations, tend to concentrate on achieving the perceived desired outcomes of the event stakeholders. The answer to the key question *"Who is this event for?"*—explored in more detail in *Conferences That Work*—determines many aspects of the resulting event's learning environment.

If conferences are primarily for the benefit of participants, they must focus on creating flexible and social learning environments that adapt to specific participant needs and support optimal social knowledge construction and dissemination. To do this requires attending to a third vital component of any effective modern learning environment.

The third element

Yes, there's a third element of the learning environment that is largely overlooked. Did you spot it yet? If you absorbed the message from my earlier chapter on why meetings are a mess you probably did—we have not yet mentioned *the learning processes we use* as a key component of our learning environment. These processes are so deeply associated with our experience of learning in specific environments that we're rarely conscious of how much they affect what and how we learn.

We are the offspring of a culture that has instilled the preeminence of individual experts as purveyors of adult learning via broadcast. This largely defines the physical and motivational learning environments we routinely employ. Broadcast requires auditoriums for delivery and speakers who get paid to speak to audiences who pay to listen. Broadcast perpetuates a learning model that assumes that knowledge resides in the heads of a few rather than being a social construct. And, as we've seen, broadcast is a lousy way to learn anything, compared to participative learning.

When conference organizers start program planning with a discussion about who should be invited to speak at an event, they have fallen victim to process blindness. If we are to learn effectively at a conference we need to concentrate *first* on the processes we will use to ensure participative learning, and only then think about how we might optimize their effectiveness via selection of appropriate participants. These days, this means taking care to include a variety of participant perspectives and backgrounds, thus ensuring a rich and valuable diversity of experience, expertise, and viewpoints.

CHAPTER 4: Active learning

Using appropriate processes for effective learning is so important that most of Part Two of this book is dedicated to process techniques that enhance conditions for learning. But before you jump there, let's meet Linda, who's about to discover why using good process can be so impactful.

An attendee experience

Linda's waiting to get her badge and information packet at a conference registration table. She's nervous because she's new to the industry and has only briefly met a couple of people on the list of registered attendees. Linda likes her profession, but came principally in order to receive continuing education credits that she needs to maintain her professional certification. She also wants to learn more about certain industry issues, get some specific questions answered, and is hoping to meet peers and begin building her professional network.

Scenario 1: Linda is a first-time attendee at *TradConf*, a small annual association conference that has pretty much the same format since it was first held in 1982. She received a conference program 6 months ago and saw a few sessions listed that look relevant to her current needs. After picking up her preprinted name badge she enters the conference venue and sees a large number of people chatting with each other in small groups. There isn't anyone there she knows. She drifts over to a refreshment table and picks up a glass of soda water, hoping to be able to finesse her way into one of the groups and join a conversation.

Linda meets a few people before the opening session, but no one who she really clicks with. Still, she's grateful that she can at least associate a few names with faces.

Linda doesn't find the opening keynote especially interesting. The speaker is entertaining but doesn't really offer any useful takeaways. And sitting and listening for 80 minutes has taken a toll on her concentration. She follows the crowd to the refreshments in the hallway outside and tries to meet some more people. Linda's not shy, but it's still daunting to have to repeatedly approach strangers and introduce herself. By the end of the first day, Linda has met one person with whom she has a fair bit in common, and she bumped into one of the people she knew before the conference. She joins them for a drink at the evening mixer, but then they go their separate ways, and Linda ends up eating takeout in her room while watching the evening news. She wishes she'd been invited to dinner with one of the lively groups of folks who clearly know one another.

The next couple of days' sessions are a mixed bag. Some are a rehash of things Linda already knows, rather than covering new techniques, while another turns out to focus on something very different from how it was described in the conference program. Linda picks up a few useful nuggets from a couple of sessions, and gets one of her pressing questions answered. She connects with someone who asked an interesting question at the end of a presentation. She spends most of her time between sessions with her old connection and two new acquaintances.

The conference closes with a keynote banquet. Linda sits next to a stimulating colleague, but doesn't get much time to talk to him because the keynote monopolizes most of their time together. They swap business cards and promise to stay in touch.

Afterwards, Linda has mixed feelings about her *TradConf* experience. She met some interesting people and learned a few things, but it didn't seem to be an especially productive use of her time. She doesn't feel like she's really expanded her professional network or gained much in the way of valuable information. Perhaps things will be better at next year's conference?

Scenario 2: Linda is a first-time attendee at *PartConf*, a small annual association conference first held in 1993. It has a good reputation, but it's hard to understand what the conference will be like, because apart from an interesting-sounding keynote from an industry star and a few sessions on hot topics, the program doesn't list any other session topics. Instead, the preconference materials claim that the participants themselves will create the conference sessions on topics they want to learn about. This sounds good in theory, but Linda is quite skeptical about how this will actually work in practice.

A few weeks before the event, Linda gets a call from Maria, who identifies herself as a returning conference participant. Maria explains that all first-time *PartConf* attendees get paired with a buddy before the conference. Maria offers to answer any questions about the conference, meet Linda at registration, and introduce her to other attendees if desired. Linda asks how the participant-driven conference format works, and Maria is happy to share her own positive experience. They swap contact information and agree to meet at registration.

Linda calls Maria as she waits on line to register. As she picks up her large name badge, she notices it has some questions on it: "*Talk to me about . . .*" and "*I'd like to know about . . .*" with blank space for answers. Maria appears and explains that the questions allow people with matching interests or expertise to find each other. Linda fills out her badge, and the two of them enter the conference venue and see a large number of people chatting with each other in small groups. Linda doesn't recognize anyone, but Maria brings her over to one of the groups and introduces her to Yang and Tony. "Based on what you've told me about your interests," Maria says, "I think you guys have a lot in common." A glance at Yang's and Tony's badges confirms this, and Linda is soon deep in conversation with her two new colleagues who in turn introduce her to other attendees.

By the time the opening session starts, Linda has met six people who are clearly going to be great resources for her. She's also surprised to discover that a couple of other people are really interested in certain experiences and expertise she acquired at a previous job.

The opening session is called a roundtable (see Chapter 32). Linda has been pre-assigned to one of five roundtables being held simultaneously. Two of her new friends join her in a large room with a circle of 40 chairs. A roundtable facilitator explains how the roundtable works, and provides some ground rules for everyone to follow. Over the next 90 minutes, all get a turn to share their answers to three questions. Linda gets a comprehensive overview of group members' questions, issues, topics, experience, and expertise. Human spectrograms (see Chapter 33), held roughly every 20 minutes, get people on their feet to show experience levels, geographical distribution, and other useful information about the group. Linda notes the names of four more people she wants to talk to during the conference, and discovers that her former job experience is of interest to several people in the room.

Learning lessons from physics and programming

As an experimental elementary particle physicist in the 1970s I was fortunate to work on what turned out to be one of the most important physics experiments in the second half of the twentieth century. Exploring the rare interactions of neutrinos in a huge bubble chamber at CERN, the European laboratory for particle physics, required labs in five countries to view and hand-digitize millions of filmed particle tracks projected onto large white tables. Only a few of these images were expected to show the crucial events we were looking for, so it was important that we didn't miss anything important.

When you're staring at hundreds of similar images, one after the other, for hours on end, it's easy to overlook something. So how did we minimize the chance of missing an infrequent crucial particle interaction?

The answer is surprisingly simple. Every set of film images was scanned at least twice on separate occasions by different staff. The resulting set of information on each image was then checked to see whether all the viewers agreed on what was going on. If they didn't, other staff viewed the film again to discover who was right, thus catching missing information or interpretative errors. Statistical methods then allowed us to calculate how accurate each scan operator was, and even to predict the small likelihood that *all* viewers would miss something significant.

This approach allowed us to be confident of our ability to catch a few, very important particle interactions. The best evidence for our results—which provided the first confirmation that a Nobel Prize-winning theory unifying two fundamental forces in nature was indeed correct—was based on finding just *three* examples.

Another example of how people working together produce more reliable work is *pair programming*, a technique aimed at developing higher quality software that became popular in the 1990s. In pair programming, two programmers work together at one computer. One writes code while the other reviews the code as it is typed in, checking for errors and suggesting improvements. The two programmers switch roles frequently. Pair programming typically reduces coding errors, which are generally difficult and expensive to fix at a later stage. Many software companies creating complex software find that the value of the increased quality is well worth any additional cost.

While these two examples of cooperative work are aimed at reducing critical mistakes, it doesn't take much of a leap to see that working together on a learning task may well increase the accuracy and completeness of learning. As a bonus, the two (or more) learners involved receive an opportunity to get to know each other while they share an experience together. With the right design, there is little downside but much to be gained from learning with others rather than alone.

At the first evening social, Linda enjoys getting to know her new colleagues. Everyone spends some time proposing and signing up for "peer sessions" to be held over the next few days, using a simple process involving colored pens and sheets of paper. Peer sessions can be presentations, discussions, panels, workshops, or any format appropriate for participant learning and sharing. Linda suggests several issues she is grappling with and two of these sessions get scheduled. Although another topic hasn't garnered sufficient interest to be formally scheduled, she notes the names of the people interested and decides to try to talk with them between sessions. She signs a topic sheet, noting that she

PART 1: Eliminate Attendees at Your Meetings!

Next practices, not best practices

There's nothing wrong with learning about and comparing different approaches to solving problems or satisfying business requirements. This helps us avoid reinventing the wheel or repeating mistakes that others have made.

But when we limit ourselves to the best that others are doing, two things happen.

First, we blind ourselves to the reality that our world is constantly changing, that the best practices of today may become quickly obsolete. As examples, we only need look at how the music and publishing industries continue to cling to outmoded business models as digital distribution becomes commonplace.

And second, we don't think about next practices: ways we might come up with something better. Example? Unlike the rest of the airline industry, Southwest Airlines has been profitable for over 40 consecutive years, not by implementing well-established best practices of the fiercely competitive air transportation business but by introducing new ways (flying out of smaller airports, standardizing airline fleets, employee profit-sharing, etc.) to satisfy customers and grow their market.

Learning about best practices is fine for novices who need to get up to speed on what an industry currently does. And implementing next practices can be scary, because they may require us to do things that we, and perhaps no one else, have ever done before.

But, if we restrict ourselves to best practices, then at best we'll maintain the status quo, with the ever-present danger that at any time a competitor could make our industry's best practices second best. Instead, focus on next practices. Doing this allows us to be open to reinventing our work, leading us to the potential of a profitable (and interesting) future.

So think about the participation techniques described in this book as *recipes*. While the recipe for a classic dish includes standard ingredients and a set of procedures to follow, every experienced cook experiments: a little less sugar, a pinch of cinnamon, more time in the oven at a lower temperature, and so on. Your experiments with the participative processes in these pages will lead to the next practices of tomorrow's events.

has expertise in that area, and is surprised to find that enough people want to learn from her former job experience that she is scheduled to facilitate a discussion on the topic the next day.

The final conference sessions are designed to provide Linda an opportunity to think about what she has learned and what she wants to do professionally as a result. She now feels confident about beginning a major initiative at work, sketches out the initial steps, and gets helpful feedback from her colleagues. She even has some time to reconnect with now-familiar peers and make arrangements to stay in touch. The last session starts with a large group evaluation of the entire conference: what worked well and what might be improved. Linda makes several contributions, gets a clear idea of how the conference has been valuable to the different constituencies present, and several great ideas emerge on how to make the event even better next year, together with next steps for their development.

Linda returns home with very positive feelings about her conference experience. She found the conference sessions productive and useful. She got her questions answered, learned much of value, and built the solid beginnings of a significant professional network. And she's certain *PartConf* will be even better when she returns next year!

The impact of good process on the learning environment

Linda's story illustrates the tremendous effect of good process on the learning environment. *PartConf*'s participation-rich process gave Linda a learning experience that was much more tailored to her and the other attendees' *actual* needs and wants than the predetermined program at *TradConf*. Linda also made useful connections with many more people at *PartConf* compared to *TradConf*.

The *PartConf* design also allows participants to make changes to the conference processes, both at the event itself and for future events. The learning environment at *PartConf* extends to the event design—the conference can "learn" itself through participant feedback and suggestions to become a more effective vehicle for participants' needs and wants.

I have been running conferences like *PartConf* for over twenty years. Perhaps it's not surprising that the vast majority of those who attend greatly prefer such designs over the *TradConf*s that have been the rule for hundreds of years.

Why we should use active learning at conferences

We've covered a lot of ground in this chapter. Let's finish with this: *what we know about how we learn makes a compelling case for active learning.*

In April 2014, the National Academy of Sciences published the largest, most comprehensive meta-analysis of undergraduate science, technology, engineering, and mathematics (STEM) education studies comparing traditional lecturing with active learning. Biologist Scott Freeman and his colleagues found that:

> ". . . average examination scores improved by about 6% in active learning sections, and that students in classes with traditional lecturing were 1.5 times more likely to fail than were students in classes with active learning."
> —Scott Freeman et al., *Active learning increases student performance in science, engineering, and mathematics*[70]

Considering that exams only evaluate learning on a single occasion close to the original learning experience, and, as we'll see, there is ample evidence that active learning enhances the retention and accuracy of *long-term* learning, the 6% increase in exam scores likely significantly underestimates the overall superiority of active learning. As Eric Mazur, a Harvard physicist who teaches large classes interactively, comments: *". . . the impression I get is that it's almost unethical to be lecturing if you have this data. It's good to see such a cohesive picture emerge from their meta-analysis—an abundance of proof that lecturing is outmoded, outdated, and inefficient."*[71]

The changes required to maintain optimum learning environments over the last 30 years parallel those occurring in retail shopping during the same period. Factual information and retail staple goods are both commodities that can now be delivered in ways that bypass organizational forms of the past. Many small retail stores have been replaced by large efficient supermarkets or by online stores working with delivery services that can bring almost anything to my rural Vermont home. Similarly, you don't need to get information at a "conference store" anymore; you can Google it or watch a lecture on your computer screen without ever leaving your chair.

Consequently, retail businesses that survive and prosper provide niche services not offered by giant corporations, such as timeliness (superior speed and availability) and advice (specialized and/or customized). Increasingly, *conferences that survive and prosper will be those that can give participants learning that they cannot obtain online*. Rather than concentrating on information transfer, these conferences will focus on providing a superior learning experience—active learning—that cannot be supplied by broadcast and has sufficient value to persuade conference participants and stakeholders to attend.

Finally, an important value-add of active learning is its ability to supply *just-in-time* learning to participants. We've seen how just-in-time learning improves learning retention because learning is delivered when it's needed, rather than years in advance when it's far more likely to be forgotten. In addition, the days when a conference program could be determined 6 months beforehand without concern that the sessions would be irrelevant by the time the event took place are, for the most part, over. Such pre-planned events should be restricted to training on slow-moving concerns: for example, learning the impact of new government regulations on a profession or business. Active learning, with its emphasis on allowing participants to determine *what* is discussed, allows conferences to dynamically focus at the event on whatever is currently timely and relevant.

CHAPTER 5
Connection

> "Of all the domains in which I have traced the consequences of social capital, in none is the importance of social connectedness so well established as in the case of health and well-being."
> —Robert Putnam, Bowling Alone, Simon & Schuster, 2000

I believe that the great majority of people hunger for connection with others. Without it, our lives suffer. Indeed, Robert Putnam in *Bowling Alone*, his sobering opus on social change in America, states that about half the observed decline in life satisfaction among adult Americans over the last 50 years "is associated with declines in social capital: lower marriage rates and decreasing connectedness to friends and community."[72] And the sociologist James House tells us that "the magnitude of risk associated with social isolation is comparable with that of cigarette smoking and other major biomedical and psychosocial risk factors."[73]

And yet, when we hold a conference in our culture—an occasion when we bring together people with a common interest in a subject—we give low priority to the potential for connection with our fellow conferees. Our sessions are mostly broadcast, with little or no opportunity for attendees to connect with each other. This is so even though we have an ideal requisite for directly enjoying each other's company—sharing a common interest!

As we discovered earlier, the need for connection with others is becoming increasingly important as we move to a world where people's knowledge and expertise are a function of the networks—both face-to-face and online—they possess rather than the contents of their heads. *If in our work lives we are spending more time learning socially than being trained in the classroom, our meetings must provide the same relative opportunities.*

How social media (especially Twitter) strengthens my connections in the world of events

Despite being one of the first people to use the commercial internet (I sent my first email in May 1994), I was a relative latecomer to social media, only joining Twitter in June 2009. Like many, I thought Twitter was a place for people to talk exclusively about themselves or read breaking news.

When I began to market my first book I quickly realized that broadcast-style advertising and search-engine optimization were not effective tools for reaching meeting planners who might be sparked by my work. Discouraged, I wondered whether Twitter would be a good place to research the questions, thoughts, and conversations of meeting professionals. In just a few hours I stumbled on the nascent and—in hindsight—highly influential #eventprofs Twitter community, many of whose members turned out to be interested in my meeting design ideas. It didn't take long to learn that Twitter could help me find and connect with others who shared my interests, people all over the world whom I would have never otherwise met.

Many individuals and organizations attempt to market via social media by using it as a broadcast tool—"Here's our new product!"—thereby missing why it's called *social* media. Twitter's power arises from three factors:

- Almost all tweets are public and searchable;
- Twitter includes methods to mention individuals and groups/topics (the latter via the use of hashtags); and
- You can retweet and add comments to someone else's tweet, allowing you to highlight, share, and strike up conversations with like-minded people.

Other social media platforms allow similar functionality, but Twitter is especially flexible and efficient in providing these features once you understand how to take advantage of them.

By becoming an active member of the #eventprofs community—posting links to interesting blog posts (including some of my own), answering questions, initiating and joining conversations, and hosting weekly Twitter chats—Twitter enabled me to discover and form relationships with members of the meetings community. Today, when I attend face-to-face meetings industry events, I invariably meet people that I first "met" online; often more than via chance meetings or third-party introductions at the meeting itself.

Traditional conferences leave connection time to the breaks, meals, and socials. This is why so many people report that hallway conversations during breaks are the best parts of such meetings. When sessions fail to meet our connection needs, we connect outside the official schedule. The broadcast design of most meeting sessions relegates connection with peers to an afterthought, as something you're supposed to do on your own. And this is not easy. Even if you somehow know exactly the new people and old friends you want to meet, arranging to do so is hard enough without also competing with loud dance music, fixed meal seating, and lunchtime entertainment or talks. And if you expect to readily meet the most interesting people (to you) at such events by chance from a crowd of hundreds or even thousands, then you have not been to many conferences.

The advantages of supporting connection during meeting sessions

Our consistent demotion of connection to second-class status must be reversed if meetings are to effectively support the social learning that's now essential for performing our jobs well. *We need to provide opportunities for participants to connect and share in the sessions themselves.* This doesn't mean turning sessions into speed-dating or adding irritating "icebreakers." Instead, it means taking advantage of:

- Improvements in learning that result from actively engaging with others around content rather than listening to it or watching it.
- The rich and extensive knowledge and experience of participants in the room.
- Increased opportunities to meet like-minded peers via discussion of session content, ideas, and questions.

We've already seen in the previous chapter how active learning increases the quantity, quality, accuracy, and retention of knowledge. Active learning is inextricably entangled with connection; you can't really learn *from* your peers without simultaneously learning *about* them. Because making connections is a powerful and important motivation for attending events, providing appropriate opportunities to connect during sessions is attractive, smoothing the way for the active learning that follows.

Connecting with peers during a session allows participants to access expertise and experience beyond what an expert at the front of the room can provide. Using participative techniques that uncover and develop useful connections to those with relevant knowledge, participants can discover and take full advantage of the collective wisdom in the room.

Finally, it's likely that among the connections you make while participating in conference sessions will be some that are mutually beneficial, leading to an ongoing relationship. In 2011 I ran a two and a half hour participative techniques workshop on the last afternoon of a four-day conference. After we ended, a participating supplier came up to me and told me that he had made many more useful connections in that one workshop than during the 3 days preceding it.

Movement and sharing

In his book *Contagious*,[74] marketing professor Jonah Berger describes an experiment in which he compared the likelihood that people would share an article with others right after they had either sat quietly or jogged lightly in place for 60 seconds. Seventy-five percent of the joggers shared the article—more than twice as many as those who had sat. Berger concluded that physiological arousal boosts sharing.[75]

More recent research by Andrew Knight and Markus Baer[76] indicates that even simply standing while meeting "increases group arousal, while at the same time decreasing group idea territoriality." We are

The classroom as a network

In a 2012 article, technologist and commentator David Weinberger writes about making the digital classrooms known as MOOCs—Massive Open Online Courses—"smarter than the [individual students]," so that they don't become "cyber lecture halls." His suggestion is that "you make a room smart by enabling its inhabitants to create a knowledge network." Here are his attributes for such a network:

- [This] network would at a minimum connect all the participants laterally, as well as involving the teacher
- It would encourage discussion of course topics, but be pleased about discussions that go off topic and engage students socially.
- It would enable the natural experts and leaders among the students to emerge.
- It would encourage links within and outside of the course network.
- This network would enable students to do their work online and together, and make those processes and their traces fully available to the public.
- All the linking, discussions, answered questions, etc., would be fed back into the system, making it available to everyone. (This assumes there are interactions that produce metadata about which contributions are particularly useful.)
- It would encourage (via software, norms, and evaluations) useful disagreements and differences. It doesn't always try to get everyone onto exactly the same page. Among other things, this means tolerating—appreciating and linking to—local differences among the students.
- It would build upon the success of existing social tools, such as liking, thumbs upping, following . . .
- Students would be encouraged to collaborate, rather than being evaluated only as individual participants.
- The learning process would result in a site that has continuing value to the next students taking the course and to the world.

—*David Weinberger, MOOCs as networks*[78]

Everything Weinberger suggests can, of course, be implemented in a face-to-face class or session. You'd expect this to be easier to do than online, since everyone is physically present. And yet, it's rare indeed to see more than a few of these simple ideas put into practice at our meetings.

starting to learn more about how the simple act of *Getting On Our Feet* improves the quality of our meetings and events.

Connecting early and often

There's one more outcome—perhaps the most valuable—when we build connection into sessions throughout a conference. People start meeting people earlier and more frequently than at a traditional event. Here's a typical experience from a report by meeting industry veteran Howard Givner on attending EventCamp, a participatory conference I facilitated in 2010.

CHAPTER 5: Connection

> "I easily established triple the number of new contacts, and formed stronger relationships with them, than at any other conference I've been to." —*Howard Givner*[77]

The sooner and more frequently we supply opportunities to connect around content and discussions at our events, the greater the number of useful connections we're likely to make, and the more likely we are to build relationships after the initial contacts.

CHAPTER 6
Engagement and community building

ENGAGEMENT AND COMMUNITY BUILDING are joined at the hip. At events, *engagement builds community*. And active participation in event experience is key to creating both. So let's further explore engagement and community building.

What is engagement?

I think it's telling that we use the word *engagement* to describe not only a promise to be married but also a hostile encounter between enemy forces. Although a few unlucky souls (not me) may see no discrepancy between these two meanings, I conclude that the word depicts an *emotional* involvement or commitment. When we're engaged, we're caught up in the associated work, relationship, or effort because we care, rather than for rational reasons such as a paycheck, material security, or social pressure.

But all too often, "engagement" is used as a shorthand declaration that things are fantastic: as a slippery feel-good word. Engagement is one of those words like *love* and *empowerment* that represents something so desirable that it's in perpetual danger of being hijacked for nefarious purposes. Businesses say their employees are engaged, marketers speak of brand engagement, schools boast about student engagement, and functionaries praise big donors for their civic engagement. This is unfortunate because the word loses its power when it is applied glibly with no real justification or follow-through.

Nevertheless, I believe that most people would agree that genuine engagement exists, even if a rigorous definition evades us to the extent that we only know it when we experience it.

What can we say about engagement? One characteristic is that, at its core, engagement is an in-the-moment experience. EventCamp 2010, the participative format meetings industry conference mentioned in the previous chapter, frustrated many of those who couldn't attend because very little was shared on social media about what was happening during the event, unlike many other similar conferences at the time.[79] The reason was that participants were so engaged in what was going on that they didn't share much, as exemplified by this quote:

> "As an attendee, I never felt that I wasn't ALLOWED to share information socially—No offense to the remote attendees, but I just didn't WANT to. I was SO DEEPLY ENGAGED and encapsulated by the relationships and information I was sharing one on one and with others in groups that I felt that I would be compromising my own experience by trying to share it real time."
> —Eric Lukazewski, participant at EventCamp East Coast[80]

Another characteristic of engagement is that it builds community. Engagement, by its very nature, bonds people around a shared interactive experience, as well as making and strengthening connections through discovered and shared commonalities. Such bonding—and the desire for more of it—is the bricks and mortar of community building.

Finally I'd like to make a case for dividing engagement into two forms. One is predominantly passive, characterized as *entertainment*. We can be engaged by a moving performance of a speaker, play, or concert; let's call this *broadcast-style* engagement. The other is engagement that occurs through active participation in an experience with one's peers, which I'll call *active* engagement. I'll say more about these types of engagement at the end of this chapter.

We can't directly measure the amount or quality of engagement at an event. Does this mean that we should avoid using the term? At the very least, I maintain that we can meaningfully compare indirect measurements of engagement *between* two similar events—for example, two annual meetings of a conference—and this is worth doing. Even so, it's important to keep in mind that although the following approaches to measurement can be informative, they are all subjective and only capable of revealing specific aspects of engagement. Ultimately, such measurements have to be correlated with an event's specific goals, adding further uncertainty to their value. Consequently, beware of anyone claiming that they can objectively measure engagement at your events, and take any comparative statistics with a grain of salt.

That said, here are two approaches to measuring engagement at events.

Measuring event engagement via participant ratings

The most obvious way to attempt to measure engagement at events is to ask people to rate certain aspects of their experience that we believe correlate with their level of engagement. Here are four measures we might use:

- Satisfaction with the event experience.
- Advocacy for the event.

- Likelihood of attending the event in the future.
- Pride in being associated with the event.

To gauge *satisfaction*, attendees are asked to rate components of the event such as logistics, content, connections, and perceived value.

Advocacy is often measured using the question: "How likely is it that you would recommend our conference to a friend or colleague?"[81]

Asking attendees to rate their *likelihood of attending the event again* can provide a useful data point, though in my experience such self-reporting usually supplies an overoptimistic response when compared to actual return rates.

Pride in being associated with the event can be measured indirectly by evaluating how much attendees share about their event experience with others, typically online via blog posts and social media. The level of engagement this reflects will depend dramatically on the kind of event—an exclusive invite to party with a celebrity is far more likely to be shared than an intimate 3-day self-help workshop, even though the latter may include much more significant engagement than the former.

Using outcomes to measure event engagement

Besides asking attendees for ratings, we can also evaluate event engagement by assessing consequent outcomes, both for individual participants and/or the group or organization involved. Such outcomes can sometimes be quantified—for example, "participants volunteered 70% more hours per month after the event," or "post-event online community messages tripled over the next 6 months." Even when they cannot, a simple count or listing of action outcomes (perhaps weighted in some appropriate way) may provide a useful rough comparison measure of generated engagement of one event to the next.

Should you attempt to measure engagement?

If you are planning a one-off event, putting effort into measuring engagement is of limited utility unless there are outcome-based measures that will be useful post-event to justify the value of the event to sponsors or participants. One can make a stronger case for measuring engagement for repeated events, as the results can be used to compare different formats, sessions, and content with a view to improving the event on subsequent occasions. If you decide to measure engagement, what's most important is that you agree beforehand on the metrics you will use and how they relate to your events' goals. Just as scientific research requires a hypothesis to be tested before carrying out experiments, having measurement metrics in place before an event will help you to avoid the reduced learning that occurs when hindsight is 20/20.

CHAPTER 6: Engagement and community building

From engagement to community

Engagement creates the possibility of community. Yet community building calls for more than the experience of genuine engagement at an event. Successful communities require ongoing support for their members' needs: a common interest or purpose, an appropriate structure for interaction, and maintaining consequently developed resources. Let's examine these prerequisites.

What is community?

We are social creatures. We would never have the incredible benefits (and some of the curses) of our lives today if we weren't driven to come together and meet, learn from each other, build alliances, and share. We call the formal and informal groups that emerge, whether bonded through blood or mutual interest or desire or pragmatism, *communities*, and they are essential and central to our existence.

> "Communities of practice are groups of people who share a concern or a passion for something they do and learn how to do it better as they interact regularly." —*Etienne Wenger*[82]

Most meetings are held by what educational theorist Etienne Wenger calls "communities of practice," as defined by three key elements: a shared domain of interest; a group whose members interact and learn together; and the development of a shared body of practice, knowledge, and resources. Such entities can take many forms: artists who rent a communal space to work and grow together, programmers linked online for the purpose of creating or improving public domain software, or a group of people with a common professional interest meeting regularly over lunch to swap ideas and experiences.

Community should not be confused with organizational membership. Membership is an attempt to formalize who is in a community and who is not. I can be a faithful dues-paying member of an organization—a nonprofit whose mission I support, for example—without feeling in any way a part of a community. An organization may support a community by supplying useful structure and process, but it is not the community; at best, it reflects or represents an embodiment of the community. In the rest of this chapter, I use the terms *member* and *membership* in a looser way; to describe either the self-reported identification of such a "member" or as an observation based on the regular voluntary and fruitful interactions with a (somewhat) consistent group of people.

Membership is a fluid construct. Some communities experience relatively infrequent membership changes—examples from family communities include birth, death, and estrangement—while many communities of practice and professional communities see a constant movement of members in and out of the community due to job changes, shifts in personal interests, and retirement.

Community, then, is something that cannot be defined by an organization or a founder. From the outside there are plenty of clues that a community exists, such as regular face-to-face meetings and online interactions, but the existence of a community ultimately depends on the collective experience of its members.

The value of community

Community is important to me because it allows me to connect with others in ways that are personal, fascinating, and useful. One of the reasons I like working with people in the meeting industry is that they are often "people-persons"; fulfilled by creating events where people come together and meaningfully connect, even if the community that is created is transitory. But not everyone intrinsically values community in this way.

Even if you experience little personal satisfaction from creating or being part of a community, it's easy to see its commercial value. A strong ongoing community provides income opportunities from its members' willingness to pay for relevant products and services, including attendance at its events. Loyalty to the community makes it likely that members will return repeatedly to ongoing events, and enthusiastic members will market the community to new potential members and recruit them via word-of-mouth. In a healthy community, some members will volunteer their time, experience, and expertise, reducing the financial resources needed for community maintenance. And if you are a paid organizer or administrator of a community of practice, putting energy and resources into skillful community facilitation simply makes good business sense.

Communities and associations

Associations are organizations that formalize communities of practice. Typically they are founded when a community of practice becomes sufficiently established and large enough to generate compelling reasons for an administrative structure that supports and fosters the community. Associations are often—but not always—membership-based, and they use a wide variety of membership models and levels. Most associations include a significant volunteer component combined with paid administrative staff.

Associations can experience problems in representing and supporting their community. Some associations attempt to expand the communities they serve, and in the process weaken their core connection with certain constituent member groups. Others take their direction from board members who may not provide good proportional representation for all the association's members. Small associations often suffer from limited financial and professional resources, while large associations can become too removed from the needs of their communities.

Communities of practice do not necessarily need the formal structure of an association in order to flourish. Some examples: A community of practice I cofounded in 1992 for administrative information technology staff at small schools existed happily for 10 years before we incorporated as edACCESS, a 501(c)(6) association; I am a member of the Consultants and Trainers Network, a

Vermont group of self-employed service professionals who have been meeting monthly since 1996 with no formal association structure; and I also moderate several large private online communities with no underlying legal basis that have been around for many years.

Forming and developing associations that effectively support their communities of practice is more of an art than a science, and a topic worthy of a book of its own. I'll restrict myself here to mentioning some of the most important components of this challenging task:

- Creating and maintaining a clear association mission that accurately reflects its community's current needs;
- Providing the right level of support for the association's community (too little and the community becomes drifting and disorganized; too much and the staff takes over the community);
- Listening intensely to member needs and responding appropriately;
- Maintaining excellent communication between staff and members;
- Supplying significant opportunities for community members to learn, share, and connect with each other; and
- Using volunteer contributions and resources effectively and skillfully.

Building and maintaining community

Communities aren't "built" in the same way as a supermarket. A building is designed to meet objectives determined before construction, does not fully exist until the last phase of construction is over, and once built, exists as a static, physical construct. In contrast, a community is rarely "designed," exists in a useful way as soon as a small (six?, seven?) number of people find each other and decide to stay connected, and remains a dynamic, immaterial construct throughout its life.

> "Communities that instill a sense of belonging in their members are by definition mature and capable. Those who belong feel productive and empowered, and they form the firm foundation of your community." —*Jono Bacon, The Art Of Community*[83]

A community is not solely a collection of members. Rather, it is what's generated by the interactions among them. Viable communities require an environment that allows and supports these interactions—what community manager and author Jono Bacon calls a *social economy*. Bacon defines *belonging* to community as "the positive outcome of a positive social economy.... In the same way that we judge a strong financial economy by prosperity, wealth, and a quality standard of living, belonging is the reward of a strong social economy."[84]

There's no clear distinction between building and maintaining a community. Because a community is composed of ever-changing relationships between a fluid cast of members, continual effort is needed to keep the community reflective and responsive to its members' needs and open to pertinent outside influences. A healthy, vibrant community is maintained by constantly being rebuilt, responding to the ebb and flow of members, needs, relationships, and external circumstances.

Communities and meetings

Communities start with meeting. I can't overemphasize this essential truth.

A group of people that shares a common trait, interest, or passion is not a community if its members have never met. Before meeting, such a group is merely a statistic, a potentiality for community that can only be sparked and blown into a flame if meeting happens.

Consequently, all voluntary events start with a group of people who have something in common and want to get together to (pick one or more):

- Learn
- Share
- Connect
- Belong
- Celebrate
- Determine future actions
- Have fun

The word *voluntary* in the previous sentence is important. Every day, organizations hold meetings that employees or customers are expected to attend, on pain of some kind of penalty if they do not: for example, losing a job, or not being allowed or qualified to sell a product or service. Obligatory meetings such as these, often called "corporate events," exist for the primary benefit of the organization itself, not the people who attend. You can still build community at such meetings, but it's harder because the primary drive to attend arises from a third-party's dictate rather than an individual's choice.

New kinds of meetings

Online synchronous meetings became possible with the invention of the telegraph and the telephone—the conference call is still with us—but burst into full flower with the rise of the internet, allowing us to be part of communities whose members may be located anywhere with an internet connection and whom we may never have met face-to-face. Such communities can use an appropriate mix of synchronous (text and video chats, messaging) and asynchronous (listservs, discussion boards, blog posts and comments) online meeting technologies.

The power of search in the online world makes it much easier for people who share an interest, whether mainstream or obscure, to find one another. In addition, the availability of free or inexpensive environments to meet online removes the often significant time and money commitment to meet face-to-face, especially when travel is involved.

As a result of all these changes, it's now possible and common to build community online. The question then arises: How does the emergence of online communities affect the need for face-to-face meetings?

The value of face-to-face meetings in building community

I moved to Vermont in the late 70s, just as the first primitive solutions for remote personal computer access were becoming available. Using dial-up connections over phone lines was slow and frustrating, but it allowed me to effectively provide information technology consultation and support to distant clients. Some of those clients I never met face-to-face. Today, it's easy to video chat with anyone in the world with internet access and I routinely consult for clients whom I'll probably never meet in person. Yet, despite my current ease and the benefits I find in working and connecting with others online, I strive to meet people face-to-face whenever possible.

Why do I make this effort? Because, apart from my core need for direct human connection, I learn much more about and from people when I meet them in the flesh, including things of which I may not even be consciously aware. Throughout our lives we learn to interpret body language, voice inflections, and a rich variety of social cues. When we're in someone's presence, we use this information to guide our interaction. We might, for example, detect hesitation that implies reluctance or disagreement, signs of boredom or inattention, embarrassment, or pleasure. The subtle body language involved in this process is absent from written and voice communications and can't be read reliably in even the highest resolution video conferencing systems currently available.

The lack of such information has even a greater impact for groups than for one-on-one communication. Online we can't scan the room to see who's involved in a discussion and who's tuned out, reliably gauge the emotions that accompany an ongoing discussion, observe the relaxation that indicates a group reaching consensus on a topic, and so on.

These observations lead me to believe that online and face-to-face meetings best support community building when used in combination. Online meetings provide wonderful opportunities to readily meet and get a sense of new community members without the expense of having to travel to a common meeting destination. They can also help maintain prior relationships that have been developed in person. What they cannot do—at least until Star Trek holodeck technology is readily available—is substitute for the intimacy, power, and consequent effectiveness of face-to-face meetings.

In my experience, communities of people who only meet online don't attain the intensity of those that supplement online interaction with regular face-to-face encounters. And over time, relationships formed in person fade without follow-up by other than electronic means.

The value of online connection is that it provides immediate contact when needed, allowing longer periods between in-person meetings before jeopardizing the strength of the community. (This, of course, assumes that group members have access to and are comfortable using online channels.) Although it's impossible to generalize, I've found that an annual face-to-face meeting coupled with plentiful opportunities for online interaction provides an adequate framework for maintaining community in many associations and communities of practice.

Community building, engagement, and participation

If we agree that face-to-face meetings are an essential component for building and maintaining community, will any kind of in-person event suffice? No! Community building is predicated on engagement—and engagement is, as we have seen, about creating and strengthening bonds and connections through shared experience and uncovered commonalities.

I believe that the most effective community building occurs predominantly through participation that generates active engagement. We are exposed to experience our entire waking life, but unless we participate in what is going on around us, our passivity denies anything more than transitory engagement. Without participation, engagement is, at best, a product of entertainment, and while entertainment has its place, it rarely leads to long-term change.

At a 2011 conference, I heard an inspired motivational speaker, Bill Toliver,[85] give an amazing 20-minute speech.

But 3 months later, I didn't remember a thing Bill said.

Now, this could be simply because my memory is declining with the passage of time. But I don't think my dying brain cells are to blame.

As a counterexample, I still have vivid memories of a workshop I attended in 2002.

Why do I remember what happened at that workshop, but not what Bill said? *Because in the workshop I was participating.* I was interacting with other participants, receiving feedback and insights about what I said and did. This led to deep learning that has stayed with me for over 13 years.

In my experience, it's rare for even the best motivational speakers to create engagement that endures, compared to the lasting outcomes I routinely witness when appropriate participation is built into the meeting design.

This isn't surprising.

Take a moment to identify the non-family relationships that are important to you. How many of them came about through active participation in a shared experience with others, and how many came about through listening to that person teach or present?

If you're like me, the former greatly outnumber the latter.

If we want to build strong, engaged communities, we need to incorporate active participation into our meetings, so we can provide the same opportunities for our participants as well.

CHAPTER 7
Action

PEOPLE MEET TO LEARN, CONNECT, ENGAGE with others, have a good time, find that significant other, celebrate, be entertained, and reminisce.

That's fine. But many meetings have another core goal.

Make something happen!

Which leads to the question:

What value does your session, conference, or meeting have if nothing significant changes as a result?

To which the answer is:

Not much.

The organization holding the meeting may hope that new directions and strategies get discussed, decisions get made, plans with clear next steps are formulated, and the necessary resources are allocated to make what's been decided happen.

Your boss, who pays for you to go, probably expects you'll get some valuable new ideas, solve a current pressing challenge, and make some useful and lucrative new contacts.

You might love to leave with a dozen great new ideas running through your head, ways to handle problems you've been worried about, important resources and contacts stored safely on your smartphone, and the energy and resolve to take full advantage of everything that you've learned and experienced.

In another words, *there's a good chance that everybody wants some kind of change to occur as a result of the meeting, and wants that change to be translated into effective action.* When there's insufficient action, organizations, bosses, and participants will inevitably experience increased levels of frustration, resentment, and unhappiness.

Unfortunately, many meetings ostensibly held for the purpose of producing actionable outcomes—whether at the meeting or "back home"—fail to do so. There are a host of reasons why this happens. For example, some meetings:

- Appear to invite discussion, while in reality the outcome has been predetermined.
- Are about asserting status rather than doing useful work.
- Become hijacked by attendees to fight unrelated battles.
- Lack crucial information needed to meaningfully proceed.
- Delay the unpleasant consequences of making decisions by avoiding making them.
- Don't include key decision-makers, thus rendering decisions pointless.

Even when meetings do not suffer from such factors, few of us are taught about good process for exploring possibilities, making decisions, developing plans, and allocating resources. Though a significant portion of our working lives may be spent on these activities, little or no time is spent on learning and experiencing such skills during our primary and secondary education—in fact, learning about running meetings is pretty much restricted to business school curricula. Everyone else is expected to learn how to do it by osmosis.

As a result, many meetings that are held to determine future action use traditional meeting structures and process: Robert's Rules, environments in which it may not be safe for everyone to share candidly, inviting anyone who might have an opinion, vague agendas, letting only a few people contribute, unstructured discussions, mixing the "what" with the "how," and so on. In Chapter 2 I explained why meeting process has stayed largely unchanged for hundreds of years. The same reasons account for the poor outcomes of most action-oriented meetings. Even when decisions are made and plans developed, it's not necessarily the case that the end product is satisfactory, either to the meeting organizers or participants.

What can we do to get more effective action outcomes from our meetings?

If we don't participate during a meeting, it's unlikely we will be especially involved in any post-event action. At most we may passively accept an end product dictated to us by "leaders" of the meeting. When chosen by a minority, such outcomes are less likely to contain creative ideas or be accurately focused, do not reflect genuine community energy, and have minimal legitimacy. Consequently they are less likely to be implemented successfully.

By contrast, when a majority at the meeting actively discuss and decide on action outcomes, these barriers are reduced, making it more likely that they will actually be carried out.

Nevertheless, the participative processes and techniques described in Part Three cannot guarantee that your session, conference, or meeting will lead to effective actions. As illustrated above, numerous factors—some of which may be outside your control—can sabotage the approaches included in this book. To minimize or nullify these factors we need to do two things:

- Create a comfortable, safe, and fertile environment to develop suitable action plans.
- Use the right techniques to elicit pertinent ideas, planning, decision-making, and next steps.

Create a comfortable, safe, and fertile environment to develop appropriate action plans

If your participants are sitting in uncomfortable chairs in a hot, crowded room, they're going to be distracted from the work they're asked to do. If the technology they need—A/V, flip charts, pens, cards, Wi-Fi, etc.—is inadequate or absent, they will struggle or give up. These considerations are, of course, important for all meetings, but they are especially relevant when participants are being asked to perform what is often difficult, high-consequences work that requires continued concentration, thinking, and creativity. Minimize their stress by supplying a *comfortable* working environment that anticipates their needs.

A *safe* meeting environment is one in which participants feel safe to:

- share their thoughts and ideas
- ask questions
- talk about how they're feeling about what's going on
- make "mistakes" that lead to learning

In my experience, the best way to create a safe environment is to introduce *explicit* ground rules, to which all participants agree at the start of the meeting. Part Two of this book includes a set of ground rules I've used for many years that support the goals listed above. Explicit ground rules are needed because, without them, participants' *implicit* ground rules reign: that is, different participants have different ideas about what is acceptable behavior.

You've probably experienced what can happen when participants don't share a common set of ground rules. Typically, a minority dominates discussion, while the rest feel unwelcome or reticent to contribute. But another important, yet largely invisible outcome is that group members tend to be reluctant to speak out: to express their opinions, ask questions, or talk about how they're feeling. For example, if someone is explaining something to an audience whose members mostly don't understand what is being said, each person is quite likely to think that it's "just me" and say nothing. Ground rules that explicitly grant the freedom to do these things have a startling effect on a meeting's quality and level of interaction.

Another important ground rule for many events is an agreement about confidentiality of statements and opinions that are expressed by individuals during the meeting. I explained this in my earlier book as follows:

> "Crucially, a conventional conference offers no expectation of or agreement to privacy for anything that is said. As a result, only the most confident or highest status attendee is likely to be comfortable revealing a lack of knowledge in some area, sharing a problem that he has, or asking a 'stupid' question. Without a public group commitment to confidentiality, participants fear that what they say at the conference may make its way to their superiors or colleagues in their organization. This leads people to censor themselves on many topics."
> —Adrian Segar, Conferences That Work: Creating Events That People Love

Finally, your meeting environment must be *fertile* if you want new ideas, initiatives, and outcomes to emerge. If action implies change, then we need to generate as many creative ideas about the future as possible before reviewing them critically, choosing the best, and deciding what we will do. As described below, a fruitful and productive conference environment makes it possible for a rich variety of changes to be proposed, evaluated, and turned into action.

Use the right techniques to elicit pertinent ideas, planning, decision making, and next steps

Sadly, during our formal education we don't spend much if any time learning directly how to draw out potential ideas, and develop high-quality, well-informed decisions and appropriate next steps. Instead, if lucky, we may stumble upon aspects of useful techniques, camouflaged among numerous poor approaches. For example, classic brainstorming is still taught as a useful technique for developing new ideas, even though we know that people who work alone and later pool their ideas come up with many more suggestions than if they brainstorm together as a group.

The guided discussion techniques described in Part Three of this book provide effective step-by-step methods that can be used to develop action outcomes. They begin by encouraging individual creative thinking to elicit a wide range of responses, avoiding the self-censorship that normally occurs when people are asked to propose ideas in public. Small groups then review and refine these ideas. Combined with the freedom of expression fostered by appropriate ground rules, these approaches supply the right tools for moving from ideas to action.

CHAPTER 8
Wishes

I SEEM TO WRITE BOOKS BACKWARDS. My first book and this one have three parts, and in both cases I completed Part Three first, then Part Two, and now here we are at the end of Part One.

The final chapter of Part One of *Conferences That Work* was called *Wishes*, and that feels like a good title for this chapter too.

Despite sitting in classrooms for many of my formative years, I finally discovered that I learn best when I'm *active* in the world: asking questions, having conversations, and staying open to new experience. When I do this, I make more connections with others and I'm more likely to act on opportunities for action that satisfy my needs, including working to make the world a slightly better place.

If my benevolent fairy godmother appeared (just as she did in *Conferences That Work* at this point) and granted me three wishes for you at this moment, they would be that you are:

1. Convinced that turning attendees into participants at events has significant value.
2. Inspired to learn more about how to create an environment for participation (Part Two).
3. Eager to read about a plethora of practical techniques you can use to integrate appropriate participation into your conferences and individual sessions (Part Three).

I hope your list is similar. I write my books backward because it's always been easier for me to start with the practical details and, only later, figure out how to communicate the underlying *why?* (That's probably why, long ago, I became an experimental particle physicist rather than a theoretician.)

Now, on to the practical details. Enjoy!

PART 2
Creating an Environment for Participation

CHAPTER 9
Introduction

Increasing participation during a session or event can be as simple as *changing the environment*.

For example, consider a meeting dinner. At a traditional sit-down dinner, you're stuck with the people sitting near you for the whole meal (unless you employ "Seat Swap," described in Chapter 29). To make things worse, when assigned seating is used attendees don't even get to choose the people they sit with!

If, however, you choose buffet-style service and don't assign seating, you'll improve the environment for interaction and connection between attendees. Explicitly encourage people to not feel tied to their initial seat and instead use the meal time to meet both those at their starting table and those seated elsewhere. Giving participants opportunities to mingle during a meal both allows them increased flexibility to meet more people and also lets them pick who they want to spend time with.

Even the seating layout you use for the dinner influences the amount of interaction. Large round or wide rectangular tables keep diners apart, making it harder to start, overhear, and join conversations. Small tables provoke intimate dining, increasing the likelihood of connecting and conversing.

These are just two examples of environment-changing opportunities that improve the ease and likelihood of participation at meetings. Embedding such techniques into a participation rich event environment builds events that support participation throughout. It's easier and more natural for people to connect, engage, and learn when an event's sessions *and* environment consistently live and breathe participation.

Creating a participatory event environment

This portion of the book addresses ways to create and improve the participatory environment during a session or event. Some of the changes concern *logistical* aspects of the event, like the dinner example above, while others are about *process* changes.

Logistical changes involve:

- Badge design
- Meals
- Event space
- Seating
- Information display
- Timing

Process changes involve:

- Giving up control
- Safety
- Play and fun
- Ground rules
- Facilitation
- Group selection
- Asking questions
- White space techniques
- The conference arc
- The conference metaphor

The following chapters describe how to enhance each of these domains to maximize meaningful event participation.

CHAPTER 10
Badge design

IN 2010 I WROTE "Anatomy of a name badge,"[86] sharing my criteria for effective badges at events. Ever since, it's been one of my most popular blog posts, earning me a mention on the front page of the Wall Street Journal in 2013.

FIGURE 10.1 • *Examples of poor[87] and well-designed badges*

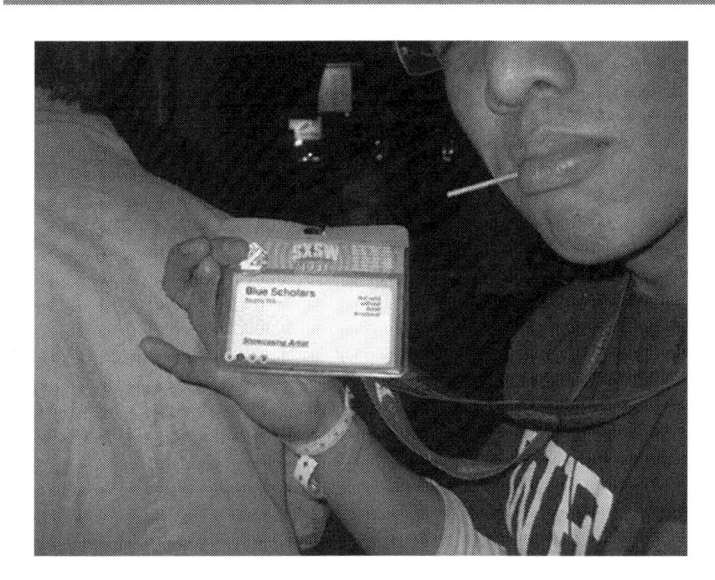

Too often, the humble name badge is an afterthought. Yet when designed correctly, name badges can improve interactivity and participation at any event.

Aside from security management at some events, the most important function for name badges is to make it easy to discover and learn people's names. This may seem obvious, but one of the most common mistakes I see is badges with attendee names in a type size that can't be read from more than a few feet away. The tendency is to use a small badge and shrink the font size so the longest attendee name can be shown without truncation on a single line. Why should Jacqueline Cornelious-Tomlinson's long name determine the tiny type printed for everyone?

To avoid this, use large badges (4″ × 6″ vertical badges are my favorite) and *print first and last names on separate lines*. In North America, for all but the most formal events I suggest making the first name larger than the last name. If the badge is small, don't reduce the font size for everyone to fit a few long names; instead, print those badges separately using an appropriately smaller font. At informal events ask attendees at pre-event registration for the name they'd like on their badge.

I suggest including both attendees' affiliation and Twitter ID, if available, on badges. The Twitter ID allows attendees to find out a lot about one another, and encourages interaction and connections via social media during and after the event.

It's helpful to include a badge wearer's role(s) at the event. Organizer, volunteer, first-time attendee, returning attendee, speaker, panelist, and session facilitator are just some possible event roles. I use color-coded shapes and/or symbols rather than the array of colored ribbons that are sometimes used to differentiate roles. Similarly, if you are dividing participants into predetermined subgroups, add a symbol for the specific group to each badge.

I am not a fan of including organization title on badges, because some people may feel reluctant to speak up when with someone whose badge says they're a director or vice president. I favor event environments that don't provide this kind of potentially prejudicial information up front. Your choice.

Don't waste badge space on large event logos. Event identification should be as small as possible consonant with the reason(s) you're adding it to the badge.

If the badge is big enough and you're supplying a lanyard for attachment, consider adding a schedule to the back. Make it as large as you can without omitting any schedule details. If you don't print an agenda on the back of your badge, consider duplicating the front there. Then it won't matter which side shows!

Finally, *badges can supply other useful information that can spark connections and engagement between attendees who are just walking around*! See the *Badge It!* Technique described in Chapter 29 to learn how.

CHAPTER 11 Meals

In *Conferences That Work* I gave this simple advice:

> *"Offer the best food and refreshments you can."*

Communal meals are one of the most elemental ways for people to meet, connect, and bond. Providing fine food and refreshments, well prepared, and attractively served at your event is, therefore, an obvious way to support and strengthen connections and community building for your participants.

This doesn't mean your meals and refreshment breaks should be elaborate formal affairs. What's important is to use these occasions *to create an environment that supports meeting people*. Here are some simple ways to encourage this.

Avoid entertainment during meals and breaks

I have nothing against entertainment at conferences, even though I'd often prefer to choose my entertainment outside the event, rather than have it chosen for me by event organizers. But I'm saddened and disconcerted by the common practice of adding a speaker, presenter, conference business, or entertainment at every major meal break. Since meals present a great opportunity for people to meet, why make it impossible to do so by supplying competing sound and spectacle whenever attendees have a chance to get together?

If your event is focused on connection and engagement, my experience is that most attendees would much rather spend their time doing just that than "being entertained."

If you feel you must supply entertainment at an event, make it *active* entertainment that involves participants in fun and/or socially responsible activities. And *make it optional*, by providing a publicized, quiet alternative location with convivial seating where participants who want to deepen connections can hang out.

Don't assign seating

Assigned seating forces attendees to sit next to people that others have chosen. Consider asking people to sit next to folks they don't know, or allow them to sit where they want at mealtimes.

Serve buffet rather than formal sit-down meals

Formal sit-down meals create an environment in which it's hard for people to move around and meet others during the meal. Buffet-style dining makes it easier for people to leave their current neighbors, perhaps while getting more to eat or drink and join new conversations.

If you want or need to hold a sit-down meal, consider using *Seat Swap* (Chapter 29) to encourage seating changes during the meal.

Serve brain-healthy food

We now know that the food we eat affects our ability to learn. The meeting breakfast staples of pastries and doughnuts cause blood glucose levels to rapidly increase, followed by a sharp decrease below normal. The resulting low blood sugar makes it hard to concentrate. Instead offer less sugar and white flour and more whole grains, fiber, fruit, vegetables, and lean proteins (e.g., eggs, fish, yogurt, and chicken) in the meals you serve. Brain-healthy foods are a smart choice at your meetings, and they do not cost more than traditional offerings.

Consider group preparation of a meal

In 2009 I attended (and facilitated part of) a 4-day Oregon conference, *Fixing Food*, at which every meal was created and served by groups of attendees, guided by professional chefs. The pleasure, networking, and bonding that resulted was incredible! You also can create food together as a group. Provide food and equipment (and probably some expert guidance) for a group to cook a meal for itself or a larger group. Anything from a casual barbecue to an elaborate feast will provide an enjoyable and effective participative experience.

CHAPTER 12
The event space

I HAVE FREQUENTLY BEEN LOST IN SPACE. No, not outer space but event space. I still vividly remember searching for my room late at night, making my way through a deserted maze of twisty little passages at a well-known conference center. The buildings, attached to each other by hard-to-find connecting passages, were so confusingly alike that the center painted colored lines on the floor in an attempt to guide you through its labyrinths. Despite clinging to my map, I repeatedly found myself at dead-end corridors, forced to turn around and retrace my steps. It was like being inside an early 90s video dungeon game, and my heart was beating furiously by the time I finally found my room.

The physical space in which you hold your event has a large impact on its effectiveness. Since most event planning books extensively cover logistical considerations for choosing an appropriate venue, this chapter concentrates on factors that affect attendee participation during the meeting.

The key to successful event logistics is attending to *everything* necessary for a satisfactory participant experience. A single failure—long lines at registration, inaudible presenters, inadequate signage, poor quality meals, rooms that are too hot or cold—can doom the overall event experience, even if everything else is topnotch. As a result, attention to detail, and the ability to react effectively to unexpected circumstances (which have come up at *every* event I've ever run) are essential qualities for any successful event producer.

Here then, in no particular order, are essential event space issues that must be considered and managed appropriately if attendee participation, connection, and engagement are to be maximized rather than thwarted.

Venue layout

Endeavor to hold all significant conference activities as close to one another as possible. If any locations you're using are isolated, think carefully about the effect this will have on activities held there. Keeping everyone near each other throughout the event means a more communal feeling, with higher energy levels, less disruptive trips for missing materials, and greater likelihood of keeping your conference on schedule.

If at all possible, provide on-site accommodations for participants and encourage everyone to use them—even local attendees—for events lasting more than a day. After-hours conversations and activities make a big difference to the connections that participants form, and, if accommodations are more than a few minutes' distance from the venue space, people tend to go to their rooms to freshen up or pick up something and decide not to return until the next day.

Make sure that your event's navigational and information signs are complete and unambiguous. Navigational signage ensures that participants have the information they need to move between any of your conference locations without getting lost. Informational signage identifies locations clearly (e.g., "Exhibits," "Buffet Lunch," "Peer Session Room A") so people know what's going on where.

Physical environment

An attractive event space can make a big impact on the enjoyment and consequent success of your event. Much of an event's physical environment is predetermined by the specific venue chosen, which is why it's important to be clear about desirable venue features as you start the site selection process. As described in *Conferences That Work*[88] I'm a fan of nontraditional conference spaces for the smaller events I run. However, professional venues have their own advantages and are sometimes the only practical option.

What aspects of the physical event environment should we focus on?

Comfort

Most of us have had to endure disagreeable conditions during events: uncomfortable seating, chairs aimed away from the activity in the room, rooms that are too hot or cold, dim lighting, obstructed sight lines, poor sound, external distractions, upsetting odors, and so on. Such circumstances make it hard for attendees to give full attention to what is going on, invariably sapping both participation and learning. Paying attention to these details will pay rich dividends.

In addition, listen to comfort concerns that arise during the event and be prepared to deal with them, rather than relying on one's own experience. Veteran presenter Naomi Karten told me of a time she presented at a summer conference where the attire was shorts and tee-shirts. "Everything went fine, but afterwards, a few people said they liked the presentation but it was too bad the room was so cold. Cold? Moving around as I do during presentations and failing to observe my audience, *I* was comfortable."

Natural light

While I've participated in many powerful sessions held in windowless rooms, research indicates that exposure to daylight, which is rich in the blue-green frequencies of the visible spectrum, helps to regulate circadian rhythms, which affect our mental and physical health.[89] Attendees will appreciate and benefit from access to daylight, especially if your sessions are solely illuminated by artificial light.

Color

Color plays a surprisingly significant role in our perception of place. Though color associations are frequently culturally specific, there is evidence that certain colors have psychological effects. Bubble-gum pink, for example, has been found to have a calming effect, warm colors (e.g., red, orange, and yellow) support detailed work, while cool colors (e.g., blue and green) are good for creative activities and increased alertness.[90] In addition, too much color can overload participants, making it hard to process information.

Some event planners, especially those with experience in special and large events, have an intuitive feeling for colors that will support specific participant activities. In some venues, room colors can be changed with appropriate lighting. Consider obtaining a consultation if color options are feasible.

Novelty

An interesting and unusual venue will pique participant interest, help maintain energy, and keep people alert. This is one of the reasons I like to use non-traditional venues, such as private schools, museums, and parks, when possible. A number of years ago I arranged for a presentation to be held in a small planetarium, which certainly added to the interest of the session! For an example of a novel commercial event space, check out the description of Catalyst Ranch in Chapter 19.

Flexibility

Attendees are far more likely to propose and engage in a variety of session designs—presentations, panels, small group work, workshops, outdoor activities, etc.—if the event space is flexible enough to accommodate the different needs of these formats. Fixed seating auditoriums and classrooms do not handle participative approaches well.

Instead, look for a variety of rooms and meeting spaces in a mixture of sizes that can handle plenaries, breakout sessions, and small group meetings. Participative plenaries require spaces where large numbers of people can easily move about and re-form in different groupings. Participative sessions require more floor space than lectures and panel presentations, so don't take the room capacity charts supplied by venues at face value. Consult the relevant chapters in Part Two of this book to determine the room area you'll need.

Supply some quiet places for participant reflection and reenergizing. If you're short of space for human spectrograms (Chapter 33) consider using nearby hallways. Don't overlook the possibilities of using outdoor space if the weather is conducive, but make backup plans in case it's not.

Confirm that the spaces you'll be using have no sight line obstructions, such as structural pillars; these can significantly interfere with participants' ability to see each other. Also, check that appropriate seating is available (see Chapter 13).

Places to post session materials

A number of the techniques covered in this book require posting generated materials on the walls or somewhere groups can readily review what's been produced. Don't assume that this will be straightforward in your venue—a surprisingly high percentage of event spaces neither permit wall posting nor offer alternatives. Chapter 14 covers this topic; keep your needs in mind when choosing an event space.

Safety

Personal safety is, of course, a requirement for any venue, but participants also will be distracted if they are worrying about the safety of their personal effects. Consider providing a staffed property-check area for attendees, so that people can drop off personal items they don't need for a while. This allows participants to circulate freely without having to lug their possessions around.

Privacy

Under the right conditions, in my experience, most individuals will share surprisingly intimate stories and information with people they have just met. Arrange a variety of spaces for personal conversations, scattered throughout the venue, so that it's easy for participants to find places to meet and connect privately.

Minimizing distractions

Minimizing distractions at your venue will allow participants to focus on your event. This is another consideration in favor of using venues located in interesting places "away from it all," rather than those in the middle of cities with lots of tempting diversions just outside the door. When selecting a venue, be sure to ask about other events scheduled the same time as yours and consider the effect this may have on your event. At one conference I heard about, a dog conference was scheduled in the adjoining meeting room. These were not quiet dogs. Making matters worse, despite requesting sleeping rooms in a quiet location, participants were given rooms next to rooms with dogs (yes, barking ones). Also, look out for noisy heating and air conditioning systems, sound pollution (see below), and unpleasant odors.

Sound considerations

Excessive ambient noise can be extremely distracting at an event. Noisy heating and air conditioning systems, buzzing light fixtures, loud adjacent sessions, and street traffic are common culprits. Perhaps the worst offenders are noisy heating and cooling systems that turn on and off, making it impossible to maintain the right volume level without continual adjustments throughout sessions. Inspecting sites in advance will allow you to check for and ask about undesirable background noise.

Effective sound reinforcement (audio systems that make live or pre-recorded sounds louder) is essential for all but the smallest events. Unless a room is extremely quiet, I ask for sound reinforcement for any group sizes larger than around twenty people. Check that sound systems work well *before* you begin—even slight distortion, clipping, or pops can ruin a session experience. Wasting hundreds of people's time waiting for an audio technician to come replace a faulty mike occurs far more frequently than it should.

Make sure there are quiet places available close to the principal session spaces for pair and small group informal, impromptu get-togethers.

While there is little research on using music during event sessions, there is some evidence that music can improve memory of presented information,[91] increase creativity when played at moderate levels,[92] and distract us from fatigue.[93] Personally, I only use music as a lead-in before a session begins, but if you think that any of these effects might be beneficial for your sessions, feel free to experiment!

Lighting

Naomi Karten told me a story about a presentation that was scheduled in a gazebo outside the conference hotel to allow hotel staff time to do some rearranging inside. The presenter had a PowerPoint presentation. Because of the bright light coming off the ocean, his slides were impossible to see. When images or video are used, facilitators often dim room lights or shut out daylight with curtains or shutters so that projected visuals are visible. Venue projector brightness is often chosen assuming that general room lighting will be dimmed for a presentation. Participative work, however, requires participants to be able to see other individuals' faces and body language and to move about the room without bumping into others. To avoid this situation, make sure that projectors are bright enough to display visuals in normal room or day lighting.

Room set

More than once I've arrived to run a session requiring an open space to discover a projector neatly installed, with cables taped to the carpet, in the middle of the room. I've also turned up to find the promised room area reduced by a third due to the unannounced addition of a stage and rear projection. And the chance that chairs are set up as requested are depressingly low. Venue staff are often unfamiliar with the needs for participative exercises and overlook or ignore associated room setup requests. As a result, I highly recommend facilitators arrive well before a session is due to start, so that problems like these can be corrected or, at least, adapted to better meet session needs. Whenever possible, these issues should be resolved in advance via a pre-event site visit.

You don't always get what you set

In 2012 an association of meeting planners asked me to give a presentation at their annual conference on incorporating participation into events. After requesting and receiving a floor plan of the room I would be using, I requested an initial chair layout of curved theater-style seating, as shown in Figure 12.1, and returned this diagram, superimposed appropriately on the floor plan. The conference organizer assured me that this arrangement would be in place.

FIGURE 12.1 • *Curved theater-style seating*

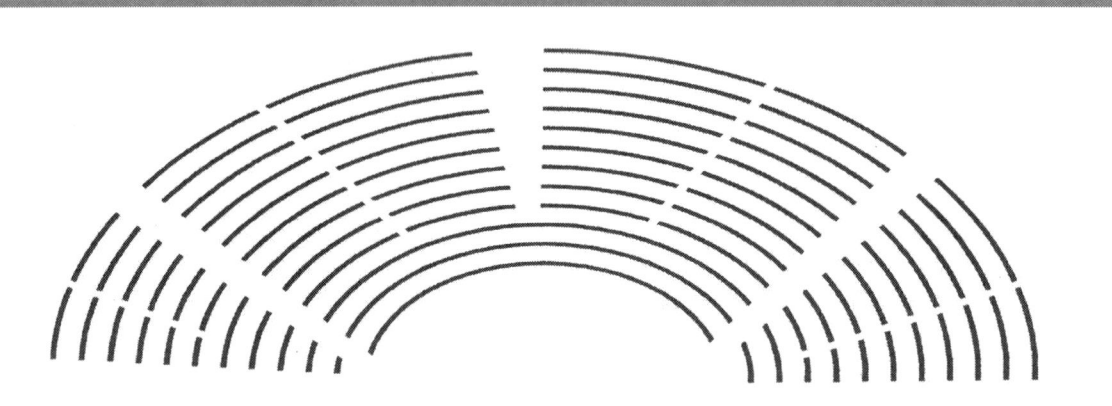

Arriving at the conference center an hour before my session started, I was concerned to see that the room had been set up in chevron style, as shown in Figure 12.2.

FIGURE 12.2 • *Chevron (aka herringbone)-style seating*

Unfortunately, chevron-style seating, while a slight improvement over traditional straight row theater seating, still requires most seated attendees to rotate their lower backs or necks throughout the session to face the presenter, and makes it hard for nearby audience members to see each other.

When I checked with the conference operations manager, she showed me her "approved" seating diagram for the event. Chevron. When I told her that I had requested curved theater-style seating, she showed me her binder of "approved" sets. Curved theater was not among them, so she had simply substituted the nearest alternative.

CHAPTER 12: The event space

Luckily, with only 120 chairs in the room there was enough time to adjust the chairs to the layout I had requested. During the session, the participants were comfortable and able to see and interact with each other.

Sadly, situations like this occur all too often. Despite years of requests like mine, many venues still don't understand how the right chair arrangement can enhance a session and aren't ready to deal with seating requests other than the few standards described in the next section.

Remember, don't take satisfying your seating needs for granted. You don't always get what you set!

CHAPTER 13 Seating

MOST PARTICIPATIVE PROCESS INVOLVES people sitting at some point, even if it's only while they're learning what they'll be doing. Although I've held sessions in meditation and exercise rooms that have comfortable mats and pillows that attendees can use for sitting, you should never assume that all participants will be comfortable without a chair. *You must be prepared to provide a comfortable chair for any participant who needs one.*

Because so many participation techniques require people to move into multiple and flexible seated groupings, it's important to create an event environment that can adapt to these needs. In most cases this means movable seating.

Avoid fixed seating

Auditoriums, lecture halls, theaters, places of worship, and cinemas can be impressive and tempting venues. But because they are designed with fixed seating to focus an audience's attention on a presenter, a play, a minister, or a movie they are poor candidates for participation-rich events. Rooms with fixed seating are not suitable for the great majority of the participation techniques described in this book. Avoid them whenever possible.

If you are nevertheless forced to work with fixed seating, some participative techniques can still be used. They include: *pair share*, *hand/stand voting*, and *card voting*. See the chapters on these techniques to see how they can be employed to maximum effect in a fixed seating environment.

Use comfortable, lightweight chairs

In 2008, Louis-Thomas Pelletier of Sid Lee[94] published "Fleeting Seating: The Slightly Uncomfortable Chair Collection," a short booklet of chair designs that discourage sitting for any length of time. This is an intriguing and occasionally tempting approach to keeping meetings short, but Pelletier could have just walked into many classrooms and meeting venues and found existing chairs that achieved the same purpose. This unfortunate reality is another reason for keeping participants sitting as little as possible.

Nevertheless, people need to sit for significant periods at most events. The majority of event venues will provide their own chairs for your sessions. Ask whether a choice of movable seating is available, and, if so, pick the most comfortable, lightweight chairs. Features to consider when evaluating seating comfort include: back support, seat and back padding, seats with a shaped front edge, and comfortable armrests.

Exercise ball chairs, often available for rental, offer an interesting alternative to conventional seating. Many people report that these chairs improve their posture, attention, and energy level during sessions. Because not all enjoy them, however, consider replacing only some of your seating with these chairs.

Soft seating and lounge spaces are attractive and useful ways to offer interesting and comfortable seating. But these seating choices are not easily movable, so they should be placed outside session rooms in varied arrangements for informal small group discussions.

Normally, venue chairs are lightweight, with individual chairs easily moved by one person. That's fortunate, since during a participation-rich session chairs may need to be moved multiple times, and you will be asking participants to help move chairs into each new grouping. Making this a communal effort ensures that the room change gets done quickly, even if some people cannot physically move their own chair or momentarily have something else to deal with.

If you have access to lightweight chairs with *functional* castors that roll easily over the floor surface in your session rooms, use them. Participants appreciate not having to lift their chairs when moving them or turning around.

Provide just the right number of chairs

Unused chairs add extra obstacles to and sap energy from a session room. It's rare to know exactly how many people will be present at a session and so the usual approach is to provide the maximum number of chairs that fit into the room. Unlike traditional lecture-style sessions, participation-rich sessions do not scale—more time is needed to work with 200 participants than with 40—and so the maximum size of a participation-rich session should be determined in advance. The room can then be set initially with this number of chairs.

Once the session is underway, if less than the maximum number of participants are present, remove extra chairs from the active areas in the room as soon as possible. You may be able to do this yourself if there's an exercise involving individual or small group work, and you may be able to enlist participants' help at certain points, for example, if you ask the group to form a single circle of chairs.

Although it's a little extra work to provide just the right number of chairs, it's well worth the effort.

Seating Matters

As the title of Paul Radde's excellent book on the subject proclaims: "Seating Matters."[95] What is often overlooked when considering seating is the arrangement of chairs in the room, known in the event industry as the *room set*.

Any venue that regularly hosts meetings will know what you mean if you ask for a room set in theater (straight rows of chairs), classroom (narrow tables in front of chairs), chevron (see Figure 12.2), banquet (chairs around round tables), or crescent (chairs around the front-facing portions of round tables) style. Unfortunately, *none of these traditional room sets are especially conducive to audience comfort or participative techniques.*

Radde proposes "five principles to set or troubleshoot any room." Here they are:

1. Set room to the long side.
2. Face each chair toward the presentation.
3. No middle aisle.
4. Cut single chair access lanes.
5. Place the last row on the back wall.

The rationale behind each of these principles and their detailed application can be found in Radde's book, but I'll outline the two most vital principles here.

The first—setting the room to the long side—is key. For some reason, event planners tend to do the opposite, with the result that those sitting at the back of the room are as far away from the front as possible. Having participants' chairs face the midpoint of a long edge of a room creates a much more intimate environment. I have used such a room set at several longtime venues where it had never been done before, and the venue management, after seeing how well it worked just once, became instant converts.

FIGURE 13.1 • *Set to the long side of the room . . .*

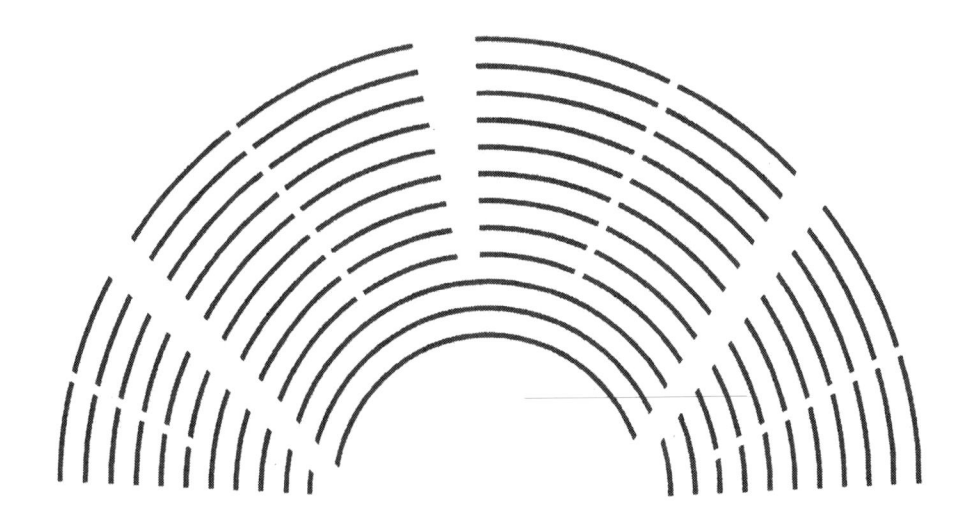

FIGURE 13.2 • *. . . not to the short side*

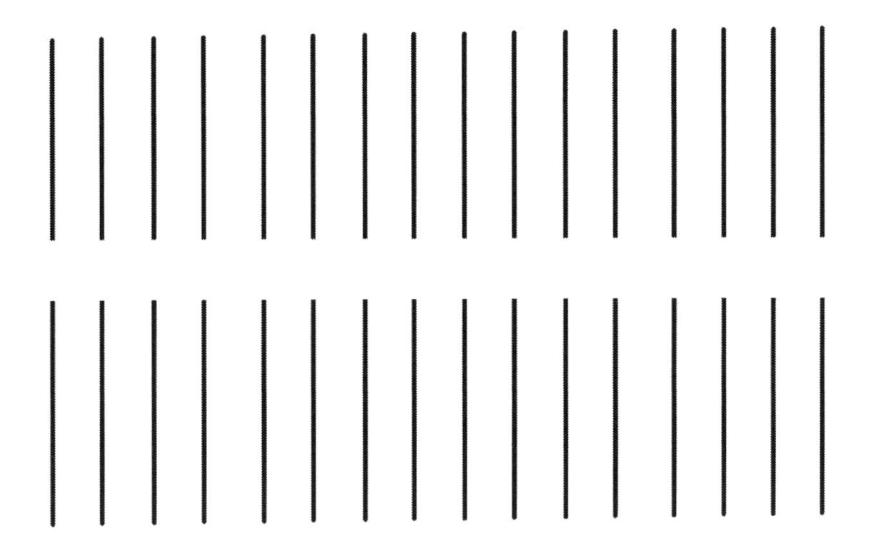

Radde describes his second principle as the one "that is most comprehensive, that includes the overall intention of all the principles."

Even when a session is participation-rich, there will almost always be some time, normally at the start, when a presenter will be introducing her topic, giving instructions, or showing visuals. During this time, *participants will be most comfortable if they are seated directly facing toward the presenter.* This principle may seem obvious, but none of the traditional room sets listed earlier follow it! Setting every chair facing the presenter provides the following three benefits:

- *Comfort*: The most commonly used room set, straight row theater seating forces most participants, especially those at the ends of rows, to turn their necks or lower backs permanently anywhere from 20 to 80 degrees to face a presenter. According to Radde, *sitting in such a twisted position will start to cause noticeable discomfort within 15 minutes.* Setting each chair facing the presenter maximizes the blood flow to participants' brains and their overall comfort.

- *Participants can see each other*: As Radde points out: "Does a meeting occur if people cannot see each other?" Straight row seating minimizes the visual connection between adjoining audience members. By facing each chair toward the presenter *the resulting curved row of chairs allows participants to see their neighbors' faces and body language.* Being able to pick up non-verbal cues and responses of those nearby significantly improves participant communication and interaction in a session.

- *Room capacity is maximized*: Many venue managers still believe that straight row seating maximizes the number of people a meeting room can hold. This is untrue. In fact, curved row seating, with every seat facing the presenter, often increases seating capacity by 5 to 15%, because curved row sets make better use of the front corners of the room.

Provide explicit seating instructions

Audience members are not accustomed to moving their chairs at meetings. As a result *it's important to give explicit instructions to move or turn chairs when needed*. A group that is asked to create a single large circle of chairs will rarely create anything closely resembling a circle without some verbal coaching and feedback. Participants who are asked to form small circles of chairs for group discussions will frequently create ragged arrangements with gaps, widely spaced chairs, or some chairs closer than others; ask them to tidy up or tighten up their circles. And when a session switches from small, seated, group discussion circles back to presentation mode, you'll need to direct participants seated with their backs to the presenter to turn around to face the front of the room.

Seating arrangements influence individual and group experience

There's a reason why I specify what might seem to be overly directive seating setups for the techniques described in this book. How we are seated influences our experience of an event. We intuitively know this: Humankind has used circle seating for group meetings throughout recorded history, while theater/classroom-style seating is thousands or more years old. My own experience facilitating hundreds of meetings has reinforced the influence of seating arrangements on group interaction.

Scientific research on this topic is minimal, but here's part of the conclusion of a 2013 study:

> "Circular shaped seating arrangements prime a need to belong while angular shaped seating arrangements prime a need to be unique. The shape of a seating arrangement, a subtle environmental cue, can activate fundamental human needs . . ." —*Rui (Juliet) Zhu and Jennifer J. Argo*[96]

Sit next to someone you don't know

When people enter a meeting room for a session they will naturally tend to sit next to people they already know. When you ask them to participate in group exercises, most people choose groups where they already know someone.

One of the easiest ways to increase connection in a session is to invite people to work with people they don't know. A session presenter or facilitator can act like a good host at a party by giving permission and the opportunity for strangers to meet. Simply instructing participants to sit next to people they don't know when they take their seat, or to work with people they don't know for a small group exercise creates great opportunities for new valuable connections.

Finally, before starting small group work, once the groups have been created (human spectrograms are excellent tools for this), request that people from the same organization join different groups by switching with someone from a different group if necessary.

When to use tables

Tables should only be used with participatory techniques when they are needed for the technique itself. Extraneous furniture removes intimacy from a room; it acts as a distracting barrier to direct connection. If you are holding a small group discussion, for example, have participants sit in a simple circle of chairs; don't fill the empty central space with a table.

During meals, participants usually will be seated around tables. That's another reason why sessions or presentations should not be scheduled during meals (for more, see the chapter on meals and refreshments).

If you need to use tables, use the smallest possible. Avoid the large rounds that facilities traditionally use for meals. Large tables make it impossible for people to have conversations with everyone at the table—the larger the table, the smaller the number of people any one person can talk to.

Regardless of table size, if people are to be seated at a table during a presentation, it's preferable for the seating to be only on the side facing the speaker. Otherwise, people on the other side have to crank their heads around to see the speaker, or turn their seats to face the speaker, thus losing the use of the table to take notes.

Use round tables whenever possible. Square tables are rarely available, but provide an adequate substitute. Rectangular tables can enhance status for the people sitting at the narrower ends and are best avoided.

Tables are appropriate when they:

- are covered with paper for communal notes, questions, mindmaps, and drawings.
- are needed to hold participation props and toys.
- serve as places to assemble for voting.
- do not interfere with the participatory activities in the room and are needed to hold refreshments for participants during long sessions.

Otherwise, avoid using them!

Rounds

Round tables, known as "rounds" in the meeting industry, are ideal for group work *when tables are needed*. The right table diameter depends on the number of people in each group. Tables that are larger than needed reduce the intimacy of the group, so choose the optimum group size and arrange for the correct size rounds in advance, as shown in Table 13.1.

TABLE 13.1 • *Optimum number of chairs to use for group work at round tables*

TABLE ROUND DIAMETER	OPTIMUM NUMBER OF SEATS
36"	4
48"	6
54"	7–8
60"	8
66"	9
72"	10

Personally, I find that 60" tables provide a subpar conversational experience. I strongly recommend not using group discussion tables larger than 60" for multiple table room sets, because they make it difficult for many people to hear those sitting across the table, even if the room has exceptional sound-deadening acoustics and the tables are spaced more widely apart than usual.

Note that this seating chart applies solely to group work not requiring extended or repeated attention given to front-of-the-room activity. When attention is being divided between table work and a presenter or visuals, participants whose chairs don't face the front of the room will need to frequently change position to stay engaged; something to be avoided. If your session requires this kind of adjustment, consider having participants face forward for an initial presentation of any visual components. Then have them face their tables and provide any subsequent facilitation orally.

Remember that setting a room with tables takes time (check with the venue). You may need to order a separate room for your session that can be set with the tables you need in advance.

CHAPTER 14 Information display

Attachment solutions

See the notes at the end of the book for references to specific products mentioned in this section.

Masking and painter's tape

If allowed by the venue, masking or painter's tape is a convenient method to hang paper and cards on a wall. I recommend 1 inch wide, fresh, name brand (e.g., 3M, Scotch) tape. A couple of 3-inch strips of tape placed at the corners will hold a piece of flip chart paper securely. To hang many sheets of paper, use a continuous strip of high quality double-sided masking tape.[97] Run the strip horizontally at about a six-foot height, and hang paper anywhere along its length.

Repositionable spray adhesive

Repositionable spray adhesive[98] can be used in a pinch to create a sticky note-like backing to paper and light cards. Spraying a large number of cards can be a trying and sticky process that should be carried out in a well-ventilated room. Test your spray beforehand on the product and venue wall surface to check that it has sufficient tack to keep items on the wall for your entire session or event.

Self-adhesive pads

Although much more expensive than plain paper pads, flip chart pads with a 2-inch strip of tacky adhesive at the top of each sheet enable you to quickly hang flip chart paper without masking tape.

Self-adhesive paper rolls

One way to create large drawing surfaces is to tape roll paper to a wall using continuous strips of masking tape. If the drawing surface has to be moved a few times, consider using an adhesive backed paper roll. Two such products are manufactured by Pacon: GOcraft! and GOwrite!

GOcraft! banner paper is available in 12 inch × 40 foot and 24 inch × 25 foot rolls. The paper is backed with a Post-it®-like adhesive. The manufacturer claims it will adhere indefinitely to a clean, hard surface and to textured surfaces such as fabric-covered walls for several days. While I haven't tried this product myself, Pacon claims that permanent markers can be used on this paper with no bleed-through.

GOwrite! is available in 18 inch × 6 foot or 20 foot, and 24 inch × 10 foot or 20 foot rolls that provide a surface that can be used with any dry-erase markers, and, according to the manufacturer, erases cleanly without whiteboard shadowing. The product is attached by removing a peel-off removable liner sheet and will adhere indefinitely to most hard surfaces, but not on textured walls for extended periods. Pacon claims that it will not ruin surfaces when removed, and can be moved "two or three times" before its adhesion deteriorates and the corners start to curl.

Sticky notes

Sticky notes are a great tool for "cards-on-the-wall" group techniques, like affinity grouping, and they are often the only material that venues will allow to be attached to walls. For small groups, 3″ × 5″ notes may be large enough, but I prefer to use 6″ × 8″ sticky notes[100] for large groups.

Pins

Thumbtacks, if allowed by a venue, are a convenient method for attaching paper and cards to bulletin- or corkboards. Buy map-style, not flat head, pins. At a pinch, straight or safety pins can be used to attach flip chart paper to draperies.

Cloth panel adhesive strips

For mounting to fabric-covered walls, use mounting squares,[101] which provide an adhesive side that attaches permanently to paper or card and a velcro-like side that provides strong yet removable adhesion to fabric-covered walls.

Cloth panel wall clips

Cloth panel wall clips[102] provide another convenient method for attaching paper and card to fabric-covered walls. They are more expensive than adhesive strips, but they can be moved and reused over and over again.

CHAPTER 14: Information display

Please let us post!

In the space of one recent month, no less than three venues (two hotels and a conference center) told me that posting anything on the walls of the room I was meeting in was not allowed. No flip chart paper, no masking tape, no stick pins, no thumbtacks, no sticky notes, and no wall clips.

To add insult to injury, none of the venues apologized or offered any suggestions on alternative ways to display materials on a vertical surface. Nor did they have available substitute surfaces, such as large portable notice boards, easels for flip charts, or whiteboards.

One meeting planner wondered whether I could use tables instead. Unfortunately, tables are rarely a reasonable substitute for walls for two reasons:

- *On walls, notes or cards can be placed anywhere in a 7-foot band between the floor and where people can reach; whereas on tables, human reach limits us to a 3-foot band.*
- *Information placed on a wall can be easily seen by many more people than that displayed on a table.*

Some of the most powerful group problem-solving techniques require displaying multiple pieces of information to an entire group, whose members can then easily and publicly move items around to cluster, list, sort, and map relationships. Schools have used blackboards for 200 years to display information to students, thumbtacks have been around for over one hundred years, masking tape was invented in 1925, and we've been using Post-it® notes for over 30 years. To venue managers reading this: These are not new technologies, folks; why are they now being banned from the walls of the spaces where your customers pay you to meet?

I understand that venues are used for many different purposes, and wall damage results from incorrect use of attachment technology or marker bleed-through. But "wall work" is an essential component of group problem solving, and for a venue to prohibit its use while offering no alternatives means that many meeting organizers will look elsewhere.

In the following chapter I describe some ways to post on walls that avoid wall damage and should be acceptable to any venue. Many of these methods are described in The Big Book of Flip Charts *by Robert Lucas,*[99] *an exhaustive guide to what can be done with those pads of 27″ × 34″ pieces of paper that we know so well. I've divided the methods into two groups:* attachment solutions *and* wall treatment solutions. *The latter need to be adopted by venue managers. If you are one, I hope you'll consider adding these options, making your rooms more meeting-friendly and adaptable for meeting facilitators.*

Vinyl dry-erase pads

Vinyl dry-erase pads[103] are 27″ × 34″ white sheets, packaged in a roll, that stick to a wall by static electricity. They will not stay up indefinitely, but work fine for temporary use. Because they stick to everything, they are not easy to install and should be put up before a session begins. They can be written on with either permanent (preferable) or dry-erase markers, but like most inexpensive whiteboard substitutes they are hard to erase completely, so plan to replace sheets after a few uses.

Wall treatment solutions for venues

IdeaPaint

IdeaPaint[104] is a treatment that turns any smooth flat wall into a dry-erase surface. It has to be applied correctly and is not cheap ($175–$200 for 50 sq. ft. coverage), though IdeaPaint's price compares favorably to the cost of a high quality whiteboard.

Steel or corkboard or wooden wall strips

One of the simplest ways to make a venue wall attachment-friendly is to install horizontal strips that can be used to attach flip chart paper. Such strips are available in various materials: steel (use magnets to attach), wood or metal-framed corkboard (use pins), and wood (use appropriately spaced straight pins or nails on which binder clips can be hung). Steel and wood can be painted to match the wall decor, while corkboard strips are generally attractive and unobtrusive.

Whiteboards

Whiteboards offer a permanent solution for writing and posting on venue walls. They are not inexpensive, but they offer perhaps the ultimate flexibility for meeting activities that require a vertical posting or drawing surface. The older (and less expensive) melamine surfaces suffer from "ghosting" of dry-erase markers over time and are not recommended for institutional use. Nowadays, most whiteboards use a hard porcelain finish over steel, which both reduces ghosting and allows the use of magnets to hold materials on the surface.

When working with small groups, small portable whiteboards are a helpful tool. Some portable whiteboards can also be hung on a wall, providing an effective way for participants to review multiple groups' work.

Pens

Although it sometimes seems that there are more kinds of pens in the world than there are people who write with them, you should be familiar with a few different categories of writing implements and when to use them. The three criteria that affect your choice are: color, stroke width, and writing surface.

Different colors can be used to:

- Visually indicate a specific group's work.
- Make it easier to read flip chart notes by alternating colors between adjacent lines.
- Highlight specific notes or flip chart points for further review.
- Make posted participant contributions more visually appealing.

Stroke width determines how easily a piece of writing can be viewed at a distance. When writing for a group, use wide chisel tip markers in *dark* colors. Write big, reserve all caps for headings, and use sentence case elsewhere. If you're using venue-supplied markers, check that they work before the start of the session (as well as the number of sheets remaining on any flip chart pads provided).

Writing surface determines the kind of writing tool used: permanent or non-permanent marker.

Ballpoint/rollerball pens or ultra fine point markers

Use these kinds of pens when attendees need to write notes for themselves. Ultra fine point markers are more expensive but can add a dash of color to notes.

Fine tip marker pens

Supply fine tip marker pens when attendees need to write notes that can be read at short distances: for example, on sticky notes that are posted on a wall for a small working group or for participants who will walk up to the wall to view them.

Permanent markers

Permanent markers are used to write group flip chart bullet points or diagrams. The resulting writing can be read 30 to 50 feet away.

Non-permanent/dry-erase/whiteboard markers

If whiteboards are available at the event venue, be sure to use dry-erase markers on them, not permanent markers!

Navigational aids

Much valuable meeting time is wasted when attendees are confused about where they should go. Navigational aids—in the form of location identities and navigational signs—are essential for all but the smallest venues, and should be carefully planned and installed before the event.

Make sure all navigational aids are easily readable (and multilingual if appropriate) and that outdoor elements will withstand local weather conditions (spoken like the Vermonter I've been for over 35 years). Physical landmarks, colors, thematic elements, symbolic objects, signs, banners, and logos can be used to indicate that an attendee has reached her intended destination.

Navigational signs should be posted at all path decision points. When creating navigational signs, put yourself in the position of an attendee who has never visited the venue before. Start with the directions you distributed to registrants. As they pull up to the venue entrance, where should you place signs and directional arrows so attendees know they've arrived at the right place and can see where to go next? Once they've parked their cars in the correct parking lot, are there signs pointing to the registration location? From registration, they'll need directions and appropriate signage so they can find their rooms and make their way to the conference sessions. Finally, attendees will need signs that direct them, in either direction, between any two session locations.

Planning in advance where and when locational identities and navigational signs need to be posted will greatly reduce attendee confusion, questions, and annoyance.

Apps

Since *Conferences That Work* was published, the availability and adoption of conference apps has mushroomed. Every week I receive solicitations to review new conference apps, whose prices range from free to tens of thousands of dollars with a concomitant wide range of functionality.

Many conference apps allow conference organizers to readily prepare a list of attendees, together with headshots and, optionally, contact information. Such functionality can potentially replace the paper face books I've been using for years during opening roundtables (see Chapter 32), although such a digital face book rarely allows real-time note-taking tied to specific attendees.

There are many aspects to consider when deciding on a conference app that is appropriate for your meeting(s): cost, support, app type (see sidebar), and features. A good comprehensive free resource is The Event App Bible.[105]

Native and web apps

Make sure you understand the difference between the two kinds of conference apps—*native* and *web*—before choosing a conference app.

Native apps are programs installed directly on a mobile device; they must be designed specifically for the mobile devices on which they're installed. This means that the developer of a native conference app must supply a version for each of the major mobile platforms. In 2015, this means one or two versions for Apple's IOS (iPad/iPhone), an Android app, and perhaps a Windows phone app. Once installed, native apps work largely independently of an internet connection, except when updates are needed. They are therefore preferable if internet access at the conference venue is intermittent, low bandwidth, or otherwise problematic.

Web apps are effectively mobile websites. They will work on any device with a web browser, but require constant connection to the internet to operate. Web apps, therefore, do not require any additional app to be installed on an attendee's mobile device; however, they will rely on a reliable internet connection.

CHAPTER 15
Timing

Staying on time

Sadly, many conferences are marred by poor timekeeping. While conference organizers, presenters, and facilitators understand the importance of staying on time, all too often, they don't follow through. Being short-changed on the time for sessions, suffering limited or eliminated breaks, and having published schedules altered with no advance warning due to earlier overruns lead inexorably to unhappy attendees. Apart from emergencies, I see no good reasons to depart from a clearly communicated session and break schedule. Having an explicit ground rule about staying on time, as described in the previous chapter, helps maintain a close correlation between a published schedule and reality.

This chapter provides timekeeping methods to monitor and communicate the passage of time in conference sessions. If this job is done well, the entire resulting event is much more likely to remain punctual.

Timekeeping for balanced sharing in groups

Many small group techniques require giving each participant an equal amount of time in turn to work with the rest of the group. You probably won't be surprised to learn that participants rarely accomplish this goal without clear guidance. When people are discussing a compelling topic in a small group, they don't notice how much time has passed and will happily overrun any given time limit unless it is gently but firmly enforced.

I find it helpful to provide two alerts; the first after ~80% of each participant's allocated time has expired, the second when the time is up. So I'll give a first alert for a 3-minute exercise 30 seconds before time is up, while a minute or more warning is appropriate for a 6–10-minute exercise. Use a different sound for the warning and final alert.

Ideally, assign a dedicated timekeeper to monitor the passage of time and sound the relevant alerts. In my experience, few people can provide reliable timekeeping while simultaneously participating in a session. If you, as session facilitator, have to take on the timekeeping function, I strongly recommend using timing software as described below, because it's very difficult to stay focused on what's happening in the room if you are also monitoring elapsed time on a watch or clock.

When small group members are asked to share in turn, there is a distressingly common propensity for groups to descend into their own private freewheeling discussions in which some people take more than their share of the time available, or interrupt other members who are sharing. Don't underestimate this tendency! Attendees are usually so happy to have the opportunity to talk with each other about topics of mutual interest that they quickly lose track of time. I suggest prefacing small group sharing sessions with the following instructions:

- You will hear a warning alert [number of] seconds before each participant's time is up and a final alert. <Demonstrate the alerts.>
- Do not move to the next group member's sharing until the final alert is heard.
- If a group member finishes before his or her allotted time, the others in the group should ask more questions and promote additional discussion. If time still remains, it can be used to further discuss earlier group member sharing.
- Groups that are smaller than [the default group size] should use their extra time for general discussion after all group members have taken their turn to share.

When calculating the amount of sharing time available for each group member, reduce the calculated time for each participant by 15–20 seconds. This time will be used to switch to the next group member.

Recommended timekeeping methods

A watch with a seconds hand, plus manually made warning and "time's-up" sounds.

Using a watch is the simplest timekeeping method but requires the most attention. You will need a dedicated timekeeper who will not participate in the session. As each attendee starts to talk, the timekeeper notes the position of the seconds hand and figures out when the two alerts should be given. The timekeeper must keep looking at her watch, so it's hard for her to concentrate on what attendees are saying.

You can use small Tibetan hand cymbals or a struck metal chime to make the alert sounds. I prefer a chime, since it can be sounded with one hand, while the cymbals need two. If you don't have anything available to make a sound, an extrovert timekeeper can usually be found to say "beep" or something similar.

Two inexpensive digital timers

You can use two inexpensive digital timers or timer apps running on smartphones to provide audible alerts. Timers must be able to count down in minutes and seconds (some can only count down minutes). The timekeeper sets Timer A to count down the time until the first warning. She can either start Timer B at the same time as Timer A, set to count the full attendee time, or she can set it to 30 seconds and start it when Timer A sounds. I prefer the second approach, with only one timer running at any moment.

Managing two digital timers is less distracting than using a watch, since once a timekeeper sees that a timer is counting down she doesn't have to keep checking to see whether an attendee's time is up. Unfortunately, most digital timers beep annoyingly while being reset and do not reset themselves to the original countdown time if stopped before the time period has expired. This means the group is subjected to distracting beeping whenever a participant does not use his full time.

A multiple event digital timer

Some digital timers can time multiple events in a single unit (search for "lab timers"). Most are not well suited to timing small group process. Common problems include: having to press multiple buttons to start and reset two event timers, a small display, buttons that become unreliable after a short time, and timers that start to count up after time is up.

A computer-based timer

You can use a laptop computer to run timing software that provides all the ideal functionality listed above. There are plenty of timer programs available for computers running the Macintosh and Windows operating systems, but few provide exactly what we need for small group timekeeping. An exception is the Macintosh program *FlexTime* from *Red Sweater Software*. FlexTime. It allows you to quickly create a custom sequence of a 30-second warning sound, a "time's-up" sound, and, if needed, a "you've overrun your time" sound. You can use any sound sources you want for the sounds. See the FlexTime sidebar for more details.

I'm not aware of a comparable program for Windows computers. Please contact me if you find one (or write one)!

Digital music player and pre-built audio timing recordings

I've used the FlexTime timer to create a series of audio tracks, available on www.conferencesthatwork.com, that can be played on an iPod or other digital music player through some small portable speakers. This is a convenient way to provide correctly timed alerts for small group timekeeping. If you are using an iPod, once you've chosen the correct timing track, I suggest you place it in an On-The-Go playlist by itself (highlight the track and press and hold the Select button until the title flashes) so other neighboring tracks don't play by mistake during the roundtable.

How to use FlexTime for group sharing timekeeping

FlexTime, version 1.2.6 at time of writing, is available for download from Red Sweater Software,[106] requires Macintosh OS X 10.4 or above, and works on both PowerPC and Intel Macintoshes.

Because FlexTime can play any Macintosh alert sound, you can use any sounds you like for your roundtable alerts, as long as they are in AIFF format and installed correctly. An Apple article[107] describes how to convert a sound to the AIFF format using iTunes, and explains how to add the sound as an alert to OS X. Many suitable sounds are available on the Internet. You can obtain chimes and other sounds for no cost from *freesound.org* (registration is required).

Use a different sound for the warning sound and the "time's-up" sound, so attendees know whether they need to wind up their answers, or stop. For a large group running The Three Questions or a Roundtable (see later chapters), it's a good idea to add a "you've gone over your time and must stop now" sound. I like to use a chime for the 30-second warning, an old-fashioned telephone ring for the "time's-up" sound, and a klaxon for the overage reminder.

I use FlexTime with two scripts, one that I use to demonstrate the sounds when introducing the timed technique, and one to play the sounds at the right times for each attendee. It's easy to create two or three alerts by adding additional timers after the first.

The first script, *Demo sounds*, plays the warning sound when started, waits 7 seconds and plays the "time's-up" sound, and waits 7 more seconds and plays the overage sound.

To use the second script, *Group sharing timer*, set the first timer to the time required before the 30-second warning. When started, the timer waits for this time before sounding the warning sound, plays the "time's-up" sound 30 seconds later, and after another 20 seconds plays the overage sound.

The scripts are available from *www.conferencesthatwork.com*.

You can export the audio from these scripts to iTunes and then transfer the audio to an iPod or other music player. If you create a set of timed audio tracks, each using a different attendee speaking time, you can use an iPod and small portable speakers to provide timed chimes for your roundtable. A set of these audio recordings is also available on *www.conferencesthatwork.com*.

CHAPTER 16
Giving up control

YOUR EVENT'S ENVIRONMENT IS SHAPED by *the level of your control*. I suggest you consider ways to give up control of your event and share decision-making with participants.

Let's be clear about what I mean by "giving up control." I am not suggesting that you abandon control over *logistical* aspects of your event. Gatecrashers, long registration lines, bad food, cold rooms, inaudible presenters, and a myriad of other annoyances that mar the conference experience are not appreciated by attendees. But using *process* that minimizes control over participant behavior is another matter altogether.

I like to tell participants at the start of my events that *we will be treating them as adults*. I explain that this means that although we have created a packed schedule, we expect participants to actively decide what they will be doing during our time together. This includes *not attending sessions* because they want to rest or do something different, and *advocating for and creating alternative formats and sessions* that meet individual or small group needs.

I also say that the event's organizers will, whenever possible and practical, support such needs if and when they arise during the event.

Why do this?

When you explicitly release control over some of what happens during your conference sessions, you are saying two things:

- "I believe that you possess valuable knowledge and experience, and are willing and able to share it with others.
- I am confident that you can decide what you want to learn, with whom, and how."

Telling participants that you will be treating them this way is refreshing and empowering for them. It increases the likelihood that they will think about what they want to have happen at the event and ask for and/or act to bring about the conditions necessary to satisfy their own needs and desires.

I believe it's important to be explicit about giving up control. Although participants will skip sessions without us giving them permission, and a few may ask whether the event can accommodate something special they'd like to do, I've found that giving people explicit permission to do these things makes it more likely that they'll take place in a positive way for both participants and the event as a whole.

If your participants are adults, why not treat them that way?

The Myth of Control

"Misconception 7: Conflict is bad. . . . The reality is that whenever you have more than one living person in a room, you'll have more than one set of interests, and that's not a bad thing." —*The Change Handbook*[108]

Why do we cling to traditional event structure? One powerful reason is because we want to avoid dealing with messy differences of opinion. When we give attendees the power to choose what happens at our conferences, people are going to disagree. And when people disagree, there's the possibility of controversy and conflict. Who'd want that at their event?

Perhaps you believe that learning is some kind of linear process that happens to you. If you do believe that conference learning should be passive, let me ask you this. Think for a moment about the most important things you've learned in your life. How many of them came to you in the absence of disagreement, pain, or conflict? And how many of them did you learn while sitting in a room listening to someone talk for an hour?

Do you want your conferences to maximize learning, even at the cost of some disagreement or discomfort? Or would you rather settle for a safe second best?

We are anxious about not having control in our lives and at our events. That's why we lock down our conferences, forcing their essence into tightly choreographed sessions. Attendees are carefully restricted to choosing, at most, which concurrent session room they'll sit in.

The reality is that you never had control to begin with, just the semblance. You've been kidding yourself all these years. Unless your constituency is bound to your event via a requirement to earn CEUs, members can withhold their attendance or avoid sessions at will. And these days, many can be there in body, while their minds are on whatever they're doing with their cell phones.

Fortunately, there are multiple ways to give up the unnecessary control exercised at traditional conferences and give attendees the freedom and responsibility to make the event theirs. All participant-driven event formats treat attendees like intelligent adults.

What's amazing to discover is how liberating participant-driven designs are for conference organizers too. When we give up over-control, we become largely freed of the responsibility to choose the content, format, and instigators of our conference sessions, concentrating instead on supervisory, facilitation, and support roles. Yes, the result is an event that is less predictable, and often more challenging. But the richer experience, the creation of an event that reflects what participants truly need and want, and the joy of uncovering valuable, unexpected, relevant learning make it all worthwhile for everyone involved.

CHAPTER 17
Safety

> "... [B]rain research suggests that the brain learns best when confronted with a balance between stress and comfort: high challenge and low threat. The brain needs some challenge, or environmental press that generates stress ... to activate emotions and learning. Why? Stress motivates a survival imperative in the brain. Too much and anxiety shuts down opportunities for learning. Too little and the brain becomes too relaxed and comfortable to become actively engaged. The phrase used to describe the brain state for optimal learning is that of relaxed-alertness. Practically speaking, this means [we] as designers and educators need to create places that are not only safe to learn, but also spark some emotional interest through celebrations and rituals." —*Jeffery A. Lackney*[109]

The word *safety* has a couple of meanings. The first is *objective*: the degree of protection from undesirable environmental hazards. At events, we increase the objective safety of attendees by eliminating or minimizing the likelihood of tripping, slipping, falling, falling objects, food poisoning, and so on.

The kind of safety covered in this chapter is *subjective* safety: *How safe do attendees feel?* As the quote above indicates, if we are to optimize learning at a meeting we want participants to be relaxed but alert; in a state I like to call *nervous excitement*.

It's easy to create a meeting environment that feels unsafe for most if not all attendees. Without careful preparation, asking people to dress up in costumes and dance on stage, or give impromptu talks to a large audience will evoke feelings of discomfort and fear in almost everyone.

It's also easy to create a safe event environment by treating people as a passive audience, not required to participate in the proceedings in any meaningful way. Unfortunately this is often the choice made by many meeting organizers who are, themselves, afraid of what might happen if attendees are subjected to something "new" and perhaps not predictable.

So, how do we strike a balance between unduly scaring attendees and treating them as inactive spectators?

It's not easy.

Creating the right amount of nervous excitement for a group of people is challenging, because each of us responds uniquely to different situations. For example, meeting someone new at a social break might be easy for John and scary for Jane, while Jane has no problem skydiving from an airplane at 12,000 feet, a prospect that terrifies John—and probably most of the rest of us too.

Ultimately, *we can't control other people's feelings* (let alone, often, our own)! Consequently, *we are unable to guarantee that any particular individual will feel safe* during a meeting session. But there are some things we can do to improve participants' experience of safety when they are faced with the new challenges invariably associated with learning and connecting.

Create an environment in which you can feel OK about making mistakes

> "Learning is fun when errors don't feel like failures."
> —Laura Grace Weldon[110]

Why is feeling OK about making mistakes important? With traditional broadcast learning, your comprehension of the material presented—or lack of it—is something that happens in your brain and is essentially invisible to everyone but yourself. In a social context, this creates a great deal of safety; no one can easily see what you don't understand.

But because experiential learning requires us to do something external, like talking to our peers about our understanding or ideas, or physically performing an activity, we lose this invisibility safety net. This brings up the possibility that others may experience us doing something "dumb," "awkward," "slow," and so on.[111]

As someone who was educated in a school where knowing the "right answer" was praised and lack of knowledge or understanding denigrated, I felt ashamed about "making mistakes" in public for many years. Unfortunately, this is a common experience that almost every child who attends school learns to some degree.

So how can we create an event environment in which it's easier to make mistakes? Here are three suggestions:

1. Keep the ball in the air

One of the first games used to introduce improvisational theater (improv) to those with no prior experience is *keep the ball in the air*, usually shortened to *ball*. Players stand in the circle and a

~12" diameter hollow rubber ball is tossed into the air. The object of the game is for the group to keep the ball in the air with any part of their body, with the game ending if anyone contacts the ball twice in a row or the ball touches the ground. Holding the ball is not allowed. Each ball touch adds one to the group's score, which the group shouts in unison after each contact. A game rarely lasts more than a minute or two, so many rounds can be played in a short time.

Games of *ball* get a group working together on a goal, provide a challenge (reach a higher score than in prior games), include physical movement, and are fun to play. While each round of *ball* ends because the ball hits the floor or is touched twice in a row by the same person, the thought that the last person who contacted the ball failed in some way doesn't matter the way it does in an actual competition. Everyone just wants to play another game of *ball*.

There are many variants of *ball* used in improv, including playing with one or more imaginary balls. When you are tossing and receiving multiple imaginary colored balls to people in your circle, everyone *will* "make mistakes" (if they don't, the leader just increases the number of balls), and again *it doesn't matter*. Everyone making mistakes is simply part of the game.

Games such as "Keep the ball in the air" and other improv exercises provide wonderful opportunities for people to get used to making mistakes. That's why they are increasingly used for leadership development and organizational team building. Games such as *ball* provide an enjoyable transition to environments where making mistakes is the norm, rather than something to be ashamed of.

If you decide to use improv to ease participants into getting comfortable with making mistakes, here are two tips:

- Consider having an experienced improv teacher who is clear on what you want to achieve guiding the session.
- Don't call what you're doing improv. Don't call it games. Just ask people to take part in the activity. An experienced teacher will know how to do this.

2. Tell participants that it's impossible to make mistakes

Another way to create a safe environment for what participants might otherwise feel is risky is to simply tell them that *whatever they do is the right thing*.

For example, when I introduce the opening technique *The Three Questions* (Chapter 31) at an event, I tell participants that it's impossible to answer The Three Questions incorrectly. Whatever answers they give are the correct answers. This sounds almost too simple—but it works surprisingly well!

3. Model being comfortable with messing up

It's crucial that facilitators and leaders of conference sessions model the behaviors they wish participants to adopt. If I am not comfortable with facilitating new or impromptu approaches that may or may not work, how can I expect my participants to be comfortable attempting them? This doesn't mean, of course, that I should deliberately mess up, or decide not to prepare adequately, which is sure to result in mistakes. But responding in a relaxed manner when I do take a wrong turn provides a reassuring model for participants to adopt and follow.

The right to not participate

It's important to explicitly give attendees the right not to participate. When starting a new activity, clearly state that people do not have to take part, for example, "You are welcome to participate or not in any activity. It's entirely up to you." When working with a group, do not put specific individuals on the spot to participate; ask the group as a whole for feedback/ideas/answers/volunteers instead.

At the start of an extended (adult) event, I want to be sure people understand they're going to be treated as adults, unlike experiences they may have had at other events. I encourage them to make decisions about how and when they will participate, and explain that they are entitled to take time out from scheduled activities, or devise their own alternatives when desired and appropriate.

However, it's also fine to set limits on nonparticipants—a common example would be to ask nonparticipants to leave the session for the duration of an activity rather than staying to watch.

Provide clear instructions

I've found that providing clear instructions is one of the hardest things to do well when leading a participatory activity. After many years it's still not unusual for someone to complain that they don't understand the directions I've given. I recommend writing out a narrative for exercises beforehand and practicing until it feels natural and unforced. However, this won't cover *ad hoc* situations when unexpected circumstances arise and you need to improvise.

In addition to sharing instructions verbally, consider displaying them on a screen or wall posters, or providing a printed copy for each participant. Once you've shared your instructions, *ask whether there are any questions*, and then *pause long enough (at least 20 seconds) for people to formulate and request clarification of what they don't understand.*

Learn from participant feedback. Remember what was not clear and revise your instructions as soon afterwards as possible, so that the next time you run the exercise you will, hopefully, be better understood. It may take several attempts before you find the right choice of words, so keep at it!

Consider providing explicit ground rules

In the next chapter I make a case for providing explicit ground rules at the start of sessions and events. In my experience, doing this can significantly improve participants' sense of safety while working together.

Conclusion

> "There are people who prefer to say 'Yes', and there are people who prefer to say 'No.' Those who say 'Yes' are rewarded by the adventures they have, and those who say 'No' are rewarded by the safety they attain."
> —*Keith Johnstone, Impro: Improvisation and the Theatre, Routledge, 1987*

As Keith Johnstone reminds us, people choose to participate or not for their own reasons. *Respect their choice*, while making it as easy and safe as possible for them to take the risk of trying something new.

CHAPTER 18 Ground rules

Traditional conferences and conference sessions have no overt ground rules. I think that this is an unfortunate oversight. Here's why:

Explicit versus implicit ground rules

Many people are surprised when I advocate for the need for explicit ground rules at sessions and conferences. "Why do you need them?" is a common response.

So perhaps it's worthwhile pointing out that every traditional conference has ground rules. We just never talk about them. They're *implicit*.

Here are some common implicit ground rules for attendees:

- Don't interrupt presentations.
- Don't ask questions until you're told you can.
- The time to meet and connect with other attendees is during the break, not during the session.
- Applaud the presenter when she's done.
- Don't share anything intimate; you don't know who might hear about it.
- The people talking at the front of the room know more than the audience.
- Don't talk about how you're feeling in public.
- If you have an opposing minority point of view, keep quiet.

And a few more for conference organizers (a little tongue-in-cheek here):

- Don't reveal your revenue model.
- Never explain how a sponsor got onto the program.
- Don't publish attendee evaluations unless they're highly favorable.

You can probably think of more.

Of course, each of us has slightly different interpretations or internal beliefs about implicit ground rules like these, and that's what causes problems.

When explicit ground rules aren't agreed to at the start of an event or session, no one knows exactly what's acceptable behavior. Think about what it's like when you have to go to a conference and don't know the dress code. The result is stress, much like when we want to do something that might not be OK, such as ask a question, let a presenter know we can't hear properly, or share a personal story. We're social animals, and most of us don't want to rock the boat much. The end result: We play it safe; we'll probably remain silent. And an opportunity to make our experience better and more meaningful is lost.

A common misconception about explicit ground rules is that they restrict us from doing things. ("Turn off your cell phones." "No flash photography.") Actually, good ground rules do the opposite; they increase our freedom of action. That's because, by making it explicit that certain behaviors (e.g., asking questions) are permitted, they remove stressful uncertainty and widen our options.

Crucially, a conventional conference session offers no expectation of or agreement to privacy for anything that is said. As a result, only the most confident or highest status attendee is likely to be comfortable revealing a lack of knowledge in some area, sharing a problem that he has, or asking a "stupid" question. Without a public group commitment to confidentiality, participants fear that what they say at the conference may make its way to their superiors or colleagues in their organization. This leads people to censor themselves on many topics.

I have been amazed at what occurs at a session when attendees agree to keep confidential what is shared. Giving people permission, encouragement, and a safe environment in which to express themselves and take risks makes a huge difference. It becomes easy and natural to ask important questions, reveal oneself, and be vulnerable, exploring beyond one's habitual boundaries. Many participants find that taking risks can be rewarding, less scary than they'd imagined, and even fun.

Feeling safe is a prerequisite for attendees to be open to intimate sharing and making connections. So my conference sessions start by supplying a set of ground rules that define a supportive and safe environment. After these rules are briefly explained, attendees commit to them, establishing a secure and comfortable environment for what is to come.

As attendees experience and practice sharing while supported by the framework of the ground rules, intimacy, respect, comfort, and excitement develops as they begin to make meaningful connections with the people they are with.

The ground rules I use send participants the following powerful messages:

- "While you are here, you have the right and opportunity to be heard."
- "Your individual needs and desires are important here."
- "You will help to determine what happens during this session/conference."
- "At this session/conference, you can create, together with others, opportunities to learn and to share."
- "What happens here will be kept confidential. You can feel safe here."

FIGURE 18.1 • *Six suggested explicit ground rules*

The Four Freedoms
In an empowering environment, everyone has the following freedoms:

1. You have the freedom to talk about the way *you* see things, rather than the way others want you to see.
2. You have the freedom to ask about anything puzzling.
3. You have the freedom to talk about whatever is coming up for you, especially your own reactions.
4. You have the freedom to say that you don't really feel you have one or more of the preceding three freedoms.

These four freedoms are deceptively simple but effective. It is our hope that this conference will provide you with such an empowering environment. You can help us by exercising your four freedoms while we are together.

The two other ground rules

5. What we discuss at this conference will remain confidential. What we share here, stays here.
6. We ask that you start and end all sessions on time.

Reproduced with permission from www.conferencesthatwork.com

What ground rules should I use?

Facilitators of a group that plans to work together for an extended period of time will sometimes have the group establish its own ground rules, not only because group-developed ground rules will handle the specific needs of the group, but also because the process of development creates buy-in for the rules that are chosen. For single sessions and short conference, it takes too much time to brainstorm and negotiate ground rules. Consequently, I've chosen to use the rules shown in Figure 18.1. I have refined them over many years and find them to work extremely well.

I *do not* claim that these six rules are the definitive or only possible set of ground rules. But my experience is that this set of rules is effective in creating an environment in which participation and sharing flourish.

If you are running a single session, you may not have enough time at the start to explain these rules as completely as described below. If so, introduce the relevant ones briefly (e.g., "feel free to ask questions at any time"; "please treat everything said at your table as confidential") as needed.

I provide these ground rules to participants on a card describing the *Four Freedoms*, a rule about *confidentiality*, and a rule about *staying on time*. I explain the rules at the start of the session or conference, and attendees are asked to commit to them while they are together.

The Four Freedoms

All of us have a comfort zone for our interactions with others, a social space inside which we feel comfortable. The boundaries of this zone vary, depending on who we are interacting with, our context (home, professional, social, etc.), and the level of safety we feel in a specific situation.

The Four Freedoms are ground rules derived from the work of family therapist Virginia Satir and further refined by Gerald Weinberg, Donald Gause, and Norman Kerth.[112] Here they are:

- You have the freedom to talk about the way you see things, rather than the way others want you to see.
- You have the freedom to ask about anything puzzling.
- You have the freedom to talk about whatever is coming up for you, especially your own reactions.
- You have the freedom to say that you don't really feel you have one or more of the preceding three freedoms.

The Four Freedoms invite attendees to be fully present with each other.

The first offers the gift of talking freely about what a person sees and understands, despite what others may think or say.

The second offers the gift of asking freely about what a person does not understand.

The third offers the gift of freely expressing feelings in response to what is happening.

The fourth offers the gift of freely discussing the lack of any of the other three freedoms.

In my early conferences I did not offer Four Freedoms to attendees. Since I started including them, my sessions have felt more intimate and empowering. The Four Freedoms create a supportive, safe environment for people to take risks and speak about subjects, beliefs, questions, and feelings that they would not normally share. This environment encourages attendees to commit to and engage in the conference experience, rather than remaining passive observers and occasional contributors.

I end my introduction to the Four Freedoms by asking each attendee to help all of us by exercising their four freedoms while we are together.

In my experience, *offering these Four Freedoms at the start of a conference or session encourages attendees to interact beyond their normal comfort zone.* This is a heady experience for many attendees who have never before felt empowered to be either proactive or revelatory while at a conference.

There are three conditions that enable these freedoms to become an integral part of the conference or session culture.

1. The Four Freedoms have to be clearly communicated. Participants must understand up front that they are free to express their point of view, it's okay to ask any question, it's fine to talk about how they're feeling, and they can speak up at any time they feel these freedoms aren't available to them.
2. The conference or session presenter(s) must model using the Four Freedoms during the conference. (I frequently invoke the second freedom: "I'm sorry, I don't understand *XYZ*.") If you don't do this, attendees will rightly conclude that the Four Freedoms are empty words, and the conference or session environment will suffer.
3. Attendees must actively commit to the Four Freedoms and the two other ground rules listed below. How this is done is described below.

Confidentiality

The confidentiality ground rule further enhances attendee safety:

> *What we discuss at this conference will remain confidential. What we share here, stays here.*

Adopting this rule frees participants to talk about many intimate topics. Difficult situations and associated feelings, relationships at work, questions unasked for fear of revealing incompetence, even the simple enjoyment in meeting kindred souls are common examples of what may be shared at peer conferences.

It surprises and saddens me how rare it is for such a ground rule to be adopted. Being able to safely share and be heard is often of the greatest importance to attendees, sometimes far more important than even conference content. This ground rule provides an environment for attendees who may have no other avenue to communicate confidentially and safely with their peers.

Staying on time

How many conferences have you been to where sessions started late or ran late, wasting the time of the people who were punctual, and cutting into later sessions? Breaking the tacit agreements promised by a published schedule irritates attendees, and reduces their trust in the value of the event. When schedule times prove unreliable, people are more likely to arrive late and leave early. This causes further problems—arriving late at a session is disruptive in itself, and latecomers may want to ask time-wasting questions about content they missed.

We can't prevent people from arriving late to a session. But we can publicly request that sessions start and end on time, and ask the people who are organizing sessions to honor this desire. (A conference can also *support* staying on time by having someone available to remind session presenters to begin and end at the times when their sessions are scheduled to start and end.) I've found that simply having attendees agree to the following ground rule:

> *We ask that you start and end sessions on time.*

together with appropriate reminders during a conference, ensures punctuality.

Committing to ground rules

Imposing ground rules on attendees, no matter how well chosen, is an empty gesture unless there is group buy-in. Providing a list of ground rules, asking whether anyone has any objections, taking silence as assent, and hastily rushing on to the next agenda item implies that the rules are just a formality and needn't be taken seriously. But, given that we have little time to spare, how can we get some kind of commitment from participants?

I like to use a brief ritual requiring active attendee participation. I say:

> *"I would like all of you who commit to using Four Freedoms, maintaining confidentiality, and staying on time to stand."*

(People who have difficulty standing can raise their hand instead.) Simply asking attendees to change their physical stance to demonstrate their commitment to the conference ground rules may not seem like a big deal, but it's an unusual enough request to get everyone to think, if only for a moment, about what they are committing to and to help cement the ground rules in their minds. If anyone doesn't stand, say, "Everyone standing sit, everyone sitting stand," ask those standing to explain what they feel they can't commit to, and, if necessary, work on an agreement as to how to proceed.

Treating participants like adults

Although it isn't a ground rule, I'll often mention at this point that we will be treating participants as adults during the session or event. For more about this, see Chapter 16 on *giving up control*.

Conclusion

It takes no more than a few minutes to present and adopt the above ground rules. The positive effect on a participative conference session can be dramatic. Try them and see for yourself!

CHAPTER 19
Play and fun

> "If you watch a small child explore the world, they don't need to be told to study, explore, experiment or learn; they do it naturally. Schools today have been insistent on dividing work and play, holding them out as opposites and confining play to a 40 minute break in the day called 'recess.' One of the things we think is the most important about the new culture of learning is that play be seen as a critical part of all learning." —*Steve Denning*[113]

When I run an experiential learning workshop I usually show a family movie clip, chosen more or less at random from YouTube, that shows a little girl playing with her older sister in a wading pool. As the movie plays I point out the continuous learning that is taking place in this 30-second snippet of a child's life. The small girl tries to catch a toy, improves when thrown a ball, experiences what the water feels like on her flapping hands, and turns toward her mother, who is filming, when she hears a sound of encouragement.

Every child learns like this. *And adults do too*—if we let it happen!

> "As the pace of change increases, games become an increasingly attractive occupation, playfulness an increasingly valuable asset. Play is how we have learned to learn.
>
> Instructions? We don't need no stinkin' instructions. We play our way to understanding. We learn how to use a new browser, not by reading about it, but by using it, playing with it. That's how we learn how to work our smartphones and iPads, microwaves and multi-function thermostats. We use them, we play with them."
>
> —*Bernie DeKoven, The Need to Play*[114]

CHAPTER 19: Play and fun

We have evolved to learn through play. Our ability to play as a vehicle for learning does not magically vanish as we grow older. Yet in our society play has become, to a large extent, something that only children are routinely expected to do. For adults, play invariably needs to be ritualized to be acceptable, through vehicles such as parties, festivals, organized games, and carnival. We are embarrassed by playing in public, as if we cannot be adults when we are being childish, even though learning through playing is one of the most powerful learning modalities available to us.

You can't force people to play, but you can create an environment that's friendly and supportive of play and fosters learning while people are having fun. Here are three ways to do this:

Be alert for opportunities for spontaneous play and fun

While talking to a trade show vendor at a conference, somehow I discovered that he played the bagpipes. "Wow," I said, "it's been years since I heard someone piping." "Would you like to hear me play them?" he replied, with more than a little eagerness. "I've got a set in the trunk of my car."

How could I refuse? The trade show space had an entry lobby where I quickly organized a space for my impromptu piper to play and made an announcement that a surprise show would be happening during the next break. The piper was a big hit, adding nicely to the informal and relaxed feeling of fun at the event.

People like surprises like this, and many good event producers manufacture them to delight participants. While there's a lot to be said for this, I'm always on the lookout for serendipitous opportunities that might be turned into enjoyable additions to what's been planned.

Laughter

Welcome and foster laughter at your events. Not preprogrammed professional humor, but spontaneous laughter that bubbles up at all sorts of unexpected moments. Why? John Cleese says it well:

> "A wonderful thing about true laughter is that it just destroys any kind of system of dividing people."
> —*John Cleese, TV Club interview*[115]

Supply a physical environment that suggests and encourages play and fun

If you're ever in Chicago with an hour or two to spare, check out the Catalyst Ranch event space. (Or take a virtual tour.)[116] Words can't really do it justice, but the venue is full of bright colors, hundreds of different chairs and seating options, artwork, ethnic furnishings, toys, music options, flexible room layouts, breakout spaces, and plentiful food options.

Without question, event environments like this stimulate and support creativity, play, and fun. It's hard to spend any time at Catalyst Ranch without finding just the right chair for your current activity, an irresistible toy to fiddle with, and the room space that works for your task of the moment.

Can't take advantage of a venue with all this built in? There's still plenty you can do at any event. Set up places where participants can play and have fun. Then provide some gentle encouragement (or plant a few willing volunteers) to start playing. Install flip charts with plenty of pens everywhere, set up play areas stocked with items like silly putty, finger-paints, and office toys.[117] Perhaps you can set up an art wall with a vertical sheet of Plexiglas®, where people can draw on both sides simultaneously. And, maybe, just maybe, you'll declare a zone where water pistols and Nerf™ guns are available and may be judiciously enjoyed.

Your choice.

Games

Games, when done right, can be one of the most effective ways to:

- help participants to get to know one another in ways that are more fundamental than via professional protocol.
- increase participant energy levels and alertness quickly, enjoyably, and effectively.
- create a relaxed environment for learning.

I am not a fan of the recent trend toward "gamification" of events (see sidebar). Instead I recommend quick lighthearted games that can act as transitions and energizers between session activities.

Bernie DeKoven is an incredible resource for these kinds of games. He reached millions of people as the co-director of the New Games Foundation in the 1970s, consulting on the design of the New Games Training, and helping to create an alternative to competitive sports that now is taught at elementary schools all over the world. His website[118] contains a wonderful repository of pretty much any kind of game you might want to play.

And having said that, I'll let Bernie have the last word.

> "In the process of growing up, most people lose touch with the sources of their personal power. Those sources: play and laughter, especially when they are whole-hearted, whole-minded, whole-bodied. When people play and laugh, and play and laugh fully, and especially when they play and laugh playfully, they are engaged, involved, in charge. That's it. That's all you need to know."
>
> —Bernie DeKoven, *Play, Laughter, Health And Happiness*[119]

Thoughts about gamification

I am not the only person who has serious reservations about the introduction of "gamification" into events. Gamification can be defined as applying game design to meeting or session activities with the aim of making them more fun and engaging. The hope is that this will lead to improvements in learning, connection, or other associated goals. Gamification is typically done by integrating scoring systems (points, badges, levels, etc.) into a task, adding competitive elements, and providing a combination of incentives, positive feedback, and rewards for "playing." For example, location-based games—in which teams have to check-in to locations, solve puzzles and clues, and complete challenges—can help participants get to know each other via a fun activity.

Increasing the amount of fun and engagement while people are learning or connecting is a worthy goal. The crucial question is whether adding extrinsic motivations to a task replaces or corrupts participants' intrinsic motivations. If we are focused on getting to the next level or beating another participant or team, this may well detract from the intrinsic joys and rewards of learning itself. In a sense, the points obtained become the focus of the experience rather than the achievement goal(s) they attempt to represent.

Perhaps the strongest positive aspect of gamification is its potential to provide feedback about the quality of individual participant's learning and competency. For this to work, the feedback best originates from a third party, such as expert judges or realistic consequences built into the game by independent observers. However, unless this feedback is anecdotal and detailed I believe it is unlikely to significantly improve participant learning.

Gamification is probably most useful as a tool for improving abilities at rote tasks, such as improving selling skills, for which acquiring proficiency is not much fun under any circumstances. Such work, however, is becoming a smaller and smaller portion of important adult learning.

CHAPTER 20
Facilitation

WE ARE ALL FACILITATORS OF HUMAN INTERACTION AND PROCESS. Even when conversing with one other person we are facilitating, to some extent, our interaction via our listening, responding, noticing feelings, giving and receiving feedback—in short, via all the subtleties of human communication.

I say this because I'm frequently asked about the need for expert facilitation of the process and techniques covered in my books. "Should we hire trained facilitators, or can we do this ourselves?" is a common question.

After more than 20 years working with a wide variety of adult groups, my observation is that such groups almost always contain enough people with sufficient facilitative skills—gained like mine through life experience, experiment, practice, and reflective learning—to run the vast majority of the techniques described in this book at an adequate and useful level. (The exceptions are the case studies and simulations described in Chapter 53, which generally require extensive planning and, ideally, appropriate training or prior experience.)

I have also found that those people who have the necessary facilitative skills are usually realistic about their abilities. They may be a little reluctant to agree to lead a process that's new to them, often feeling normal nervous excitement about doing something they haven't done before. But with a little coaxing and friendly encouragement they will generally try it out, with a very high likelihood of good outcomes.

That said, if you have access to experienced facilitators, they are clearly prime resources for implementing the techniques shared in this book. If not, trust your own judgment or that of the group that is organizing the relevant session or event.

Thousands of books have been written about facilitation and facilitative leadership[120] and I will neither do the topic justice here nor comprehensively tackle conveying such a subtle human skill in writing. Instead I'll touch on some facilitation issues that are especially relevant for successfully implementing the techniques covered in this book.

The task of facilitation

> "The role of government is to create the appropriate infrastructure and then get out the way."
> —Angus King, Governor of Maine (1995–2003)

In a similar fashion to King's perspective, I see the task of facilitation as providing the right amount of structure, process, and support and otherwise staying out of the way.

Too much structure, process, or support leads to excessive formality that gets in the way of productive participation, while too little leads to chaos, frustration, and dissatisfied participants. Sadly, the right amount is not something that can be clearly defined in advance. Rather, it is a constantly changing goal that every conscientious facilitator constantly strives for, intervening here, fading into the background there, always with the goal of creating an optimum experience for the group with which she is working.

> "The way to get things done is not to mind who gets the credit of doing them." —Benjamin Jowett

This dance of balance requires that when you are facilitating a group, the focus needs to stay relentlessly on the people in the group and the work they are doing together—not you! They gain benefits from their participation in group activities and their interactions with each other—not you! Your role is to provide the structure, process, and support they need to be successful. Acting on the desire to be in the spotlight detracts from the value of the experience for everyone.

Facilitation as leadership

> "... Jerry Weinberg describes organic leadership as leading the process rather than people. 'Leading people requires that they relinquish control over their lives. Leading the process is responsive to people, giving them choices and leaving them in control.' Jerry's resulting definition of leadership is 'the process of creating an environment in which people become empowered. . . .'
> I also find Dale Emery's definition of leadership helpful. Dale describes leadership as 'the art of influencing people to freely serve shared purposes.'"
> —From my first book, Conferences That Work: Creating Events That People Love[121]

These definitions of leadership for peer conferences are also helpful for facilitators of participative group process. Creating an environment in which people become empowered is, to my thinking, the fundamental goal of good facilitative leadership. The various processes described in this book are some of the tools that will well serve a skillful facilitator.

A common misconception is that facilitative leadership is the sole responsibility of a single individual. Yes, I think it's important to have at least one person who takes overall responsibility for running a session, technique, or process—but a healthy participative environment allows the possibility of leadership temporarily devolving to an appropriate participant.

Process leadership is different from content leadership

The techniques described in this book can be applied in almost any meeting environment. It doesn't matter whether the participants are community activists, owners of independent garden centers, financial conference planners, association managers, or camp counselors (some of the groups with whom I've had the pleasure of working). These techniques are relevant because they involve *process* leadership, not *content* leadership.

A content leader has experience or expertise in the content of the session, and will generally contribute and affect the content shared there. The extreme example of a content leader is a traditional presenter who provides all the content.

A process leader, in contrast, concentrates on managing the process of the session and is neutral on the content. This is why a facilitative leader can work effectively with people with expertise in topics that she knows nothing about—her ability to facilitate group process is independent of content knowledge and experience.

While specific content knowledge can be helpful when working with group process—familiarity with content terminology is often useful—I haven't found it to be a prerequisite when facilitating group process. And if facilitative leaders with relevant content expertise and experience switch from a neutral to a contributory role they should be sure to explicitly point this out to the group.

Giving directions

It's surprisingly hard to give clear, unambiguous directions when facilitating. No matter how hard you try to be clear, some participants will misunderstand aspects of what you say, or be distracted as you speak.

Rehearsing your directions in advance, preferably with someone who can give you feedback about anything that's unclear, will help. In addition, while running the technique, check that your directions are heard and understood, both when they are given and subsequently as participants carry them out. Strive to create an environment in which questions are welcomed, ask for questions before a process begins, monitor participant activity once the process is under way, and quickly clear up any misunderstandings or confusion that you notice.

Using *permissive language* makes it easier for people to follow directions. Phrases such as "I'd like you to . . ." (rather than "I want you to . . .") and "You might . . ." can help reduce the natural resistance many people experience when asked to do something.

Bringing people back on track

We all digress from time to time. Conversations can change focus in a moment—Bill is holding forth about Californian wines when Juan jumps in talking about the best meal he ever ate at a restaurant in San Francisco, then I switch to a story about the incredible improv conference I attended in Fort Mason Center (which is in San Francisco) last year and Susie asks me whether I've met her brother-in-law who does improv and I say . . .

This is fine when you're shooting the breeze after work, but it's counterproductive if you're attending a conference session that's billed as a discussion of the latest North American culinary trends. If you're a session facilitator, one of your responsibilities is to steer the proceedings appropriately. Here are a few suggestions that can help.

- Notice participant body language. Are people looking frustrated, zoning out, or fidgeting? Or are they energized by the new direction the session has taken? Use this information to decide what to do. For example, you might ask whether it's time to move on to another topic, or propose a 15-minute break.
- If you decide an intervention may be needed, draw attention to what is going on. You might say something like "I'm noticing that we're digressing from our session topic right now." This may be all that's necessary to bring participants back on track.
- If the topic shift has some energy and focus behind it, after drawing attention to the shift you may want to add, "Do you want to continue discussing Y or should we park it and go back to our original topic X?" Get a few quick representative suggestions and facilitate an appropriate resolution, which could include general agreement that those present would really rather be talking about Y for the remainder of the session.

Facilitating effective communication

Our lives would probably be a lot less frustrating if we understood exactly what everyone who ever speaks to us means to convey. Unfortunately, until we develop Star Trek's mind-meld it ain't gonna happen, so when group members interact there is going to be a certain amount of bafflement, confusion, and misunderstanding going on much of the time. As a facilitator, you can improve effective communication between group members in three ways.

- Provide an environment in which it's OK and easy to ask questions. The easiest way to do this is by having participants agree in advance to an appropriate ground rule (see Chapter 18).
- Speak up if you hear people using acronyms or jargon that others may not understand. You can simply ask what it means—even if you know.

- Notice when confusion or misunderstanding may be occurring, check whether your observation is accurate, and ask for clarification. Watch participants' body language and rely on your own experience—if you don't understand something, perhaps others don't either.

Supporting engagement

The techniques in this book gently encourage and support *every* participant to contribute to the learning and interaction in a session. Nevertheless, you will probably encounter people who are reluctant to engage in what you're offering. What should you do if someone is not participating?

Recognize that you cannot force people to become engaged in what you are offering. Ultimately, each person gets to decide for himself. What you can control, however, is the potential effect on those who *are* participating. Because "observers," especially those who make it clear—often nonverbally—that they question the value of an activity, may inhibit active participants, it's perfectly reasonable to politely ask them to leave the room while the activity is going on.

The gift of listening

I was facilitating a roundtable when a young man began speaking. He was obviously nervous: his voice a monotone, when it wasn't quavering. I was peripherally aware that some people didn't seem to be listening. He paused for a moment and his eyes swept around the circle, searching for a sign that anyone cared about what he had to say. He found me.

I was leaning forward, looking directly at him, giving him my full attention. Our eyes locked and I nodded slightly. He took a breath and continued. His voice became stronger. I saw people turn back to him and he finished well.

I had just given the gift of listening, and this young man had been nourished by it.

When I am facilitating, it's my responsibility to actively listen to what is going on, focusing my full attention on what others say and do. When I'm successful, those who are present know that there is at least one other person who is listening to them and who takes seriously what they have to say.

Listening like this is hard work. To conscientiously listen to participants for over 2 hours at a large roundtable is extremely challenging for me. But it's worth the effort. People need to be heard, and if they sense they will not be heard, why should they bother to speak? By offering good listening, I model and encourage a conference environment in which openness twinned with receptiveness becomes a safe option for participants.

There's a wider benefit from the cultivation of this skill. Practicing listening when required by my role has helped me to be a better listener in other parts of my life—when I'm a participant, or with my family, or as a customer. You, too, may find that developing your ability to fully listen pays rich dividends.

CHAPTER 21
Small group selection

MOST PARTICIPATORY TECHNIQUES REQUIRE SMALL GROUPS. Deciding how these groups will be formed should not be an afterthought. This chapter explains why it's a good idea to guide group selection, lays out selection criteria, and describes various ways to perform effective group selection.

Why you should facilitate small group selection

Here are two reasons why you should use a thoughtful process to form small groups.

First, leaving it up to participants to choose their other group members tends to lessen learning. When allowed the choice, we naturally tend to create groups with people we already know. Though having friends or colleagues in your group is comforting, it can limit open sharing and resulting learning, especially about intimate or controversial issues. Psychologically it is often easier to share with strangers who we may well never meet again, as we are spared any future consequences or repercussions arising from what we say.

Second, one of the principal advantages of small group work is the opportunity and ease of making new, useful connections with others. The practice, common in some cultures, of requiring an introduction by a third party before meeting and conversing with someone still has force in today's meetings. A group selection process essentially acts as a third party, giving people who do not yet know each other a formal introduction by assigning them to the same group and then guiding them into activity together.

Goals for small group selection

Before dividing people into small groups you need to be clear on the reasons for forming them. Those reasons determine the selection strategy. Here are the most common objectives.

Have people meet and connect with new people

It takes time for two people to meet and start to get to know each other through conversation. Add a third person, and this process takes two to three times longer. Why so much longer? Because two people need only *one* conversation, but three people need *three* pairs of conversations, less some time saved because some of what one person says to another in the trio might contribute to connection with the third group member. Four people need six conversations, five people ten, ten people 45, and so on.

Dividing participants into small groups helps to ensure that everyone will connect with a minimum number of others for a chosen quantity of time and/or process. By selecting the group size used, we can control the level and amount of person-to-person interaction that's appropriate for the participation technique we've chosen.

Performing activities that require groups of a certain size

Many of the techniques described in this book require group sizes in a specific range, either because the technique itself demands it, or due to the time constraints of the associated session or event. For example: opening roundtables (Chapter 32) become unwieldy and tiring with more than 60 participants, pair share in a fixed seating auditorium would not work with more than two people per group, and affinity grouping with 500 people would take too long to be effective.

Growing communities of practice

Educational theorist Etienne Wenger coined the term *communities of practice*, defined as "groups of people who share a concern or a passion for something they do and learn how to do it better as they interact regularly." Events are usually designed to meet the needs of communities of practice. To *grow* communities of practice during a session or event, members need opportunities to interact among themselves in ways that deepen their connection around their common interests.

Unfortunately, in large groups, interaction loses coherence. Either one person is talking while everyone else listens and conversation disappears, or multiple side conversations spring up in the same physical space, which is potentially distracting and dispiriting for everyone present.

The larger the group the harder it becomes to hold a genuine conversation. Typically a few people monopolize opportunities to speak, and the rest listen or tune out.

If you wish to support the communities of practice at your event, restrict large groups to broadcast-style activities where they're appropriate, such as lectures and presentations. The rest of the time, use small group activities that allow meaningful connections to increase and strengthen.

Obtain a wide variety of perspectives

A common goal for small group selection is to create groups of mixed experience, abilities, and viewpoints (aka *heterogeneous* groups). Mixed groups enable novices to interact with experts, those who have just entered a profession or field with gray-haired veterans, vendors with potential clients, academics with practitioners, and those of different political and social stripes with each other. If we want to foster new learning, catalyze original viewpoints, share restricted knowledge and experience, we need to create heterogeneous groups in which the differences encourage the kinds of creation, worldview growth, and learning that we want.

Allow similar participants to work together

Sometimes it's appropriate to create groups in which members share similar experience and/or abilities (aka *homogeneous* groups). In training situations, for example, you may wish to group novices and those with prior experience separately so they can work on a given task with others who are at a similar level. The novice groups can then practice without being embarrassed or intimidated by the superior skills of those who have performed the task before.

Another example when homogeneous groups are useful is when both industry practitioners and suppliers of products and services attend the same conference. You may wish to keep these two groups separate during small group work so that the practitioners feel free to discuss information about suppliers or their own circumstances that they would be uncomfortable sharing with the suppliers—and vice versa.

Incidentally, I avoid assigning participants to tables by geographical origin, as at most conferences people prefer meeting those they consider their true peers irrespective of whether they work near each other.

I suggest limiting the use of homogeneous groups. In heterogeneous groups, novices learn from more experienced participants and the latter usually enjoy being helpful to the former. Additionally, novices often contribute effective questions and a fresh viewpoint to even the most jaded practitioner. If it's unclear to you which kind of group would be most effective for your particular circumstances, it's unlikely you'll be disappointed by choosing groups with a variety of experience, abilities, and perspectives.

How large should small groups be?

Some participation techniques such as pair share dictate the size of a small group, but most of the techniques in this book can handle a range of sizes. Often, the desirable group size will be influenced by the time available for the technique. If time is tight, choosing a larger number of smaller groups will allow each member more time to share. On the other hand, larger groups provide a wider range of perspectives and more resources for group and individual problem solving.

In general I'd avoid creating groups of more than eight. There should be enough time for each person in a small group activity to have at least a few minutes to talk and share. General discussions can be larger, but small group intimacy is lost in larger groups.

General considerations when forming groups

Ask for a commitment to stay for the entire small group process

It can be, at the very least, disconcerting if one or more participants leave in the middle of small group process. Session facilitators need to stay alert for such incidents.

To reduce premature participant departure, make it clear that, barring unexpected circumstances, participants are expected to stay for the duration of the small group process. (Be sure to specify how long it will last!) Then give those who can't fully participate time to leave.

Although it's obviously impossible to ensure that everyone will stay throughout the life of a small group, making it clear before group formation begins that the process will suffer if people are planning to leave early will help minimize the disruption that the loss of a member can cause.

Small groups using a common process should be approximately the same size

If you're planning to run the same process with a number of small groups, they should be as close to the same size as possible. (An exception to this is if you're running small general discussion groups on topics with a range of participant interest; even under these circumstances, avoid groups of wildly different sizes—consider splitting popular groups to maintain roughly equal group sizes.) If you don't ensure similar sized groups, those in the larger groups will be short-changed with respect to the quantity of individual participation and attention they get.

In practice, successful small group sizing entails ensuring that each group either contains your target number of people or has, *at the most*, one fewer person.

This can be surprisingly hard to achieve! People tend to disregard directions when creating multiple groups. Typically, they form more groups than are needed and do not actively look for spaces in existing groups. Read the instructions for group formation below to avoid this.

Splitting large numbers of people into small groups takes time; usually more than you'd expect. Be sure to allow for this when estimating your timing for a session.

Performing group selection

Here's how to do heterogeneous (differing abilities/experience) and homogeneous (similar) group selection.

Heterogeneous group selection

The simplest and quickest way to seat more than around a hundred people in a fairly heterogeneous way is to seat them at random, asking them to sit at one of a set of tables with preset chairs or in given size circles of chairs *with people they don't know*. With fewer than a hundred participants, ask them to count off as you point to them (see below) and then sit with those with the same number. These methods usually work well enough, unless people ignore your request to sit with others they don't know.

To guarantee a heterogeneous mix of participants in each group, first decide on a participant measure that you'll use to define heterogeneity. This is nearly always the number of years of industry/field/topic experience of participants, though you can substitute another measure if it's more appropriate.

Count the number of people present, divide by the number of chairs at each table or in each circle and round up your answer to the nearest whole number.

For example, if there are 53 participants and eight chairs you'll need 6.625 tables, which you round up to seven tables. (In this case, you'll end up with four tables with eight people each and three tables with seven people each.)

It's helpful to have the tables or circles of chairs set up in advance, with a card at each displaying the table/circle number (in the example above, one through seven).

Now have participants line up in a one-dimensional human spectrogram (see Chapter 33) in the order of the measure you've chosen.

Start at one end of the spectrogram, point to each person in turn, and have people count off from one up to the number of tables or circles of chairs needed; that is, the first person says "one," the next, "two," and so on, and in the example above the seventh person says "seven," and then the eighth starts again at "one," and so on. Tell everyone to remember his or her number. When everyone has counted off, ask any who don't recall their number to figure it out by asking their neighbors.

Finally, have participants move to their respective table/circle of chairs.

Homogeneous group selection

To create homogenous groups based on a single measure, like years of experience, use a similar procedure to the one described above. Once the human spectrogram is lined up, simply split the line into groups of the desired size. For example, with 56 participants in seven groups of eight, the first eight people would be in group one, the next eight in group two, and so on.

To create homogeneous groups that are divided by industry/job description/etcetera, first ask the people in each category to move to separate places in the room. Then create the small groups from each category in turn, by asking people to move into equal-sized groups with people they don't know.

CHAPTER 22
Getting attention

You've probably attended events where the timeliness of the scheduled activities increasingly deteriorates as the day goes by. This is especially common at small events when sessions are held in a few rooms, and the tardiness of one session impacts everything that's scheduled from that point forward. Either the event ends much later than scheduled, or, more likely, the last few sessions are drastically truncated. The resulting state of affairs is always unfair to someone, usually the leaders of later sessions, and always, ultimately, the participants.

On the other hand, you'll know when your session or event is going well when people don't want to stop talking to each other to listen to you! I need to remind myself of this frequently, as it's quite frustrating trying to make announcements and being ignored. So I'll tell participants at the start of an event:

- "One of my responsibilities is to keep the program on time";
- "I often have a hard time doing this"; and
- "Please forgive me if I come across as irritatingly insistent."

Clearly, having someone whose job it is to make announcements and who is prepared for keeping sessions on time is important. So what are the best ways to get adults' attention?

Whatever strategy you choose, share and demonstrate it at the beginning of the event. I've experimented with many methods over the years, starting with props that make distinctive sounds, such as Tibetan gongs and chimes. Although this approach works quite well for a short event, I've found that over several days its effectiveness falls off. My favorite attention-getters these days are techniques that you may well have experienced in kindergarten. (Sometimes the old ways are best.) Here are the three that I use.

Raising hands

One method to get a group's attention is to agree at the outset that when you see a hand raised, you stop talking and raise your hand. As hands rise and room volume lessens, more people realize what's going on and join in. I find that this technique works better if you ask people to the raise *both* hands—it seems to be harder to continue talking if you have both arms in the air!

Clap once, clap twice

Say "If you can hear my voice, clap once," and then clap your hands once. Say "If you can hear my voice, clap twice," and then clap your hands twice. By the second clap, usually enough people will have joined to get everyone's attention. If not, continue with "clap three times." If that still doesn't work, repeat from the beginning.

Distinctive music

A workshop I've been staffing for many years uses a 1-minute version of Richard Strauss's *Thus Spake Zarathustra* (better known as the opening music of Stanley Kubrick's 1968 film *2001: A Space Odyssey*) as a signal that participants need to end conversation and be seated, ready for the next exercise, by the time the music ends. Obviously any memorable short piece of music can be used. This simple technique both indicates the ends of breaks and gives people a predictable time to make the transition back to group work.

CHAPTER 23
Asking questions

KNOWING HOW TO FRAME GOOD QUESTIONS is a skill that can make a big difference to the effectiveness of an interactive and participation-rich conference session. Many of the participation techniques described in this book rely on questions as part of their process framework. Here are some important considerations when designing and responding to questions in a participative environment.

Ground rules for questions

Although I personally like to take questions at any time during a session, others prefer that attendees save them for breaks or the end. When questions can be asked is up to the leader or facilitator of a session. *It's vital, however, that ground rules for questions are clearly communicated at the start*, whatever they may be: for example, "Feel free to ask me questions at any time," or "I'll answer questions after the next exercise." If confidentiality is appropriate, establish an appropriate ground rule at this time (see Chapter 18).

In addition, make it clear *how* questions can be asked:

- Spoken out loud (in a small group)
- Raising a hand
- Using a mobile app, website, or audience response system (ARS)
- Writing on sticky notes or cards that are then posted or collected
- Walking to a microphone
- Raising a colored card (see Chapter 47).

CHAPTER 23: Asking questions

Crafting questions

Once you're clear what you want to ask, you still need to phrase the question appropriately. Here are some tips to take into account:

- If you're *training*, it's fine to ask questions to which you know the answer (leading questions).
- But if you're *facilitating*, don't ask leading questions—simply offer the answer.
- Define any terminology *before* you use it.
- Make your questions clear and inviting.
- Ask one question at a time.
- Start with low-risk questions that put participants at ease.
- Tone is important! For an example of what *not* to do, watch the economics teacher "anyone, anyone" scene in "Ferris Bueller's Day Off."[122]
- Reduce the perceived threat of a challenging question by preceding it with "Has anyone ever . . . ," "Have you come across . . . ," "Does anyone here have experience with . . ."
- Open-ended questions generally foster more thinking than yes/no questions.
- Give people the opportunity to share how they *feel* about a topic, rather than just what they *think* about it.
- Don't FRAP—fix, repair, advise, or project.

Additional considerations in using questions

We are all accustomed to classroom teachers asking for verbal responses to their questions. Without supplying quiet time to think before taking answers, this can be a disservice to introverts, who tend to prefer thinking silently about their answer before verbalizing it. As a result, extroverts often dominate verbal discussions. You can equalize the playing field by waiting an appropriate amount of time after you've asked the question before requesting verbal responses. (Note that *if you think "appropriate" here means 2 seconds, you're an extrovert* and the introverts around you will appreciate much more time to think than you: perhaps 20 seconds.)

If the question requires significant thought, I recommend asking participants to write down their answers before discussing them. This is extremely helpful for introverts.

One of the best ways for participants to learn is to work in pairs or small groups to create written questions for each other about session topics. Once the questions have been devised, have each person ask the other group members their question(s).

When you are asked questions

In a successful interactive session, you'll be posing questions and are likely to receive a few yourself. When you do:

- Unless the questioner has a microphone or the group is small, repeat the question so everyone can hear it.
- If you're asked an especially good question, tell the questioner that it's a great question.
- If you aren't sure you understand the question, ask for clarification: "What do you mean by . . . ?" or "Are you asking me . . . ?"
- Should a question include unsupported assumptions, bring these to light and discuss them with the questioner before responding;
- It's fine to say "I don't know" or "Give me a moment; let me think about my answer" or "I don't have an answer to that right now, but I can think about your question and get back to you (by the end of the day)."
- Use the questions you are asked as a valuable source of feedback on participants' learning, experience, and comfort level with the session.

Meta-questions

Here are some useful meta-questions that explore learning and probe deeper:

- If you wanted to know whether someone got the most important point of this session, what question would you ask him?
- Can you give an example?
- If we are successful, what will it look like?
- What puzzles you about [topic/issue]?
- How would you suggest a friend handle something like that?
- What is the best piece of advice you can give?
- What do you suggest we do next?
- What questions should I be asking that I haven't asked?

Be careful with "Why?" questions

"Why?" questions are fine when asked as a genuine open question to a group. In other circumstances—especially when asked to an individual—questions that start with "Why" often come across as aggressive and/or implying fault. (Of course, sometimes, that's just what the questioner intended.) If you're tempted to use a "Why?" question, see whether you can replace it with a more specific "What?," "How?," or "When?" question. Often you'll find that the resulting question is better, and less likely to put a respondent on the defensive. Alternatively, "What is/was the purpose of . . . ?" has fewer emotional overtones than "Why?"

Be comfortable with silence

After you've asked a question, a subsequent silence can feel uncomfortable. If you break this silence prematurely, you'll reduce the amount of time participants have to think about their responses. Sit with the discomfort until someone responds, or it becomes clear that no answer is likely to be forthcoming. This is hard to do initially, but becomes easier with practice!

A (sometimes) magical question

One of the most common answers to a question is *I don't know*. (I'm not saying it's *especially* common, just more common than "cheddar," "42," or "in the second drawer on the left.") Generally, it's a good answer because it's likely to be an honest one. After all, all kinds of trouble may ensue when someone confidently answers a question about which they really haven't a clue.

But occasionally someone—let's call him Paul—answers with *I don't know* after a pause, perhaps in a hesitant manner, that makes you wonder if perhaps he *does* have an interesting answer "at the back of his mind." Here's a magical follow-up question that often gets a more specific, useful answer.

Let's suppose that a specific problem has been identified and described by Paul and you ask him:

"What would the solution look like?"

Paul, after a pause, says hesitantly:

"I don't know."

Here's the magical follow-up question, asked in an even tone:

"If you did know, what do you think the solution would look like?"

Now stay quiet and wait for an answer.

You may get another, puzzled, *I don't know*, but more often than not, this reframing of your original question will evoke a specific answer to your question.

I'm not a psychologist, but I believe that this follow-up question frequently works because we don't consciously know everything we know. The "if you did know" addition gives Paul temporary permission to ignore his stated lack of knowledge and potentially tap his experience and expertise at an unconscious level.

Note that if Paul appears confident that he doesn't know, this is *not* the right question to ask. Also, if you have a hunch that the magical question might work, don't ask it in a condescending way, that is, implying that you know Paul knows the answer but *he* doesn't.

More questions?

For additional information on effective questions and question technique, see Dorothy Strachan's book *Making Questions Work*.[123]

CHAPTER 24
White space techniques

I DEFINE WHITE SPACE TECHNIQUES as those that *increase participation by adapting, improving, or eliminating features of the conference environment.* We've already covered ways in which the event space itself can help or hinder participation; this chapter describes other aspects of the conference environment that can help or hinder participants' natural desire to network and connect.

While much of this book focuses on increasing the quantity, quality, and variety of participation during conference sessions, we *mustn't ignore the rest of the time we're together at an event.*

Far from it.

In fact, one of the best ways to improve participation at events is to rethink the amount and format of "out-of-sessions" time. Here are some ways to do this:

Provide more out-of-sessions time

Many program committees cram sessions into their event's schedule. This is understandable. Attendees often commit significant time and money to travel to an event and attend sessions, and, the thinking goes, we should give them good value for money by filling the program with as many sessions as possible.

Unfortunately, program cramming only makes sense up to a point. As we've seen in the earlier chapter on learning, we don't learn or retain learning well when we're stressed and tired. Providing scheduled downtime for attendees to rest and recharge can lead to better overall learning and a more enjoyable conference experience than if we jam activities into every available minute.

Scheduled downtime is especially appropriate if your event includes training or sessions that must be attended in order to maintain professional certification. If that's not the case for your conference, consider the following approach, which allows you to offer a full program by devolving downtime choice to the conference participants.

Give attendees explicit permission to miss sessions

Every conference attendee has different interests and circumstances, and unique energy levels and biorhythms. No matter how carefully constructed, there's no way that a conference schedule can optimally satisfy every attendee. As a result, unless a conference is very short or attendance is mandatory, just about every attendee skips one or more sessions at some point during the event.

Given this reality, one way to approach the need for personal breaks at an event is to explicitly hand the responsibility for taking time to rest and recuperate over to the participants themselves. I usually do this at the opening of the conference by saying something like:

"We have a full program over the next [number of] days. I want you to know that we expect many of you will want and need to take time off to rest and take some down time, missing a session or two, to keep your energy level high. This is completely OK. Rather than reducing the variety of sessions offered while we're together, we are turning over the responsibility to you to decide on what sessions you want and need to attend and the times that you need to take off in order to recharge."

I find that making this expectation explicit makes attendees more relaxed about scheduling their own downtime. I've also seen a significant reduction in the number of evaluation comments complaining that the conference program was too full.

Provide longer breaks

In 2011 I was invited to give a 40-minute presentation at a large European conference. When I arrived and saw the conference program I was surprised to see that the day's sessions were scheduled with NO intervening breaks. Participants were somehow expected to instantaneously teleport between session rooms—even restroom visits were not on the agenda. As you might expect, I lost 10 minutes of my 40-minute time slot because of this elementary scheduling error.

Most event planners won't make this kind of mistake, but, presuming that breaks between sessions are included, how long should they be? The answer depends on several factors:

- The time needed to move between sessions held in different locations
- The overall length of the event
- The amount of participation and interaction designed into sessions

In my book *Conferences That Work* I describe an event where, at the last minute, we were forced to schedule sessions in two buildings that were separated by a 10-minute outdoor walk. Scheduled program breaks weren't long enough, sessions started late, and very hot weather during the conference led to additional complaints. At the very least, breaks must be long enough for people to decide which session they want to attend next, figure out where it's held, take a bathroom break if needed, and get to their desired destination leisurely. Even at a one-day conference where sessions are held in adjacent rooms, I recommend at least 10 minutes between sessions; 15 would be better. If your sessions are held in rooms that are further apart, or in a building that is confusing to navigate, you need to allocate more time.

Breaks can be shorter at a 1-day event than they need to be at a 4-day event. That doesn't mean they should be. But if you have a crowded, must-do agenda you can get away with minimum breaks for a 1-day event. At longer conferences there's no excuse for not scheduling extended breaks, and your attendee quality of experience will suffer if you don't. A long lunch break—at least 90 minutes, preferably 2 hours—and a significant break between the last session of the day and dinner is a simple way to build longer breaks into the day, but having 20- to 25-minute refreshment breaks between morning sessions will also help to keep energy, participation, and learning high during a multiday event.

Finally, the amount of participation and interaction included in sessions will influence the amount of break time needed. The opening roundtable I use at my conferences can last a couple of hours, and when I first ran this session I innocently ran it with just a single midway 20-minute refreshment break. Eventually I noticed what an energy sink this was, and now I break up the session every 20 minutes with short participative exercises such as human spectrograms and pair share introductions. A refreshment table in the room allows people to grab a drink or an apple during these frequent breaks. By using multiple short breaks, the energy level in the room now remains high at the cost of very little extra break time overall.

Eliminate distracting business and entertainment during meals

In my view, one of the most annoying choices that can be made by conference organizers is overlaying meals with presentations, conference business, and intrusive entertainment. Eating and drinking with other people is one of the most fundamental human social activities, and to disrupt the connecting and networking that naturally occurs when we break bread together to squeeze in another speaker, for business considerations, or in a mistaken belief that attendees must be continually entertained is highly counterproductive.

If you need to include award ceremonies, sponsor acknowledgements, or organizational business meetings during your event, schedule them as stand-alone sessions and make them as short as possible. Very few people attend conferences for these activities (yes, those honored may be the minority exception), and to have them occurring while people are attempting to connect and socialize is irritating at best and a complete turn-off at worst.

Similarly, if you feel that offering entertainment to attendees is important, schedule it outside meals and provide quiet, attractive locations nearby where people who want to socialize can do so without having to compete with loud music or a distracting performance of some kind. Music by itself during socials, whether live or recorded, can be fine if the volume is low enough so that it doesn't interfere with conversation.

CHAPTER 25
The conference arc

THIS BOOK IS ABOUT PARTICIPATION TECHNIQUES that can be used as part or all of a conference session. If you are looking for ways to fundamentally improve a single session, you've come to the right place. But it's shortsighted to think only in terms of enhancing individual sessions.

Surprisingly, conference organizers rarely concern themselves with how to take advantage of the *flow* and *progression* of sessions during events. In many cases, more attention is paid to designing event *themes* (e.g., Roaring Twenties, Homecoming, Portraits of Success, Mad Men, Black and White). Themes provide a consistent look and feel to an event and can be a lot of fun, but they don't capitalize on the development of the event process as it unfolds.

I urge those designing conferences to think about the evolution of your event. Carefully designed *openings*, *middles*, and *endings* create a *conference arc* that provides a logical sequence for the sessions to build on each other as the event progresses.

You can find an example of how this works in my book, *Conferences That Work*. The right combination of session formats creates a powerful environment for participation, learning, engagement, and community building throughout an entire conference.

Let's take a look at how the phases of a participation-rich event can be tuned to maximize participants' experience.

Openings

Conference welcomes should cover at minimum the formalities of introducing conference organizers or hosts, and sharing necessary logistical information with attendees. Ideally, a welcome should also foster a comfortable atmosphere that reassures people that practical, conference-related needs can and will be attended to. Once these items are out of the way, traditional conference sessions get underway.

Unfortunately, such a beginning does nothing to support forming connections among attendees. Consequently, people go to sessions knowing only those other attendees they know from outside the conference. Participants are initially isolated, at best slowly building a network of connections as the conference proceeds, but missing out on the benefits of finding simpatico peers early on.

It doesn't have to be this way.

We can use participation techniques from the get-go that *build meaningful connections between participants* by providing ways for them to share all kinds of useful information. The *Openers* section of this book describes a variety of powerful techniques that:

- Increase familiarity with other group members.
- Model a participatory learning environment for the event.
- Provide opportunities for participants to meet others with similar interests and viewpoints.
- Make public the range of participant opinions on and experience with key topics.
- Increase participants' comfort level with the event.
- Uncover topics and questions that engage and excite participants.

Using the right combination of these techniques at the start of an event supplies participants with a rich initial set of relevant connections, ideas, and possibilities embedded in a safe, supportive environment for their time together.

Middles

I rarely see much sense in the placement and sequence of conference sessions. Sometimes I wonder whether a program was designed for the convenience of the presenters' travel schedules—it's hard to discern a deeper plan. Although many conferences divide concurrent sessions among specialty tracks, which helps those with specific interests attend more of the sessions that interest them, the placement of sessions along these tracks often seems to be driven largely by logistical considerations.

While there will always be practical reasons for scheduling sessions at certain times, here are two simple rules that will improve your attendees' conference experience:

- Require all sessions to emphasize interaction and connection.
- If you can't require all sessions to emphasize interaction and connection, place sessions that do so early in the schedule.

Scheduling interactive and connecting sessions at the start helps attendees meet each other productively and quickly, and supplies a smoother transition between the conference Opening and the content-richer Middle, thus maintaining the conference arc.

Endings

There will always be practical reasons—planes to catch, families to feed, or traffic to avoid—for people leaving events before their formal conclusion. However, during the interviews conducted on attendee conference experience for *Conferences That Work*, I was surprised to discover how many people either left or wanted to leave a traditional conference before it was over simply because they had concluded that it wasn't worth their while to stay.

Though personality certainly played a part in the variability of interviewees' responses—several people said that they were incapable of leaving before the end due to their upbringings—the median answer to the interview question "What is the percentage of the conferences you've attended where you either left before the end (for other than practical reasons) or wished you had?" was 25%!

Professional conference planners worry about keeping attendees until the end, and usually suggest scheduling some kind of climactic event to tempt people to stay. When the formal sessions of a conference fail to create an environment in which people want to stay to the end, such manufactured closing events can be effective. That they're so often needed is a sad commentary on the level of commitment traditional conferences generate among participants.

Instead, once attendees have come to know each other and had productive learning experiences, they won't *want* to leave. They'll want to spend as much time as possible with their new friends, even if leaving early is what they'd normally do.

In addition, there are a couple of opportunities that every conference should supply for its Ending—and I don't mean a closing banquet and motivational speaker! Rather, conferences should provide opportunities for:

- Consolidating individual learning; and
- Participants *as a group* sharing and celebrating learning, discovering commonalities, creating and developing new ideas, and moving to action.

Reviewing and reflecting on individual learning *during the event* proves to be a highly effective way to consolidate learning and identify next steps for individual action after the conference is over.

Using appropriate process at the end of the event can also uncover important group initiatives with widespread, grassroots support. Groups can generate, evaluate, and adopt promising ideas and then together come up with next steps.

Such endings support individual development and growth as well as successful organizational planning and community building. Sadly, most events take no advantage of these opportunities, wasting a tremendous opportunity for leveraging the learning, connections, and community building that has occurred.

The *Endings* section of this book describes a range of participation-rich techniques that provide these opportunities. These supply a coherent transition from the formal end of the conference to individual and collective future actions and events, once again maintaining a flowing conference arc.

CHAPTER 26
The conference metaphor

IN THEIR REMARKABLE BOOK *Into the Heart of Meetings*,[124] Eric de Groot and Mike van der Vijver describe what they call *Elementary Meetings*:

> "An Elementary Meeting has a specific name and consists of an obligatory, tacitly agreed series of actions performed by those taking part in the meeting. It usually originates in a specific national culture."

Some examples of Elementary Meetings are *weddings*, *court trials*, *Christmas dinners*, *autopsies*, *parties*, and *conversations*.

You may be thinking: "What on earth have these got to do with creating an environment for participation at meetings?"

The authors explain that the power of Elementary Meetings is in their set of conventions and behaviors familiar to all participants. We've all held conversations, been to parties, and eaten holiday meals. If we haven't attended a trial or an autopsy, we've probably seen them enacted on TV or in the movies. If it's possible to map the form of a professional meeting onto the form of an Elementary Meeting, *we can create an event where attendees possess a common underlying knowledge and/or experience of its components and flow*.

Here are three examples from *Into the Heart of Meetings* of the power of this approach.

A wedding

Suppose you are asked to design an event to prepare the workers of two companies that are about to merge. Merging two organizational cultures is a challenging task; for examples, review the history of the AOL and Time Warner or Chrysler and Daimler-Benz mergers. Most of us do not have direct experience of corporate mergers. But we are familiar with what happens at a wedding—a ceremony about the merging of two people's lives! Making this connection suggests modeling the corporate merger event on the marriage process. This could include how the couple (in this case, companies) met, "courted," and got "engaged." Other marriage components suggest themselves: "bachelor parties," rehearsal dinners, and so on, culminating in the actual "wedding" of the two companies. De Groot and van der Vijver recount how they used this particular Elementary Meeting model for a successful company merger.

Notice how the wedding metaphor brings up all kinds of creative ideas for process that can be used during the event. Not only that, but any of the matching process that is appropriated will be familiar and relatively comfortable to participants due to their existing knowledge of what the Elementary Meeting routinely entails.

A conversation

How would you design an internal corporate event to announce major changes at a company? Change is rarely easy, so you'll expect a host of questions and potentially some confrontation. The likely first thought of most meeting professionals would be to use a standard presentation setup: employees sitting in theater seating facing management making presentations on a stage at the front of the room. But here's how de Groot and van der Vijver describe the message such a setup sends:

> "Having management on the stage in the floodlight and the employees as spectators sitting in the auditorium in darkness carries a powerful message. The message is this: the employees are a passive audience of what the management wants to put across; there is a gap between management and the rest of the company and the employees are kept in the dark. The participants would feel this in an instant. It is not a message that is transmitted through words; it is transmitted through the experience they have when entering the theatre and the lights go out. They undergo a physical experience that tells them: you are mere onlookers, the important people are up there on stage. In fact, the gap is clearly visible, you can see it because there is an open space between the front row and the stage."

Instead, what if we used a *conversation* as the Elementary Meeting starting point for the event design? Here's what the authors came up with:

> "All 450 employees were seated on the stage, in two groups facing each other. This made them actors in their own play. Centre stage stood a small pedestal, with a camera mounted on it. It worked as a whiteboard. Everything that was written on it was projected directly onto big screens, visible for everyone. Those who spoke stood in the middle, between the two stands. Meanwhile, each participant was constantly facing a whole bunch of people, namely their colleagues. This gave an instant feeling of 'us'; having a conversation amongst ourselves."

See how the simple metaphor of a conversation changed the dynamic environment for this event?

Saying goodbye

The Elementary Meeting metaphor can even be employed to design a single session. This final example describes the end of a seminar using a sports-based Elementary Meeting, namely the ritual used at the start of a hockey game:

> "... the facilitator instructs participants to arrange themselves in two rows opposite each other, like ice hockey players before a match. They find themselves standing in pairs, one in front of the other. When he signals they shake hands, express a brief wish, and then step sideways to meet the next person. In just a couple of minutes, all of the 64 participants have exchanged a meaningful goodbye."

Powerful metaphors

As you can see, when designing an event it's worth investigating whether there's an Elementary Meeting that will provide a familiar format for the entire meeting or a portion of it. De Groot and van der Vijver's book is well worth reading for more examples of this approach, as well as a host of other fresh and innovative ideas about meeting design.

CHAPTER 27
And now for something completely specific

I F YOU'RE LIKE ME, AT THIS POINT you're probably itching to get to the actual techniques. "Enough of the environmental exposition," you're thinking, "I want to learn how to *obtain* all the benefits I've been reading about."

The rest of this book should make you very happy.

PART 3
Compendium of Participation Techniques

CHAPTER 28
Participation techniques overview

Introduction

> "Name one of your favorite things about someone in your family."
> "If you were an animal, what would you be and why?"
> "What award would you love to win and for what achievement?"
> —Some examples of "Good Icebreaker Questions" found on the internet

This book is not about participation for the sake of participation. Participation is not a feature that we mechanically graft onto an event and check off on a list in an event binder. Including appropriate participation into an event invariably improves the quality and value of the time that attendees are together, by increasing:

- The amount of learning
- The quality of the learning
- The relevance of the learning
- The retention of the learning, in both accuracy and detail
- The fun and enjoyment attendees experience
- The quantity of useful connections among attendees
- The quality of useful connections among attendees
- Attendee engagement at the event
- Attendee satisfaction with the event
- The strength of the event community

PART 3: Compendium of Participation Techniques

Appropriate participation

All too often, session leaders believe that they should "warm-up" the audience with a group participation exercise before broadcasting their content for the remaining allocated time. As a result, most of us have suffered through poorly conceived "icebreakers" at events. Knowing that they are not supposed to begin by sharing large blocks of content with a group of attendees who barely know each other, presenters spend a few minutes looking online or in one of the more than 700 books on "icebreaking activities" listed on Amazon to pick an exercise or two they can drop in to the start of their event. Once the icebreaker is over, the "real" presentation begins.

At best, such practices can reduce nervous expectations in the room, get participants' blood pumping a little faster, and introduce people in a non-threatening way to a few other attendees.

At worst, inappropriate icebreakers can embarrass or infantilize participants, seriously sabotaging the effectiveness of the rest of the session. Unfortunately, this is the more likely outcome. There are good reasons for the attendee groans, the "oh no" facial expressions, and the slow responses to directions the moment an audience realizes an icebreaker is nigh.

Occasional short, playful, physical, interactive exercises are a good way to reengage audience members who are losing focus—which all of us do to some extent after 10 to 20 minutes of uninterrupted lecturing. But such lighthearted games and the dreaded aforementioned icebreakers are not the only ways in which conference attendees can participate in their learning, even though an alien anthropologist might well come to such a conclusion after studying a majority of today's conferences.

In contrast, there is a wealth of effective participatory techniques that can measurably improve the conference learning environment, but are rarely used. In this chapter, I describe the categories I've used to organize the techniques in this compendium, and provide tables that will help you select the right techniques, depending on your goals, session placement in the event, and size of group.

How to use this compendium of techniques

How this compendium is organized

The techniques described in this compendium are organized by *sequence*—that is, when they are most likely to be used during an event. Some techniques, however, resist this categorization, so be sure to review the following sections in this chapter that provide a useful way to quickly discover appropriate techniques based on your *goals*, *conference phase*, and *group size*.

The four broad sequence-based categories of participation techniques in this compendium are:

Techniques for encouraging connection outside conference sessions

Some participation techniques increase participation by adapting, improving, or eliminating features of the conference environment. As such, they are continuously in effect throughout the event. I call them *white space techniques* to emphasize that they operate whenever participants' attention is not captured by the normal activities at an event.

Openers

Openers are, as you might expect, participation techniques that are especially useful during the early stages of an event. Some openers are appropriate during individual sessions as well, so don't overlook their potential to improve what happens throughout your conference.

Middles

Many participation techniques improve learning, engagement, and connection during core content sessions. I've grouped these techniques into those that facilitate productive *small group discussions*, support effective *voting*, and *create learning opportunities*.

Endings

Ending techniques allow participants to consolidate their learning from a session or an event and assist them, both individually and as a group to move to productive outcomes. These techniques provide effective closure for participants and build community.

Choosing appropriate techniques

Start with your goals for the session or event. *What are the desired outcomes? What important information do you want to convey effectively? Do you want to build connections between participants who don't know each other well? Do you want to uncover useful expertise and experience in the room? Do you want to build a community or a movement—or both? Are there action outcomes that the group needs to decide on?* Being clear about your goals allows you to zero in on techniques that will support them. You'd never use every technique in this book in a single event, so you need to pick what will work for you.

Once you've established your goals, use the tables in the next three sections to review the techniques by goals, conference phase, and group size. Then review the associated chapters for the techniques you find that fit your needs.

Read the whole chapter before making a decision to use the technique. Pay close attention to the *resources* section (see below) to ensure that your meeting environment and available resources can support the time, space, materials, and staff needed.

Preparing to use a technique

Whenever possible, give yourself plenty of time to prepare. While some techniques require little or no preparation, others will need extensive pre-work to use them successfully. If you have never used a technique before, comprehensive review and, ideally, one or more practice run-throughs are especially important, both for your confidence and the quality of participants' resulting experience.

PART 3: Compendium of Participation Techniques

Arrange for all resources to be available when and where they will be needed.

As you review the *how* section of a technique (see below), note any options given and make appropriate choices so you'll know exactly what to do to successfully implement the technique.

How each technique chapter is structured

Each of the technique chapters in this compendium is divided into four sections:

Description

This section provides an overview of the technique, helping you decide whether it's appropriate for the circumstances you have in mind.

When

Some techniques are appropriate throughout an event or session; others are clearly associated with openings, middles, or endings. This section covers the part(s) of an event when a technique is most effective.

Resources

Many of the techniques require low-tech materials resources such as pens, markers, flip chart paper, sticky notes, colored dots, and so on. Others need environmental resources, such as sufficient room space, specific chair arrangements, walls on which materials can be posted, and so on.

How

Here's where you'll learn the details of implementing each technique. Many of these sections include sample narratives that further illustrate how to guide participants through the process.

Techniques by goal

Here are the book's techniques organized by potential goals for your session or event. Many of these techniques are useful for pursuing multiple goals, so you'll find them listed more than once.

Consider the following techniques if you want to . . .

introduce attendees to each other:

Badge It!	Pair Share	Small Group Discussions
Guided Discussions	Pro Action Café	The Solution Room
Human Spectrograms	Roundtable	The Three Questions
Open Space	Seat Swap	World Café

CHAPTER 28: Participation techniques overview

uncover topics of interest to participants:

Anonymous Voting	Plus/Delta	Small Group Discussions
Badge It!	Post It!	The Solution Room
Dot Voting	Pro Action Café	The Three Questions
Fishbowls	Quiz Show	World Café
Open Space	Roundtable	

explore topics and learn from peers:

Affinity Grouping	Open Space	Short Form Presentations: Pecha Kucha and Ignite
Body Voting	Pair Share	Small Group Discussions
Case Studies and Simulations	Plus/Delta	The Solution Room
	Post It!	
Fishbowls	Pro Action Café	The Three Questions
Guided Discussions	Quiz Show	World Café
Human Spectrograms	Roundtable	

evaluate sessions of a conference:

Fishbowls	Human Spectrograms	Plus/Delta
Group Spective	Personal Introspective	Pro Action Café

poll attendees:

Anonymous Voting	Dot Voting	Roman Voting
Body Voting	Hand/Stand Voting	Table Voting
Card Voting	Human Spectrograms	

plan for the future:

Affinity Grouping	Personal Introspective	The Solution Room
Dot Voting	Plus/Delta	
Group Spective	Pro Action Café	

solve problems:

Affinity Grouping	Pair Share	The Solution Room
Guided Discussions	Pro Action Café	World Café

PART 3: Compendium of Participation Techniques

introduce new topics:

Affinity Grouping	Pair Share	Short Form Presentations:
Badge It!	Plus/Delta	Pecha Kucha and Ignite
Guided Discussions	Post It!	The Three Question
Open Space	Roundtable	World Café

Techniques by conference phase

Some exercises work well in more than one conference phase; others are best suited to the start, middle, or end of an event. The following list makes it easy to see what techniques can be used during the different phases of an event.

Openers

Badge It!	Pair Share	The Solution Room
Human Spectrograms	Post It!	The Three Questions
Open Space	Roundtable	World Café

Middles

Affinity Grouping	Fishbowls	Roman Voting
Anonymous Voting	Guided Discussions	Seat Swap
Badge It!	Hand/Stand Voting	Short Form Presentations:
Card Voting	Human Spectrograms	Pecha Kucha and Ignite
Case Studies and Simulations	Open SpacePair Share	Small Group Discussions
	Plus/Delta	Table Voting
Dot Voting	Post It!	World Café

Endings

Fishbowls	Personal Introspective	The Solution Room
Group Spective	Plus/Delta	World Café
Open Space	Pro Action Café	

148

CHAPTER 28: Participation techniques overview

Techniques by group size

Want to know what participation techniques are appropriate for groups of various sizes? Use Table 28.1 to find out. Read the associated technique chapter for more detailed information.

TABLE 28.1 • *Techniques by group size*

GROUP SIZE	2–8	9–20	21–50	50–100	100+
Affinity Grouping		✓	✓	✓	✓
Anonymous Voting	✓	✓	✓	✓	✓
Badge It!	✓	✓	✓	✓	✓
Body Voting	✓	✓	✓	✓	✓
Card Voting	✓	✓	✓	✓	✓
Case Studies and Simulations	✓	✓	✓	✓	✓
Dot Voting	✓	✓	✓	✓	✓
Fishbowls	✓	✓	✓	✓	✓
Group Spective		✓	✓	✓	✓
Guided Discussions	✓	✓	✓	✓	✓
Hand/Stand Voting	✓	✓	✓	✓	✓
Human Spectrograms	✓	✓	✓	✓	✓
Open Space		✓	✓	✓	✓
Pair Share	✓	✓	✓	✓	✓
Personal Introspective	✓	✓	✓	✓	✓
Plus/Delta	✓	✓	✓	✓	✓
Post It!	✓	✓	✓	✓	✓
Pro Action Café		✓	✓	✓	✓
Roman Voting	✓	✓	✓		
Roundtable		✓	✓	✓	
Seat Swap	✓	✓	✓	✓	✓
Short Form Presentations: Pecha Kucha & Ignite	✓	✓	✓	✓	✓
Small Group Discussions	✓	✓	✓	✓	✓
Table Voting	✓	✓	✓	✓	✓
The Solution Room		✓	✓	✓	✓
The Three Questions	✓	✓	✓	✓	✓
World Café		✓	✓	✓	✓

Techniques glossary

I can guarantee there will be at least a few unfamiliar terms in these pages, given that I invented some of them myself. This glossary contains brief definitions; see the relevant chapter or the index for more information.

Affinity Grouping: This technique allows a group to discover and share ideas that arise at a session or conference and group them into categories, so they can be organized and discussed. Sometimes called "cards on the wall."

Anonymous Voting: Any voting method that preserves the anonymity of those voting.

Badge It!: Using participant badges to share useful personal information besides the traditional elements like name, company, etc.

Body Voting: See *Human Spectrograms*.

Card Voting: Provides each participant with an identical set of colored cards that can be used in flexible ways: typically for voting on multiple-choice questions, *consensus voting*, and guiding discussion.

Case Studies and Simulations: Ways to create a classroom or conference environment in which participants can create and explore in a semi-realistic way alternative roles, points of view, puzzles, and positions. Case studies use a story as a jumping-off place for group analysis and discussion, while simulations immerse participants into an experiential situation.

Conference Arc: An approach to design that concentrates on event chronological parts—openers, middles, and endings—and the consequential progressive experience of participants.

Consensus voting: Voting techniques that gauge the degree of group consensus on a point of view or course of action.

Continuum Voting: See *Human Spectrograms*.

Dot Voting: A technique for public *semi-anonymous* voting in which participants are given identical sets of one or more colored paper dots that they stick onto paper voting sheets to indicate preferences.

Fishbowls: Provide group process that facilitates focused discussion, either by assuring that the conversation at any moment is restricted to a few clearly defined people or by allowing representatives of both sides of a point of view time in turn to listen to and question representatives of the opposing viewpoint.

Group Spectives: Closing conference sessions that provide time for attendees to collectively take stock, reflecting on where they started, the path traveled, and the journey yet to come.

Guided Discussions: Guided small discussion groups used regularly during a session to expose different answers, viewpoints, and levels of understanding and create multiple simultaneous rich customized learning environments in the room.

CHAPTER 28: Participation techniques overview

Hand/Stand Voting: In hand voting, participants raise their hands to indicate their answer to a question with two or more possible answers. Stand voting replaces hand raising with standing.

Human Graphs: See *Human Spectrograms*.

Human Spectrograms: Also known as *body voting*, *continuum voting*, and *human graphs*. A form of *public voting* that has participants move in the room to a place that represents their answer to a question. Human spectrograms can be categorized as *one-dimensional*, *two-dimensional*, or *state-change*.

One-dimensional Human Spectrograms: *Human Spectrograms* in which participants position themselves along a line in a room to portray their level of agreement/disagreement with a statement or a numeric response (e.g., the number of years they've been in their current profession).

Open Space: A simple method for participants to create their own meetings.

Openers: Participation techniques that are especially useful during the early stages of a group's time together.

Pair Share: Discussion of a topic or question with a partner during a session that develops and reinforces learning.

Participatory Voting: Any form of voting that provides public information about viewpoints in the room and paves the way for further discussion.

Personal Introspectives: Two-part closing conference sessions that guide participants through a review of what they have learned and a determination of what they want to consequently change in their lives.

Plus/Delta: A review tool that enables participants to quickly identify what went well at a session or event and what could be improved.

Post It!: A simple technique that uses participant-written sticky notes to uncover topics and issues that a group wants to discuss.

Pro Action Café: A blend of *World Café* and *Open Space* that facilitates reflection, discussion and consolidation of ideas, and moving to action.

Public Voting: Voting methods that allow a group to see the individuals who have voted and how they voted.

Roman Voting: Roman Voting is a *public voting* technique for gauging the strength of consensus.

Roundtables: Structured conference *openers* that employ *The Three Questions to* (1) define and model an active, interactive, and safe conference environment; (2) provide a structured forum for attendees to meet and learn about each others' affiliations, interests, experience, and expertise; and (3) uncover the topics that people want to discuss and share.

Seat Swap: A strategy for switching seats during a seated meal to increase conversational partners.

Semi-anonymous voting: Voting techniques in which others can only determine how individuals vote by watching them closely during the voting process.

Short Form Presentations Pecha Kucha and Ignite: Very short stylized presentations that offer a rapid introduction to a topic, an idea, or an experience and that act as a jumping-off place for stimulated viewers to start learning more via engagement afterwards.

Small Group Discussions: Techniques that use small groups to improve learning, connection, interaction, and engagement.

State-change Human Spectrograms: *Human Spectrograms* in which participants move en masse from one point to another to display a change of some quantity (e.g., opinion, geographical location) over time.

Table Voting: A technique used for polling attendees on their choice from predetermined answers to a multiple-choice question, and/or for dividing participants into preference groups for further discussions or activities.

The Solution Room: An opening or closing conference session that engages and connects attendees and provides peer-supported advice on their most pressing problems.

The Three Questions: An opener that supports and encourages a group of people in learning about each other, their wishes for the time they are together, and their relevant experience and expertise.

Two-dimensional Human Spectrograms: *Human Spectrograms* in which participants position themselves in a two-dimensional room space to display relative two-dimensional information (e.g., where they live with reference to a projected map).

World Café: A format for dialogue in small groups around questions that have been determined in advance.

CHAPTER 29
Techniques for encouraging connection outside conference sessions

THE CORE GOAL OF THIS BOOK is to provide persuasive reasons coupled with clear how-to information on improving learning, connection, and engagement by integrating participation into conference sessions. But that doesn't mean we should ignore the time participants spend outside sessions socializing, eating, and drinking. Here are two great techniques that encourage connection outside conference sessions.

Badge It!

My popular blog post, *Anatomy of a Name Badge*,[125] details the pluses and minuses of the myriad choices of badge type, size, contents, layout and design, attachment methods, and so on. Besides all these considerations, the humble name badge can provide useful information that can spark connections and engagement between attendees who are just walking around. Here's how to do it.

Use large name badges (I like 4″ × 6″ vertical badges) and design them so there's space for attendees to write on them. Then add a "Talk to me about . . ." space, or an "I'd like to know about . . ." space, or an "All we need is . . ." on your badge. Voila! Attendees now have a way to broadcast their interests and expertise and an excuse to peer at each other's badges.[126]

A slightly different approach is to have people write a specific area of interest on their badge (perhaps on the back if it's blank) and then walk around and cluster with other attendees who share the same interest. These groups can then use any of the small group techniques described in this book to further explore their common interest together.

Seat Swap

Once attendees are seated at a formal plated meal, in most cultures it's considered impolite for them to move to a different chair until the meal is over. While this can be fine for people who know each other and choose to sit together, you've probably had the experience of wanting to talk to other people in the room but having to remain in one spot, restricted to conversation with your nearby partners.

To increase conversational partners at seated meals, simply announce a seat swap between two courses (typically between the main course and dessert). If the group includes approximately equal numbers of men and women, ask all the men or all the women to stand up and choose a chair at another table. Alternatively, have everybody move whose last name begins with a letter in the first half of the alphabet. All will double their pool of conversational partners at the cost of perhaps a couple of minutes' rearrangement. At a seated buffet-style meal you can have more than one seat swap, with a commensurate increase in potential connections.

CHAPTER 30
Openers

THIS SECTION OF THE BOOK covers participation techniques that are especially useful during the early stages of a group's time together. Traditionally such techniques are called *icebreakers*, a term that has elicited plenty of groans from meeting attendees over the years. Why? Because, although getting people introduced and connected at the start of an event is important, organizers and presenters frequently choose specific activities that have little relevance to the reasons why people are present.

Icebreakers are typically presented as "fun" activities, but one person's fun can be another's turnoff or even torture. Rather than cajole everyone into playing a silly game that some will not appreciate, the techniques in this section elicit useful information about the people, interests, and resources available in the room that are directly relevant to the reasons they are there.

I'm not saying that there is no place for traditional icebreakers at events. For example, if a group of relative strangers has come together for creative purposes, icebreakers can help quickly break down some of the normal social inhibitions about working freely with people you've just met. All too often, however, a presenter will choose a more or less random icebreaker because he thinks it's what he's supposed to do.

Using the word *icebreakers* transmits the message that there is ice in the room that needs to be broken, while naming them "energizers" or "warm-ups" implies that people need to be energized or warmed up. When we name techniques like this we often end up unwittingly defining and hence limiting their scope, power, and influence.

So this section of the book is about what I call openers—techniques that address specific, relevant objectives during the early lifetime of a group. In other words, I am categorizing these techniques by when it's most helpful to use them, rather than by their purpose or implied outcome.

What are openers for?

Openers concentrate on building meaningful connections between participants by providing ways to share all kinds of useful information between group members. When done effectively, openers provide many other benefits, such as increasing familiarity with other group members, modeling a participatory learning environment, increasing comfort level, and uncovering topics and questions that have energy for the group.

Building meaningful connections

There are two fundamental requirements for building meaningful connections between attendees. You need opportunities to discover and meet like-minded people, and you need ways to move into conversation with them.

How do we discover like-minded people? We need opportunities to ask other attendees what we want to know and hear their answers. Their answers inform us about shared interests and experiences—commonalities that will provide openings for us to engage with them.

How do we provide ways to move into conversation with like-minded attendees? Appropriate participative activities offer a supportive social format. In the same way a party creates an environment in which a good host can introduce people to each other, the right participative techniques provide time and structure for people to meet and connect through shared activity.

During an event we have, at most, a few days together, perhaps a few minutes of potential interaction with each attendee. So how can we best build the above requirements into our event process?

Whatever we do, it should happen quickly, and at the beginning. No waiting to try to meet people during session breaks. If we're going to be proactive about fostering connection, let's start right at the opening of the event to maximize the opportunity.

Opening techniques . . . and more

Because the techniques described in this chapter build meaningful connections between participants, they are especially useful at the start of events or sessions. This doesn't mean that they are solely openers; employ them whenever you seek a deepening of interpersonal understanding or connection. Shorter techniques, such as pair shares and human spectrograms, are also excellent methods for boosting the energy of attendees before attention begins to fade.

CHAPTER 31
The Three Questions

Description

The Three Questions is one of the most effective ways to assist a group of people to get to know each other in the way each person wants—quite different from the common but often artificial and awkward icebreaker approach. Requiring each person to speak to others in the group using a clear format for a limited time, the technique sets up an environment for sharing that is personal, safe, supportive, and information rich. Besides being a powerful opener, The Three Questions can also be used periodically by a group that meets regularly to keep members updated and engaged.

The Three Questions format grew from my desire to create a conference session at which we could ask everyone present what we wanted to know about them. In thinking about what would fit the bill, I came up with the following types of questions:

- Open-ended questions that were appropriate for any attendee to answer.
- Questions that could be answered safely by an anxious participant.
- Questions for which there were no wrong answers.
- Questions covering the past, the present, and the future. Hearing where someone is coming from tells us about their context and their experience; it gives us baseline information. Hearing about what they want to do now and in the future, their wishes for their professional or personal life, tells us about the interests we may share and where their energy is focused.
- Questions about people's experience or expertise that might be useful to other group members. There's no guarantee that what people tell us will be useful, but if we don't ask, how will we know?

It turned out that we can satisfy all of the above requirements by asking just three questions:

- How did I get here?
- What do I want to have happen?
- What experience or expertise do I have that others may find useful?

I call the resulting framework I've developed for safely posing and answering these questions *The Three Questions*. I've been using this technique to open meetings and conferences for many years, usually embedded in a *roundtable* (described in the next chapter). The process is simple: After explaining the questions and providing time to consider one's answers, each person in turn is given the same amount of time to share his or her answers with the group.

If time is limited or many people are present, you can use The Three Questions with subgroups of a larger group—from a pair share (see Chapter 38) with one other person, in triads, in small groups, and in groups with up to around 60 other people.

When?

I recommend you run The Three Questions at the start of a conference or session following the welcome and housekeeping details. The technique shares a great deal of useful information about attendees. I suggest you inform participants in advance about the importance of being present at the opening session.

The Three Questions can also be used periodically at the start of a regularly scheduled meeting, especially if the meeting is voluntary, to recall and update the reasons why people are present. I've found this to be an effective and enjoyable way to reconnect with attendees and refresh commitment to the meeting group's purpose.

Resources

Core resources for The Three Questions are a pen and a copy of the Three Questions, printed on a 5" × 8" card (Figure 31.1), for each participant.

FIGURE 31.1 • *The Three Questions Card*

The Three Questions

How did I get here?

What would I like to have happen?

What experience or expertise do I have that others may find useful?

Timekeeping

You will need a method to equally allocate time for answering The Three Questions among participants. If the group is small, say six or fewer, this can be done informally by someone with a watch or timer. For larger groups, you'll need a dedicated timekeeper. As each person shares, the timekeeper's job is to sound up to three alerts; the first, 30 seconds before each attendee's allocated time expires, the second when time is up, and the third if an attendee goes 20 seconds over her allotted time.

Timekeeping is a surprisingly demanding job. For The Three Questions, I recommend you use Flex-Time, as described earlier in this book. This software makes it easy to set up and adjust a series of timers, each of which plays a different sound. I like to use a chime for the 30-second warning, an old-fashioned telephone ring for the "time's-up" sound, and a klaxon for the overage reminder. You'll need two FlexTime scripts: a demo script to familiarize participants with the sounds they will hear, and a script with the correct times you'll need for each participant. These FlexTime sounds and scripts are available on www.conferencesthatwork.com.

When using The Three Questions with a large group, read the next chapter on roundtables to learn about the additional resources you'll need.

Room setup

The Three Questions works best when participants can all see each other. For a small group, simply have participants sit around a table or in a circle of chairs. For larger groups, a single circle of chairs should be used if at all possible. This requires significantly larger rooms than conventional room sets, which often necessitates advance planning with the venue. See Appendix 1 for minimum room dimensions for circle seating.

Why use question cards?

The cards give attendees the opportunity to answer The Three Questions *in writing* before their sharing starts. Providing time for people to think about and write their answers is important for two reasons.

First, some attendees may be anxious about speaking up in front of the entire group, especially right at the beginning of an event. Giving everyone a quiet time to collect, organize, and write down their thoughts helps reduce attendees' unease.

A second reason involves the concept of personality types or preferences, as expressed by Isabel Myers and Katharine Briggs, who devised the Myers-Briggs Type Indicator (MBTI), a popular method of categorizing personality differences. One of the MBTI dichotomies is an individual's introvert or extrovert preference. Many people have an extrovert preference—they tend to develop their thinking while speaking, and thrive on interacting with others. However, around 25% of the general population inclines toward introversion, and in some professions this percentage is significantly higher. Introverts need quiet time to do their thinking, usually prefer to write out their ideas, and find it harder to think well when others are talking. Introverts greatly benefit, therefore, from being given time before group sharing begins to quietly gather and record their thoughts.

How?

Preparation

Before starting The Three Questions, calculate the amount of time that will be available for each participant to share her answers. Aim for around 2 minutes per person.

For a small group subtract 7 minutes from the total available time (for introduction and pondering answers) and divide the remaining time by the number of people in the group.

For a large group, perform the following steps:

- Subtract 10 minutes from the available time (for introduction and pondering answers), plus 10 seconds for each person in the group (for switching between sharers).
- Divide the remaining time by 25 and round down to the nearest whole number; this will give you the number of 5-minute breaks you'll take for every 20 minutes of group sharing.

CHAPTER 31: The Three Questions

- Subtract 5 minutes for each break, and then divide the resulting time by the number of participants.
- Round down the calculated time to the nearest 10 seconds.

Small group example

For a group of six people you will need about 20 minutes. Subtracting 7 minutes leaves 13 minutes, allowing 2 minutes per person.

Large group example

For a group of 30 people, you will need about 80 minutes. Subtracting 10 minutes and 30 × 10 seconds (5 minutes) leaves 65 minutes. Dividing 65 by 25 and rounding down tells us we will have two breaks. Subtracting 10 minutes for two breaks leaves 55 minutes, allowing 110 seconds per person.

Typically each person should end up with 1 to 2 minutes, with the shorter time restricted to groups that have met before. If you are using timekeeping software, give this information to your timekeeper so he can set up the *Group sharing timer* script with the correct time. Ask your timekeeper to announce a break after each 20 minutes of sharing.

When you're ready for The Three Questions, distribute a question card to each participant and a pen to anyone who needs one. Because participants may want to share private information, consider having them agree to a confidentiality ground rule before beginning.

Explain The Three Questions

After the cards and pens have been distributed, say something like this:

> *"Welcome to The Three Questions! We're going to use your answers to the questions on your cards to learn about each other: why you're here today, what you'd like to have happen, and the experience and expertise you have to share. First I'm going to explain the three questions. Once I've done that you'll have time to prepare your answers, and then each of you will get* [amount of time you calculated] *to share your answers with the group."*

If you're working with a large group, or a group in which some have not experienced The Three Questions before...

...say something like this:

> *"Before I go over these questions, I want to emphasize something that's important for you to keep in mind.*
>
> *There are no wrong answers to these questions!*
>
> *The first question is: 'How did I get here?' What brought you here today? We want to hear a story about how you come to be sitting here, in this room. Tell us your name to start. Then there are countless stories you could tell us. You could tell us that you got here on Interstate 91 in your Subaru. You could tell us how you heard about* [this conference] *from your good friend*

> *Bruce and that it sounded interesting. Maybe you'll tell us about yourself and how [this conference] attracted you. Tell us your name, your affiliation if relevant, what you do, what you want to do, what you're passionate about, and how that all plays into your being here. Help us know you a little, help us understand you a little, tell us about where you came from to get here."*
>
> *It's your choice how deep to go, how far to go, what to say. Don't feel constrained by what others share or the way they share. Feel free to go outside the box. Remember, there are no wrong answers.*
>
> *The second question is: 'What do I want to have happen?' The first question was about the past; this question is about the future. What do you want to have happen here, while we are together? What do you want to learn about, what do you want to discuss, what puzzles do you want help in solving or investigating, what journeys do you want to make? This is a time to tell us what you really want from [this conference]. Don't be afraid to ask for anything. There are no guarantees, but, collectively, we possess tremendous resources, and asking for what you want is the essential first step for getting it. You may not get what you want if you ask for it, but we'll never know you want it unless you tell us.*
>
> *The third question is: 'What experience or expertise do I have that others may find useful?' We're asking for information about the experience, knowledge, and wisdom you possess and that you can share with us. Many of you will have some clear responses to this question, but I encourage you to dig deeper. All of us have experience that is of value to others, but we are often surprisingly unaware of the richness of resources that each of us has to offer. If there's something you know something about, or have experience of, that's relevant to [the topic of this conference] please mention it in your answer to this question. It's common to have someone casually mention some experience and be totally surprised to discover that many people want to find out more.*
>
> *Any questions about The Three Questions?"*

Answer any questions.

If you're working with a small group, or a group that has experienced The Three Questions before...

...say something like this:

> *"Before I go over these questions, I want to emphasize that there are no wrong answers to these questions!*
>
> *The first question is: 'How did I get here?' What brought you here today? We want to hear how you come to be sitting in this room today. Tell us your name and affiliation and how you got here.*
>
> *The second question is: 'What do I want to have happen?' What do you want to have happen here, while we are together? What do you want to learn about, what do you want to discuss? This is an opportunity to tell us what you really want to happen during our time together.*

> *The third question is: 'What experience or expertise do I have that others may find useful?' What experience, knowledge, and wisdom do you possess that you can share with us? If there's something you know something about, or have experience of, that's relevant to* [the topic of this meeting/conference], *please mention it in your answer to this question.*
>
> *Any questions about The Three Questions?"*

Answer any questions.

Give attendees time to answer the questions

> *"OK, I'm going to give you 5 minutes to come up with your answers to the questions. Use the card to write down a summary of what you're going to say during the* [amount of time you calculated] *available to each of you. Remember, there are no wrong answers to these questions!"*

Attendees may need less than the time you allocate. When most people seem to be done, announce that you'll provide another minute for everyone to finish. Then ask whether anyone needs more time and wait for anyone who does.

Explain sharing guidelines

Here's an example of what you might say next:

> *"Here are some guidelines about sharing your answers.*
>
> *First, if someone shares before you do and mentions some of your own interests, desires, needs, experiences, and so on, please don't omit these items from your answers. It's important for all of us to get a sense of the levels and intensities of interests and experiences represented here.*
>
> *Second, if the person sharing asks for specific assistance on a topic along the lines of 'does anyone know the answer to X,' and you can help, it's OK to stick your hand up long enough for them to notice you and to say your name and 'I can help with that.' Don't start giving the help there and then, just make the connection.*
>
> [Include if the group is large] *Third: Please stand when it's your turn to share your answers.*
>
> *Finally, a lot of information is going to come flowing from everyone during this session. Don't expect to remember everything people say—you'll notice what's useful and meaningful for you. As each person responds to the three questions, I encourage you to make notes* [add, if you have a face book] *right next to their entry in your face book so you can keep track of who said what.*
>
> *We have* [period of time remaining] *for our sharing. So that everyone gets an equal opportunity, each of you will have up to* [time period for each attendee] *to share. You'll get a 30-second warning alert that sounds like this* [timekeeper sounds the warning alert]. *When your time is up you'll hear* [timekeeper sounds the 'time's-up' alert]. *You don't have to finish mid-sentence, but we ask that you keep to this time limit as much as possible. If you don't finish within another 20 seconds, you'll hear* [timekeeper sounds the overtime alert] *and you must stop immediately."*

Breaks

If sharing will last more than 30 minutes, provide a 5-minute break every 20 minutes. Ask that all be back in their seats (no changing seats) in 5 minutes. Use these breaks to raise group energy with:

- Appropriate human spectrograms.
- The simple instruction: "Introduce yourself to someone you don't know." This can be repeated multiple times.
- A refreshment/bathroom break every hour.

At 4 minutes, ask people to return to their seats. Multiple announcements may be necessary. Don't wait for latecomers—stay on your schedule by continuing the sharing.

Begin sharing

You have several options for beginning sharing:

- Start with a prearranged volunteer who can provide a good model for the attendees who follow.
- Ask the circle "Who wants to start?"
- If you have provided a face book sorted by name, start with the first person listed and proceed in alphabetical order.

With the first two options, once the first person is done sharing, continue around the circle, with each person taking their turn. You can ask the first sharer to choose the direction to continue.

An advantage of using the third option, face book order, is that people don't have to flip through the book to find each person's entry for note taking. However, there can be awkward silences when the next person in the book is absent. To minimize these pauses, announce the next sharer's name when each attendee finishes speaking.

Watch the time. You want people to take an average amount of time equal to or slightly less than the time you've announced. Don't allow anyone to continue long after the second alert, and cut people off if the overtime alert sounds (this is rarely necessary). Interrupt them politely but firmly and ask them to end. If a significant number of people overrun their time, point this out and ask attendees to be more concise. If people are finishing too quickly, encourage them to expand their answers, by suggesting the answers you feel they could amplify.

Ending The Three Questions

Check that everyone has shared (late attendees may arrive, or people may be missing from the face book) before wrapping up The Three Questions.

CHAPTER 32
Roundtable

Description

Read this first!

The term *roundtable* often appears on conference programs as a synonym for a breakout or discussion session. Rather, I use *roundtable* to describe a powerful structured conference opener using *The Three Questions* (described in the previous chapter).

As a roundtable is essentially a practical way to use The Three Questions with large groups, this chapter concentrates on implementation issues specific to large groups.

Roundtable introduction

A roundtable is the most effective way I know for conference attendees to learn about and share with a large number of conference peers in a relatively short period of time. I have been developing this technique since 1992, as described in *Conferences That Work: Creating Events That People Love*, and I've received thousands of evaluations testifying to its effectiveness with a wide variety of groups.

A well-run roundtable lays the groundwork for the novel concept of everyone participating actively in the conference, participation that invariably leads to rich dividends for attendees.

The roundtable may be the only time during the conference when every attendee is expected to speak publicly. Some people have a hard time speaking to a group, but by providing a supportive environment and requiring each attendee to speak, however briefly, a roundtable gives reluctant attendees a relatively safe opportunity to discover that sharing a little about themselves in public need not be a scary ordeal. Expecting each attendee to say something gently reinforces the notion that the conference's culture embraces active participation. Once they've had this experience, attendees are more likely to participate and contribute during the event.

Many interesting things happen during attendee sharing.

Obviously, you get to hear intriguing tidbits about and from people you haven't met before. I especially appreciate that I get to experience even those I already know in a fresh context through the roundtable. Sharing allows me to check in with old friends and hear what's currently on their minds.

The roundtable provides explicit feedback about the level of interest in topics. Hot subjects become evident through repetition, murmurs, and body language. Unexpected subjects come up, and are incorporated into subsequent sharing. At times it becomes clear by default that there's little interest in a topic that was expected to be popular with attendees.

But what I find to be most interesting and wonderful about roundtable sharing is how the atmosphere invariably changes as people speak; from a subdued nervousness about talking in front of strangers to an intimacy that grows as people start to hear about topics that engage them, discover kindred spirits, and learn of unique experiences and expertise available from their peers. When sharing is over, both a sense of comfort and excitement prevail: comfort arising from the knowledge attendees have of their commonalities with others, and excitement at the thought that they now have the rest of the conference to explore the connections and possibilities that the roundtable has introduced.

The roundtable is a gift to attendees, a gift to be taken and used as each person wishes, a gift that keeps on giving during the conference. Surprisingly, the roundtable is ultimately a catalyst—supplying nothing, save perhaps permission, to the interactions that participants create—a gift that people give of and to themselves.

Once participants have had an opportunity to absorb what's happened, a new dynamic sets in. They have been given both permission and the opportunity to act in a way that is new, a way that leads to meaningful interactions between people and also gives them the power and responsibility to determine what will happen next.

In my experience, people love the fresh and energizing start that a roundtable provides to a conference. You hear a loud hum of conversation as they seek out and engage with others whom they've discovered share their interests and experience.

Roundtable considerations

Roundtables, like most participatory group techniques, do not scale indefinitely. As the number of participants increases, the amount of information shared also rises, until it threatens to overwhelm our capacity to filter and absorb what's useful. After many years of experimenting, I recommend that the maximum number of roundtable participants be capped at 60.

If you have more than 60 people at your event, hold multiple simultaneous roundtables. Provided you have enough space—something that should not be taken for granted at many venues in my experience—holding more than one roundtable allows every attendee to be informatively introduced to the maximum feasible number of fellow participants.

CHAPTER 32: Roundtable

When?

Run roundtables at the start of a conference as soon as any welcome and housekeeping are complete. Be sure to inform all conference registrants in advance of the importance of being present at this opening session.

Resources

In addition to the resources required for The Three Questions, described in the previous chapter, you will need to consider the following issues:

Multiple roundtables

If you are running multiple simultaneous roundtables, you will need to make a couple of decisions in advance. Do not leave these decisions to the day of the event!

Deciding how to divide attendees among multiple roundtables

How you divide attendees among multiple roundtables can make a significant difference to their effectiveness. You want to provide an interesting peer group at each roundtable while keeping each group roughly the same size. There is a trade-off between random assignment, which can lead to interesting cross-fertilization of ideas and expertise, and division by specialty, which allows peers with much in common to find and connect with each other. Ultimately, you'll need to make this determination yourself based on the ideas below.

If your attendees have distinguishing interests, it's often best to divide them into roundtable groups that reflect these interests. For example, at a conference for medical office staff we split the 500 attendees into ten roundtables by different office specialty and practice type (obstetrics, oncology, general practice, etc.). Because we had more than 50 attendees in some of these categories, we ran several roundtables for the more popular specialties, with attendees assigned to one of their specialty roundtables at random. If you have more distinguishing interests than roundtables, you'll need to combine multiple interests into a single roundtable. Try to pick groups that have overlapping interests.

Avoid assigning roundtables by geographical origin. At most conferences, people prefer meeting those they consider their true peers irrespective of whether they work near each other. For example, a national association of summer camp organizations used roundtables based on geographic region. From the feedback they received, attendees would have preferred being grouped by job specialty: development staff, financial staff, board members, and so on.

To help decide how to assign attendees to roundtables, I suggest asking a sample of registrants their opinion. If there's no strong preference, use a random assignment.

Once you've decided how attendees should be assigned, choose a simple scheme to name each roundtable. You can use something appropriate to the theme of the conference—for example, a Christian conference might use books of the Bible—or something abstract such as numbers or colors. Before the conference, assign each registrant to a specific roundtable and individually code badges to make roundtable assignments clear.

Deciding when attendees move to individual roundtables

You have a couple of choices as to when attendees join their individual roundtables.

One is to begin the description of the exercise with everyone together in one room and have people move into their separate roundtables once they have written their answers to The Three Questions. This format is convenient when, as is usually the case, the roundtables are held immediately after welcoming the entire group. All the separate roundtable rooms should be located near the main room, and signage and staff should be available to make the room changes swift and efficient.

The other option is to have attendees start in their separate roundtables. This has the advantage that no one has to change rooms once each roundtable has started. The disadvantage is that people will not be together for the usual conference welcome and housekeeping, and general announcements will have to be made to each group separately.

Multiple roundtable seating considerations

Provide a separate room for each roundtable; otherwise, everyone will be distracted by the "noise" from the other roundtable.

If you start a multiple roundtable session with everyone together in one room you'll need a room, preferably set using curved theater-style seating, that can accommodate everyone, plus rooms for each subsequent roundtable. (The main room can also serve as a roundtable room if the seating can be changed quickly. Normally this is only practical if done by the participants themselves, which may well be possible depending on the formality of your event.)

In each roundtable room, set out a circle of chairs. If the room is much larger than the circle of chairs, position one point of the circle near a wall where flip chart sheets can be hung. Take time to make the circle as round and tight as possible, while leaving a few gaps so people can arrive and depart.

You want the smallest comfortable circle, with as few empty chairs as possible. I put out slightly too few chairs, with a pile of extras nearby. Then, latecomers can take a chair from the pile and put it in one of the gaps. This way, the circle is complete during the session, with no empty chairs at any time.

Roundtable facilitation

Select a facilitator for each roundtable prior to the session, and ensure that they read and understand this chapter and the previous chapter. All facilitators should agree in advance on the attendee sharing time allocation so they all end at approximately the same time.

Face book

Consider supplying each participant with a paper face book that contains a photograph of each person together with associated relevant information (name, affiliation, contact information, etc.).

CHAPTER 32: Roundtable

Participants can then use their face books to make notes about each person's answers while the sharing is underway.

Recording topics

It's useful to create a record of topics that participants mention during their answers to the second question ("What do I want to have happen?"). If you have a large expanse of wall-mounted whiteboard in the room, use this. Otherwise, place two flip chart stands opposite each other, just outside the circle. Ideally, the flip charts should be near a wall where completed chart sheets can be hung. If the paper flip chart sheets are not self-stick, tear off short strips of masking tape in advance and store them on the flip chart stands.

You can use a digital camera to photograph the flip chart or whiteboard topics recorded during the session. The digital photographs, or a PDF containing them, can be posted on a conference website, easily available for reference during the conference.

A third way to record topics is to use a shared public Google Doc, projected onto a screen for roundtable participants to view. Two or more scribes can simultaneously enter topics into the document, which is available to all participants during or after the roundtable. Since the link Google supplies for accessing the document is complex, I use a link shortener such as bit.ly or goo.gl to create an easy-to-type URL for the document, and add the shortened link into the document so that any participant can quickly access it.

Select two scribes to stand at the flip charts or whiteboards (or type into the shared Google Doc via laptops) and alternatively record shared conference topics and ideas. Choose people who have some conference subject expertise so they can summarize attendee responses accurately and concisely. Provide each writing scribe with two markers in contrasting colors and ask them to alternate colors between topics. Tell the scribes that if a topic is described too quickly to be recorded, they should ask the person to repeat it. And if a scribe is unclear as to how a topic can be captured in a few words, he should ask the attendee how to summarize what she said.

How?

Running a roundtable is quite similar to running The Three Questions described in the previous chapter. There are enough minor modifications, however, to warrant providing the following description.

Preparation

Before the roundtable starts, calculate the amount of time that will be available for each participant to share her answers using the following steps:

- Subtract 10 minutes from the available time (for introduction and pondering answers), plus 10 seconds for each person in the group (for switching between sharers).

- Divide the remaining time by 25 and round down to the nearest whole number; this will give you the number of 5-minute breaks you'll take for every 20 minutes of group sharing.
- Subtract 5 minutes for each break, and then divide the resulting time by the number of participants.
- Round down the calculated time to the nearest 10 seconds.

For example, suppose you have a group of 60 people with 2 hours available for a roundtable. Subtracting 10 minutes for the introduction and writing answers, and 60 × 10 seconds (10 minutes) for switching between sharers leaves 100 minutes. Dividing by 25 shows we will have four 5-minute breaks. (In this case, the last break coincides with the end of the session, so you may end a little early.) Subtracting 20 minutes for the breaks leaves us with 80 minutes of sharing, allowing 80 seconds per person.

Typically each person should end up with 1 to 2 minutes. If you are using timekeeping software, give this information to your timekeeper so he can set up the *Group sharing timer* script with the correct time. Ask your timekeeper to announce a break after each 20 minutes or so of sharing.

At the start of the roundtable, distribute a question card to each participant and a pen to anyone who needs one. Because participants may want to share private information, consider having them agree to a confidentiality ground rule before beginning.

Start to explain the roundtable(s)

Once the cards and pens have been distributed, say something like this:

> *"Welcome to our roundtable session. It provides a structured and intimate way for us to learn more about each other right at the start of this conference. During the session, we'll discover why people came and the topics that interest them. We'll also get a feeling for the depth of interest in these topics, and we'll find out who has experience and expertise that we want to connect to and explore."*

Add the following sentence if you are running multiple simultaneous roundtables but have decided to start with everyone together in one room:

> *"By the way, this group would be a little overwhelming to work well as a single roundtable, so, shortly, we'll split into* [number of] *groups, reseat ourselves and hold* [number of] *roundtables."*

Then continue as follows:

> *"We hold a roundtable by going around our circle, and answering, in turn, the three questions that are on the cards you've been given. Before I go over these questions, I want to emphasize something that's important for you to keep in mind.*
>
> *There are no wrong answers to these questions!*

CHAPTER 32: Roundtable

> *The first question is: 'How did I get here?' What brought you here today? We want to hear a story about how you come to be sitting here, in this room. Tell us your name to start. Then there are countless stories you could tell us. You could tell us that you got here on Interstate 91 in your Subaru. You could tell us how you heard about* [this conference] *from your good friend Bruce and that it sounded interesting. Maybe you'll tell us about yourself and how* [this conference] *attracted you. Tell us your name, your affiliation if relevant, what you do, what you want to do, what you're passionate about, and how that all plays into your being here. Help us know you a little, help us understand you a little, tell us about where you came from to get here."*
>
> *It's your choice how deep to go, how far to go, what to say. Don't feel constrained by what others share or the way they share. Feel free to go outside the box. Remember, there are no wrong answers.*
>
> *The second question is: 'What do I want to have happen?' The first question was about the past; this question is about the future. What do you want to have happen here, while we are together? What do you want to learn about, what do you want to discuss, what puzzles do you want help in solving or investigating, what journeys do you want to make? This is a time to tell us what you really want from* [this conference]. *Don't be afraid to ask for anything. There are no guarantees, but, collectively, we possess tremendous resources, and asking for what you want is the essential first step for getting it. You may not get what you want if you ask for it, but we'll never know you want it unless you tell us.*
>
> *The third question is: 'What experience or expertise do I have that others may find useful?' We're asking for information about the experience, knowledge, and wisdom you possess and that you can share with us. Many of you will have some clear responses to this question, but I encourage you to dig deeper. All of us have experience that is of value to others, but we are often surprisingly unaware of the richness of resources that each of us has to offer. If there's something you know something about, or have experience of, that's relevant to* [the topic of this conference] *please mention it in your answer to this question. It's common to have someone casually mention some experience and be totally surprised to discover that many people want to find out more.*
>
> *Any questions about the three questions?"*

Answer any questions.

Give attendees time to answer the questions

> *"OK, I'm going to give you 5 minutes to come up with your answers to the questions. Use the card to write down a summary of what you're going to say during the* [amount of time you calculated] *available to each of you. Remember, there are no wrong answers to these questions!"*

Attendees may need less than the time you allocate. When most people seem to have finished, announce that you'll provide another minute. Then ask whether anyone needs more time and wait for anyone who does.

If you are running simultaneous roundtables but have decided to start with everyone together in one room, this is the moment when people should move to their previously assigned separate roundtable rooms.

Here's an example of what you might say next. Adapt it to your particular circumstances:

> *"Here are some guidelines about sharing your answers.*
>
> *First, if someone shares before you do and mentions some of your own interests, desires, needs, experiences, and so on, please don't omit these items from your answers. It's important for all of us to get a sense of the levels and intensities of interests and experiences represented here.*
>
> *Second, if the person sharing asks for specific assistance on a topic along the lines of 'does anyone know the answer to X,' and you can help, it's OK to stick your hand up for long enough for them to notice you and to say your name and 'I can help with that.' Don't start giving the help there and then, just make the connection between you and the aid you're offering.*
>
> *Third: As you answer the second question, themes and topics will appear. We have roundtable scribes who are ready to capture and summarize them on* [flip charts/whiteboards/projected Google Doc].
>
> *Fourth: Please stand when it's your turn to share your answers.*
>
> *Finally, a lot of information is going to come flowing from everyone during this session. Don't expect to remember everything people say—you'll notice what's useful and meaningful for you. As each person responds to the three questions, I encourage you to make notes* [add, if you have a face book] *right next to their entry in your face book so you can keep track of who said what.*
>
> *We have* [period of time remaining] *for our sharing. So that everyone gets an equal opportunity, each of you will have up to* [time period for each attendee] *to share. You'll get a 30-second warning alert that sounds like this* [timekeeper sounds the warning alert]. *When your time is up you'll hear* [timekeeper sounds the 'time's-up' alert]. *You don't have to finish mid-sentence, but we ask that you keep to this time limit as much as possible. If you don't finish within another 20 seconds, you'll hear* [timekeeper sounds the overtime alert] *and you must stop immediately."*

Breaks

If sharing will last more than 30 minutes, provide a 5-minute break every 20 minutes. Ask that everyone be back in their seats (no changing seats) in no more than 5 minutes. Use these breaks to raise group energy with:

- Appropriate *human spectrograms*.
- The simple instruction: "Introduce yourself to someone you don't know." This can be repeated multiple times.
- A refreshment/bathroom break every hour.

About a minute before the break is due to be over, ask people to return to their seats. Multiple announcements may be necessary. If some have still not returned, don't wait for them—stay on your schedule by continuing the sharing.

Beginning sharing

You have several options for beginning sharing.

- Start with a prearranged volunteer, perhaps one of the conference organizers, who can provide a good model for the attendees who follow.
- Ask the circle, "Who wants to start?"
- If you have provided a face book sorted by name, start with the first person listed and proceed in alphabetical order.

With the first two options, once the first person is done sharing, continue around the circle. You can ask the first sharer to choose the direction to continue.

An advantage of using the third option, face book order, is that people don't have to flip through the book to find each person's entry for note taking. However, there can be awkward silences when the next person in the book is absent. To minimize these pauses, announce the next sharer's name when each attendee finishes speaking.

You want people to take an average amount of time equal to or slightly less than the time you've announced. Don't allow anyone to continue long after the second alert, and cut people off if the overtime alert sounds. (This is rarely necessary.) Interrupt them politely but firmly and ask them to end. If there is a significant trend of people overrunning their time, point this out and ask attendees to be more concise. If people are finishing too quickly, encourage them to expand their answers, by suggesting the answers you feel they could amplify.

Remind people to stand when it's their turn to answer.

Ending a roundtable

Check that everyone has shared (late attendees may arrive, or people may be missing from the face book) before wrapping up a roundtable.

CHAPTER 33
Human spectrograms

Description

I've included human spectrograms in the *Openers* section of this compendium because they provide an ideal way for participants to learn about each other early in an event. However, as you'll see, they could have been included equally well in the *Middles* or *Participatory Voting* sections of this book.

Human spectrograms—also called *human graphs*, *continuum*, or *body voting*—are one of the most versatile participative techniques. They provide an information-rich public tableau of opinions or personal information by asking participants to move to a place in the room that corresponds to their responses to questions with a range of possible answers. Human spectrograms allow session presenters, the group, and participants to directly experience the range and distribution of responses, and then explore individual responses or group outcomes as appropriate.

They can be used to:

- help attendees learn about each other;
- uncover differences and similarities;
- share the distribution of a participant attribute; for example, years of experience in a profession;
- explore opinions or display the degree of consensus on a topic;
- rate a variety of alternative options;
- create teams to discuss opposing views on a topic;
- build homogeneous (of the same kind) and heterogeneous (diverse) groups for further work; and

- allow attendees to quickly discover geographic neighbors; for example, people who live, work, or were born nearby.

Spectrograms can be *one-dimensional* or *two-dimensional*. They can also be used to display changes in participants' information or opinions over time—I call these *state-change* human spectrograms.

If all these reasons weren't enough, spectrograms are a lot of fun for participants, functioning as open-ended icebreakers during a session.

Finally, spectrograms get people moving, thinking, and interacting—features that improve learning and retention. When carefully scheduled as breaks between static activities, they offer an excellent way to maintain a high level of interest, involvement, and learning.

When?

Use human spectrograms when you want to:

- have participants learn more about each other regarding particular topics or issues.
- gain information about group and individual attributes or opinions that is more complicated than that available via a yes/no vote, for example, number of years in business, or the strength of agreement/disagreement about an issue.
- obtain geographical data and share it effectively among group members.
- create homogeneous or heterogeneous small groups.
- divide a group into teams with opposite viewpoints for a subsequent debate or discussion.
- visualize how participant information changes over time.

As I've explained earlier in this book, participatory techniques such as human spectrograms are best used as natural discovery and sharing exercises that provide a break from presentation process every 10 to 20 minutes to keep participant energy high and optimize learning. So, if it makes sense to use spectrograms in a session, rather than using the technique just once, you'll probably want to create a series of appropriate questions to be used at different points during the session. When designing your session, spend some time thinking about the order of questions you'll use. Normally, you'll move from general or warm-up questions toward more specific issues as the session continues.

Resources

As usual, if the group is large the facilitator should have a microphone. If you want to be able to interview people about their positions in a spectrogram, an additional wireless microphone can be helpful.

One-dimensional human spectrogram requirements

To run a one-dimensional human spectrogram you'll need enough completely clear room space to arrange participants into a line of bodies that reflect responses to each question asked. I call this area the *spectrogram corridor*. The line will be formed between the two walls of the room that are farthest apart (the long dimension of the room). Make the clear area at least 10 feet wide, and large enough to provide at least 10 square feet per person. Check that people can easily make their way to the open space in the room from wherever they may have been seated or standing, and that no obstacles, such as projectors, audio equipment, or podiums will obstruct the space during the process.

Some people recommend that one-dimensional spectrograms use a line of tape on the floor to show where people should stand. I don't find it necessary, but if you want to use tape, select a high quality masking tape that can easily be removed from the floor.

Two-dimensional human spectrogram requirements

Before running a two-dimensional human spectrogram, decide on the kind of geographical location you want participants to share. Usually this will be where they live or work, though you could also use where they were born, went to college, or any other useful information.

Because many participants may be unfamiliar with the local geography of the conference venue, or may simply be geographically challenged (I include myself in this category), it's helpful—though not essential—to project a map of the geographical region that will include a majority of the attendees' locations, and this map should be prepared in advance. Don't worry about including the far-off locations of a few participants; if you do, the map won't be of much use to the majority.

Search for the conference venue on a mapping service and adjust the map scale to produce an appropriate map for displaying the majority of your participants' origins. (For an optimum map, the venue may not be in the center of the resulting image.) I like to use Google My Maps: The video listed in the notes shows how to make just the custom map you want.[127]

Leave the search venue marker on the map so people can easily see their current location, and take a screen shot of the map. You can then copy the resulting image into a PowerPoint or Keynote presentation and project the image onto a screen in the room.

Finally, as with the one-dimensional spectrogram, you'll need sufficient completely clear space in the room, the *spectrogram corridor*. Allow at least 10 square feet per person, with the space's shape roughly reflecting the relative dimensions of any map you've prepared. Note that two-dimensional spectrograms generally require a wider space than one-dimensional spectrograms.

State-change human spectrogram requirements

State-change human spectrograms have no additional requirements than those described above for one- or two-dimensional human spectrograms.

How? One-dimensional human spectrograms

If time is short, you can and should introduce one-dimensional human spectrograms simply by running them on the statistic, opinion, or sentiment you wish to display. When you have time, however, I recommend you run an initial spectrogram that highlights the total amount of experience among participants.

Demonstrating the years of experience available in the room

A spectrogram of the number of years of available experience in a conference theme or session topic provides a powerful demonstration of the collective resources of the group compared to those of one or a few experts.

Say something like this:

> *"I'm going to invite you to form what's called a human spectrogram. You're going to line up in order by the number of years' experience you have in* [conference or session topic]. *So, if you've just entered the* [industry/field], *you should go to that wall* [indicate a wall at one end of the human spectrogram corridor]. *If you've been in the* [industry/field] *for many years, the sky's the limit; you should be over there* [point to the other wall of the spectrogram corridor]. *You'll need to talk to each other to figure out where you should be standing! Find your places!"*

While people move into position, estimate the number of participants in the room.

Once people have stopped moving, ask a few of those at the high experience end of the spectrogram to say how many years' experience they have and repeat their answers for the whole group. Then, walk to the middle of the line (i.e., the point where there are approximately equal numbers of participants on either side of you) and ask the people there how many years' experience they have. Use their answers to calculate the total number of years by saying something like:

> *"So the median number of years of experience here is ten* [replace by actual median] *years. Since there are 80* [replace by actual estimate of people in the group] *people here, we have about 800* [10 × 80; replace by actual multiplied figure] *years of experience in* [industry/ field] *present in this room. This is far more experience than any one or two people could have."*

If appropriate, you may want to add:

> *"We're going to tap that experience right now to your benefit."*

And if you plan to run small heterogeneous or homogeneous groups later in the session, this is the time to create them, as described in the section below.

Lighthearted and conference-specific spectrogram introductions

If you are running several spectrograms and have the time, you can introduce participants to the exercise with an enjoyable example. I like to have people line up in order of their birthday. (Just the day of the year—e.g., September 22—not the year they were born!) Before running the spectrogram ask people what they think the odds are that two people in the room have the same birthday.

Nearly everybody underestimates the likelihood that will happen. It turns out that if you have more than 23 people in the room, it's more likely than not that two people share a birthday; with 30, the probability is 70%; with 50, 97%; and with 100, 99.99997%. It's always fun to see people's surprise when they invariably discover shared birthdays; with a large group there will be several sets. In fact, with more than 88 people in the room, there's a better than even chance that there will be three people with the same birthday in the group!

Say something like this:

> *"In this session we're going to find out about each other and get some information about the group by forming several human spectrograms. To illustrate, I want you to line yourselves up in order by your birthday. Not the year you were born, just the date! But before we do this I have a question for you; what do you think the likelihood is that we'll find that two of you have the same birthday?"*

Get responses and then compare them with the statistics given above. For example, since a group of 30 people rarely thinks that any two people will share a birthday, you might say:

> *"Actually, the odds are about 70% that two of you have the same birthday. Let's find out now!"*

If the group has around 100 or more people, ask what they think the likelihood is that three people will share the same birthday. After hearing responses you might say:

> *"Actually it's very likely that there will be several groups of people who share the same birthday, and the odds are, in fact, that there will be three people here who share the same birthday. Let's find out!"*

Continue as follows:

> *"So, if your birthday is January 1, you should go to that wall* [indicate a wall at one end of the human spectrogram corridor]. *If your birthday is December 31, you should be standing over there* [point to the other wall of the spectrogram corridor]. *You'll need to talk to each other to figure out where you should be standing! Find your places!"*

Wait while people are moving into position. When everyone has figured out where they should be (and you'll probably hear the surprise of the people who discover they have birthdays in common), poll the group by saying something like:

> *"So does anyone share a birthday with someone else here? Raise your hand if you do!"*

Comment on the results, pointing out if there are three people sharing a birthday. Then say:

> *"See how quickly we figured that out? We'll be using more human spectrograms during this session."*

CHAPTER 33: Human spectrograms

It can also be fun to run one or two spectrograms about lighthearted topics: how much people like ice cream, what's their favorite day of the week (line up from Monday to Sunday with breaks between the days), how many different states or countries people have lived in, how long did it take participants to travel to the event, or how many conferences have they attended this year. Run these spectrograms quickly, don't spend more than a few minutes total, and only do this if you have several useful spectrograms planned during the session.

Finally, choosing interesting subjects, issues, or concerns that are rankable and that relate to the conference, session topic, or industry can be a great way for participants to learn useful information about each other, discover commonalities, and get a better sense of the composition of the group.

Using one-dimensional human spectrograms for various purposes

The applications of human spectrograms are limited only by one's imagination. They are useful whenever there's a reason to publicly display distributions of participant data or opinions. In addition, they provide an excellent method to effectively create similar or dissimilar teams or small groups for further activities. Here's how to run them:

Uncovering differences and similarities, exploring opinions, displaying the degree of consensus on a topic, or sharing the distribution of a participant attribute

One-dimensional spectrograms provide a great opportunity to obtain and share information about group and individual attributes or opinions that is more complicated than that available via a yes/no vote; for example, the distribution of the number of employees in participants' organizations, or the strength of agreement/disagreement about an issue. If you are planning to run a series of spectrograms, I suggest you start with easy-to-answer questions and move toward harder or more ambiguous topics. Adapt the following example for your specific needs:

> *"Let's explore how much we agree or disagree about* [statement X] *by forming a human spectrogram. The space between these two walls* [point to them] *represents a continuum of agreement to disagreement. You're going to place yourself in the space depending on how much you agree or disagree. So, if you strongly agree with* [statement X] *you should line up at that wall* [indicate a wall at one end of the human spectrogram corridor]. *If you strongly disagree with* [statement X] *you should be over there* [point to the other wall of the spectrogram corridor]. *Those are the extremes; I invite you to show us where you stand on the line between these two viewpoints. Find your places!"*

Once people have found their positions, summarize what you see. For example, if everyone is more or less in agreement, that may be all you need to observe. To find out more about participant thinking or sentiment, walk up and down the line and interview a few people (you can ask for volunteers) at representative points. Provide a microphone if the group is large, or repeat their comments.

After hearing opinions and arguments, it's possible that people may want to change their position in the spectrogram. When appropriate, encourage them to do so. Suggest that participants notice who is standing where on the spectrogram. This helps people find people in common as well as those who have different points of view.

Depending on what happens and your goals for the session, you may move into a discussion of some kind. Someone might suggest a slightly different statement and you may decide to run a spectrogram to explore it. Plan to stay flexible with what comes up while you're using a spectrogram, and be prepared to take advantage of unexpected and interesting opportunities that arise.

Rating a variety of options

One way to explore opinions about options you've developed earlier in a session or plan to put to the group is to create a series of spectrograms, one for each option. For example, you might have three different proposals to increase revenue for an organization. One wall represents unqualified approval of the option, the other represents strong disapproval. Run each spectrogram as described in the previous section, and publicly review the resulting distribution of participants. You may want to mark the median level of approval for each option on the floor of the room. This enables you to determine the level of consensus and identify who strongly favors or opposes a specific choice. Interviewing those with strong opinions can rapidly uncover important issues or constituencies to address.

Creating discussions on opposing viewpoints

If you want to create a discussion about a topic or issue, you can use a one-dimensional spectrogram to check on the degree of agreement. For example, you might ask participants whether they are in favor of increasing expenditures on local public transportation. Once the spectrogram is formed and opposing views are apparent, either interview people along the line to hear representative reasons for their points of view or partition the group at the median point of the line of participants into two teams to discuss the issue. Consider using a two sides fishbowl as described in Chapter 42 to hold a follow-up discussion.

Building heterogeneous or homogeneous groups for further work

When facilitating small group work, you need to decide how to divide participants into groups. Random selection often works well, especially if you ask participants to put themselves in groups with people they don't know. However, it's frequently desirable to create heterogeneous groups with a mixture of experience levels represented (novices through veterans). And occasionally you'll want to divide a group into homogeneous cohorts (i.e., separate veteran groups and novice groups). Spectrograms provide a fast, effective way to do this.

First, run a spectrogram for the attribute that you wish to select on. Usually this will be a "years of experience" spectrogram as described above.

CHAPTER 33: Human spectrograms

If you want *heterogeneous* groups (the most likely choice), while people are moving into position divide the number of people in the room by the desired group size. Once everyone is in position, walk to one end of the spectrogram and say:

> "We're now going to divide into [Y] separate small groups. To do this I'm going to have each of you count off from 1 to [Y] starting at this end of the spectrogram. When I point at you, say, and remember(!), the next number—that will be your group number. When we get to [Y] the next person starts again at 1.
>
> Please remember your group number! If you forget it, ask the people on either side of you what theirs is so you can figure yours out."

Walk down the line staying opposite whoever is saying their group number. If people are bunched together, point to them and check that no one is missed. When everyone has counted off, remind people one more time:

> "Please remember your group number! If you've forgotten it, ask the people on either side of you what theirs is so you can figure yours out."

If you want *homogeneous* groups, the procedure is simpler. Start at one end of the line, and count, pointing, the first × people. Tell them they are Group 1. The next × people are Group 2, and so on.

How? Two-dimensional human spectrograms

One of the most basic and powerful ways we connect with others is by living or working in the same community. As a conference attendee, wouldn't you like to be able to easily discover other attendees who live and/or work near you? Well, you can use a two-dimensional human spectrogram to do just that in a few minutes!

When it's time to run the spectrogram, if you have created the map described earlier in the chapter, display it and stand in your room's clear space in a spot facing the map, positioned in the room so that you mirror the position of the venue marker on the map. If you are using the spectrogram to show where people live or work you might say:

> "Let's find out where everyone [lives/works]. OK, this direction [point, usually from where you're standing toward the projected map] is north, and where I'm standing in the room is [the location of the conference], so if you [live/work] around the corner you'll stand right next to me. Here's a map of [the conference region/country/continent] for the geographically challenged, like me. Please move to stand where you [live/work]. You'll need to talk to each other!"

If you haven't prepared a map, point in turn to north, east, south, and west while asking people to move. If there are major cities or landmarks nearby, point to where they would be represented in the room.

Wait while people determine where to stand. Once most people seem to have found their right location relative to you and each other you could say:

> "If you've figured out where to stand, take a look at the people around you! Is there anyone nearby who you don't know? If there is, introduce yourself to them! Feel free to swap business cards!"

Give participants some time to introduce themselves to their neighbors. When talking starts to die down, comment on the distribution of people in the room. Ask anyone who is from far away where they live/work.

You can use two-dimensional histograms for any geographical mapping of participant information, such as where they were born, where they went to school, or their favorite vacation destination. You can also use them to investigate any two personal pieces of information that may display an interesting relationship when spectrogram-graphed for the group; for example, participants' self-evaluation of extroversion-introversion versus how creative they see themselves, how much control they have over their schedule compared with how productive they rate themselves, or the size of their staff versus their departmental budget.

How? State-change human spectrograms

A state-change human spectrogram displays information about how participants' opinions, answers to questions, and geographical locations have changed over time. Here are some examples of typical applications:

- Exploring how participant comfort level before an exercise compares with the level afterwards (one-dimensional).
- Seeing how group opinion on a topic or question has changed during the course of the session (one-dimensional).
- Visualizing how participants have moved their job or home locations over time (two-dimensional).

Every state-change human spectrogram needs an initial spectrogram to provide a baseline to compare one or more subsequent changes. If you are planning to run several state-change spectrograms, it may be helpful to decide on a "baseline" spectrogram that can be compared with subsequent variations.

Once you've planned how to use the state-change technique, run an initial one- or two-dimensional spectrogram as previously described. Have participants take their positions and share any relevant observations.

If you are not going to do a comparison right away, ask everyone to remember their position in the room. If the room has distinguishing features, such as posters on the walls, suggest that people remember where they are standing by using the features as a reference. Otherwise, suggest that they mentally remember their position as a number between 0 and 10. Emphasize that everyone will be asked to return to her current position later in the session.

When it's time to see how the spectrogram has changed, have all participants return to their memorized places in the room.

Once everyone is in their initial spectrogram positions, say:

> *"OK, don't move yet; listen to the instructions!*
>
> *We're now going to explore* [your response to a new question, or the same question after some session work]."

Either state the question, defining what the two walls represent, or remind participants of the original question and the two extremes represented by the walls, and say:

> *"Don't move yet! Decide where you're going to move to indicate your* [response to the question]. *Any questions?"*

Answer any questions, and then say:

> *"When I say go, move to your new spot, and watch what's happening with the group.*
>
> *Go!"*

Summarize any trends you see and ask for comments from the group.

If your initial spectrogram was a baseline for multiple state-change spectrograms, now have people return to their initial positions and run the next state-change spectrogram.

CHAPTER 34
The Solution Room

Description

Although the basic concept of The Solution Room is not new, the design described in this chapter is derived from a session at Meeting Professionals International's 2011 European Meetings & Events Conference[128] that was co-created on-site[129] by Robert Benninga, Simon Bucknall, Midori Connolly, Miranda Ioannou, Ruud Janssen, Linda Pereira, David Bancroft Turner, and Mike van der Vijver. Ruud produced a short video of the original session,[130] as well as a longer video of participant testimonials.[131]

The Solution Room is a powerful conference session, typically lasting between 90 and 120 minutes, which both engages and connects attendees and provides peer-supported advice on their most pressing challenges. By facilitating peer interaction and consultation at the start of an event, The Solution Room creates a conference environment that embodies participation, peer learning, and targeted problem solving. By the end of the session, every participant will have had the opportunity to receive advice and support on a challenge of his choosing.

I am continually surprised and pleased by the level of trust Solution Room participants exhibit. Many want to talk about difficult professional problems they are encountering, frequently involving interpersonal issues. The Solution Room gives people a safe place to talk with peers. And because each participant chooses what he wants to discuss, he controls the level of intimacy of what he shares.

A session of 20 or more people starts with a short introduction, followed by a human spectrogram (see Chapter 33) that demonstrates the amount of experience available in the room. Next, participants are given some time to think of a challenge they have for which they would like to receive peer advice. A second human spectrogram follows that maps participants' comfort level.

CHAPTER 34: The Solution Room

Participants are then divided into small equally sized groups of between six and eight people, each group sharing a round table covered with flip chart paper and plenty of colored markers. Group members then individually describe their challenge on the paper in front of them using mindmapping (described below). Each participant in turn has the same amount of time to explain his issue to the others at the table and receive advice and support.

When sharing is complete, two final human spectrograms provide a public group evaluation that maps the shift in comfort level of all the participants and the likelihood that participants will work to change what they've just shared.

When?

The Solution Room can be used at various stages during an event. My personal placement preference (say that quickly three times) is as a conference opener, because of its power to model an environment of participation and peer sharing for the remainder of the event.

The Solution Room is also an ideal session to use early during a traditional conference that does not use an initial roundtable. It can be scheduled after an opening plenary, for example. I recommend that the session be placed early in the conference program, so its benefits extend over the longest possible remainder of the event.

Interestingly, The Solution Room can also be used as a closing session. (This is how Ruud Janssen likes to schedule it.) When run at the end of a conference, you can emphasize uncovering issues that were not addressed during the event. As a closing session, The Solution Room provides an effective concluding burst of energy and some targeted next steps for participants to address when they return home.

Resources

Make sure that the room space and round table resources described below are available *before* scheduling a Solution Room session! Also be sure to satisfy the requirements for holding a human spectrogram, as described in Chapter 33.

Room space

The Solution Room requires a room large enough to hold all participants seated at 48-, 54-, or 60-inch round tables, plus enough open space along the long dimension of the room to hold human spectrograms for everyone.

To see whether a room is large enough for The Solution Room, first review the floor plan to obtain the clear room dimensions. Consult Chapter 33 for the space needs for human spectrograms. Normally the spectrogram area will be along one of the long walls of the room, but it's also possible to use a clear corridor down the middle of the room; this may be preferable if the long walls have obstacles or entrances along their length. Determine the space needed for the spectrograms and subtract this area from the clear room area. The remaining space will be used for the round tables. Now you need to calculate how many tables will fit in this space.

To determine the area required for each round table, add 5 feet to the diameter of the table. A square of this size will be needed for each round table. Thus each 60-inch table (8 people) needs 100 square feet of space, each 54-inch table (7 ? 8 people) needs 90.25 square feet of space, and each 48-inch table (6 people) table will require 81 square feet of space. See how many complete "table squares" will fit into the room's remaining table area and multiply by the number of chairs at each table. The resulting number must be equal to or greater than the proposed number of participants.

Round tables

The recommended round table diameters for The Solution Room are 48, 54 or 60 inches. Do not use tables larger than 60 inches in diameter, as participants will not be able to reliably hear each other due to their distance from the people opposite them and the noise of other conversations in the room.

Although uncommon, hexagonal or octagonal 48-inch classroom tables can also be used.

Completely cover tables in advance with sufficient layers of flip chart paper so that markers will not bleed through.

Setup

The Solution Room requires a certain amount of setup that can take some time for a large session. Be sure to provide the staff who will be setting the room with a diagram of your room set, since the combination of banquet style plus open space may not be a standard configuration.

Playing music as participants enter The Solution Room is a nice optional touch. Pick music that sets the ambiance you're seeking. And if, as described in the next section, you wish to use campfire/jungle visuals to dramatize the comfort level spectrogram you'll need a couple of projectors and screens set up with appropriate images at opposite ends of the spectrogram corridor in the room. (See the notes for two suggested Creative Commons licensed images.)[132]

Supply each table with fine tip markers in a variety of bright colors, with at least two pens per participant. If you're going to assign people to specific tables (see the next two sections) a set of plastic table numbers, displayed in table stanchions, can be useful; or simply write the table number on the paper at the center of each table before the session begins.

You'll also need a timing solution and assigned timekeeper, as described in Chapter 15. Although an experienced session facilitator can juggle timekeeping and session direction, it's better to use a dedicated timekeeper. The timekeeper will need to provide three time signals for each table member's sharing: after a minute has passed (end challenge explanation), a minute before the end (wrap-up warning), and when time is up.

The Solution Room works well with multiple facilitators; consider having more than one available, especially for a large number of participants. Having several facilitators makes it easier to guide participants to seating and to respond to questions during the exercise.

If your group is large, it's helpful to assign someone to count the number of participants during the first human spectrogram.

Small group size and session time considerations

I recommend table groups of between six and eight people. I am not a fan of larger group sizes (though nine people can be squeezed in around a 60-inch table), because that means larger tables, and it becomes difficult to hear the other participants. The number of people at each table determines the time needed for the session.

Provide enough time for The Solution Room so the session is unrushed. In practice you should allocate at least 75 minutes, and the session can be run profitably for as long as 2 hours or more with the larger table sizes and/or question/suggestion/discussion format described in the next section. The session can be split into the following components:

- Spectrograms.
- Instructions, mindmapping, and small group division.
- Sharing.

Here's how to calculate and allocate total session time.

Spectrogram timing

The time required for the human spectrograms depends on the number of participants. As a guide, allow 5 minutes for each spectrogram for a group of 50, and 8 minutes for a group of 200.

If time is short, you can omit the initial comfort spectrogram and final two spectrograms, saving 15 to 20 minutes, but I'd suggest instead cutting a minute or two off each participant's time to share. Do not omit the initial experience spectrogram—this is crucial for demonstrating the wealth of peer experience available in the room, and will also be needed if you plan to create heterogeneous small groups.

Time for instructions, mindmapping, and small group division

Allow 15 minutes to cover giving instructions and individual mindmap time.

The time required to divide people into appropriate small groups and get them seated depends on two factors: the extra time, if needed, to create table "interest tracks" of conference peers and the total number of session participants.

The simplest and quickest seating strategy is to seat people at random, asking them to sit at a table with people they don't know. An alternative quick way to produce small heterogeneous groups that only takes a minute is described in the next section.

Neither of these approaches may be the best choice if your Solution Room includes subgroups with widely varying interests. In this case, because you usually don't know in advance the mix of interests at a session, you will have to create "interest tracks" of table groups on the fly. Your goal should be to provide an interesting peer group at each table. As with roundtables, there is a trade-off between random assignment, which can lead to valuable cross-fertilization of ideas and expertise, and division by specialty or interest, which allows close peers to optimally share and support each other. If your attendees have distinguishing interests, it's often best to divide them into small table groups that reflect these interests. Avoid assigning participants to tables by geographical origin, as at most conferences people prefer meeting those they consider their true peers, irrespective of whether they work near each other.

Decide which of these three methods you will use to distribute participants to tables—random distribution, heterogeneous groups that each contain a range of years of industry/field experience, or assignment by specialty or interest—before your session starts.

Then read the description of table assignment in the following section and estimate the amount of time this will require for your session. Typically, table assignment takes between 6 minutes for 50 people in a few categories to 12 minutes for 200 attendees in five or six categories.

Finally, add a couple of minutes for a group of 50 to get seated at their tables, and up to double that for 200 people to move to their correct tables once their interest track has been determined.

Sharing time

Give each participant a *minimum* of 6 minutes to share their problem or challenge for regular table sharing. More time is preferable. Twelve minutes allows some in-depth discussion and feedback. An alternative question/suggestion/discussion format requires at least 15 minutes per person. This approach, best used with 50 or fewer participants, is described in the next section.

Timing examples

Fifty people, six people/table, small group division by interest, brief session:

> 4 spectrograms, 5 minutes each = 20 minutes
>
> 15 minutes for instructions and mindmapping plus 8 minutes for small group division and seating = 23 minutes
>
> 6 per table at 6 minutes each = 36 minutes
>
> Total time = 79 minutes

Two hundred people, eight people/table, small group division by interest:

> 4 spectrograms, 8 minutes each = 32 minutes
>
> 15 minutes for instructions and mindmapping plus 16 minutes for small group division and seating = 31 minutes
>
> 8 per table at 8 minutes (facilitator's choice) each = 64 minutes
>
> Total time = 127 minutes

CHAPTER 34: The Solution Room

How?

Before the session starts, arrange to guide people entering the room to stand facing you in the human spectrogram corridor space. If the group is large you'll probably need some assistants to steer participants to the area. If people enter the room early, direct them to sit at tables close to the spectrogram corridor until shortly before the session starts.

Once everyone is standing in front of you, introduce The Solution Room like this:

> *"Welcome to The Solution Room! This session is a participant-driven opportunity for each of you to get consulting from your peers on a professional challenge that you choose.*
>
> *Along the way, you'll also get to know a number of your peers who are here today.*
>
> *Please make a commitment to stay for the whole session. If you leave early, your peers will lose the benefit of your experience and expertise.*
>
> *The first thing we're going to do is to see how much [conference topic]-related expertise and experience we have in this room.*
>
> *I'd like each of you to think about how many years you've been involved in working in or with [conference topic].*
>
> *[Pause]*
>
> *I'm now going to invite you to form what's called a human spectrogram. You're going to line up in order by the number of years' experience you have in [conference topic]. So, if you've just entered the [industry/field] you should go to that wall [indicate a wall at one end of the human spectrogram corridor]. If you've been in the [industry/field] for many years, the sky's the limit; you should be over there [point to the other wall of the spectrogram corridor]. You'll need to talk to each other to figure out where you should be standing! Find your places!"*

While participants move into place, if you are using heterogeneous groups, have someone count the number of people in the spectrogram. Otherwise an estimate will suffice.

Once people have stopped moving, ask a few people at the high experience end of the spectrogram to say how many years' experience they have and repeat their answers for the whole group. Then, walk to the middle of the line and ask the people there how many years' experience they have. Use their answer to calculate the total number of years' experience in the room by saying something like:

> *"So the median number of years of experience here is 10 [replace by actual median] years. Since there are 80 [replace by actual estimate of people in the group] people here, we have about 800 [10 × 80; replace by actual multiplied figure] years of experience in [industry/ field] present in this room. This is far more experience than any one or two people could have. We're going to tap that experience right now to your benefit."*

If you're dividing participants into heterogeneous groups

If you have fewer than a hundred participants and will be creating heterogeneous small groups with a distribution of years of industry/field experience at each table, count the number of people in the spectrogram, divide by the number of chairs at each table and round up your answer to the nearest whole number.

For example, if there are 53 participants and eight chairs at each table you'll need 6.625 tables, which you round up to seven tables. (In this case, you'll end up with four tables with eight people each and three tables with seven people each.)

Once you have the number of tables you need, start at one end of the spectrogram, point to each person in turn, and have people count off from one up to the number of tables; in the example above, the seventh person says "seven," and the eighth starts again at "one," and so on. Before you begin, tell everyone to remember their number. When everyone has counted off, ask them whether they still remember their number; if not, they can ask their neighbors.

Deciding on a personal challenge

Next say:

> *"Now I'm going to invite you to think of a challenge that's currently occupying your professional life. Perhaps you've already been sparked by conversations you've had here. Or, perhaps you have a professional challenge you're now facing.*
>
> *This is an opportunity for you to receive consulting and support from your peers. I want this to be a safe session for you all. If there are two or more of you from the same organization I'm going to ask you to work at separate tables. And I want everyone to treat confidentially what is shared in this session today.*
>
> *If something came into your head when I mentioned a professional challenge, that's probably what you should be working on. Don't try to filter what's coming up for you.*
>
> *Now I'm going to give you a couple of minutes to decide on your challenge to work on today."*

Wait for about 90 seconds and say:

> *"You're going to have some time to think about how to share your challenge with others in a small group. Please raise your hand if you have decided on your challenge to work on today."*

Allow a little more time if a significant number of people need it. Then say:

> *"Now let's do another spectrogram about how comfortable you feel about working on this challenge.*
>
> *First, think about how difficult or easy will it be for you to solve the challenge you have in mind after this conference. Now assess for yourself, how comfortable do you feel about working on solving this challenge?"*

At this point, if you've chosen to illustrate the two comfort levels visually, turn on the two projectors showing the campfire image on "Wall A" and jungle image on "Wall B" at the opposite ends of the spectrogram corridor.

> *"To gauge your comfort level I'll give you two scenarios. Stand close to* [point to Wall A]— *think: a wonderful evening around a campfire with friends and guitar music—if you have a high comfort level about working on this challenge. At the other extreme* [point to Wall B], *you're in the middle of the jungle, you can hear wild animals around you and it's very, very dark. That would be a low comfort level about working on this challenge. Now, place yourself between these two walls to represent your comfort level about working on your challenge. High comfort* [point to Wall A]; *low comfort* [point to Wall B]."

If people seem reluctant to move, add a personal note: *"I've had challenges where I'd be standing over here, and others where I'd be standing over there."*

Wait until people have arranged themselves and say:

> *"Great! OK, this is important. Remember where you're standing!"*

Point out any visual landmarks available, such as posters on the wall, that can help people remember where they're standing in the room.

> *"We'll revisit your comfort level later."*

It's time to split participants into peer groups if appropriate (see the previous section).

If you're dividing participants into peer groups

If you decided to divide people into peer groups, here's an example of what you might say. Adapt for your specific peer group categories!

> *"I'm going to divide you into peer groups now. Let's start with the big divide: association executives over here* [point to a clear spot in the room]; *suppliers over here* [point to another clear spot]. *If you straddle both worlds, stay in the middle for a moment.*
>
> [An organizer] *gave me a list of attendee job titles and I've come up with the following categories. I'll read them one at a time; please pick the category that best fits for you. If none of these categories fit, you can let me know shortly.*
>
> [Association executives example]
>
> | | |
> |---|---|
> | *Directors* | *Events* |
> | *Chapter relations* | *Membership* |
> | *Marketing* | *Operations* |
> | *Sales* | *Other* |
>
> *Is there anyone here who feels they don't fit in one of these categories?"*

If a hand is raised, say, *"Describe yourself,"* and assign them appropriately.

Ask the peer groups to move to different parts of the room. If some groups are very small, combine them with similar groups. Then say:

> *"I'm now going to have you take your places at the tables, one peer group at a time. Please arrange yourselves next to people you don't know. If you have a choice, choose a table with people you don't know. Please fill each table before starting a new one."*

Now ask people to walk into the table area single file and fill a contiguous set of tables, one group at a time. Your aim should be to have most tables full, and have one (and not more than one) empty place at a few. Once each group is seated, if one or two people are still at a table by themselves, you can have the next group fill up their table. After the last group has taken its place, if the last table is not full, ask one person from each of the previous tables to join the table until it is almost full. When everyone is seated, every table should be full, or have, at most, one empty place.

If you're seating participants at random

Say:

> *"Please arrange yourselves next to people you don't know. Now take your places at the tables, sitting with people you don't know. Please fill tables before starting a new one."*

Guide participants in single file to fill tables. After everyone has taken a seat, consolidate tables that are not full. If the one remaining table is not full, ask one person from each of the nearby tables to join the table until it is almost full. When everyone is seated, every table should be full, or have, at most, one empty place.

Running mindmapping

Now say:

> *"You now have a few minutes to mindmap your own professional challenge. You've got paper in front of you and plenty of colored pens. Create a concise, few-word summary of your challenge, write it down and maybe place it in a circle. Then if it's helpful, add a few details around your challenge summary. Your goal should be to be ready to explain your challenge clearly and briefly in 1 minute or less. Be clear about the help you're asking for from your peers.*
>
> *If you'd like help expressing your challenge, raise your hand and* [I and any other available facilitators] *will come and help as many of you as we can. Please begin!"*

Give people 2 to 3 minutes to work. When most people seem ready, announce that sharing will start in another 30 seconds. Once this time is up, it's time for table sharing to start.

Giving away your problem

Say:

"I invite you all now to stand up and move one seat clockwise to your left."

Wait until everyone has moved.

"Congratulations! You have just given your problem up for adoption!"

Pause here; people usually laugh!

"Each of you in turn is going to have to interpret what is in front of you. You have to decipher what is there. Do so by asking open-ended questions to the person whose problem it was.

I'll explain the timing first and then what you're going to do for each person at your table. You will each have [number of minutes] for your consultation. I'll let you know when a minute remains. Please use all your time; don't go on to the next person early. If you have any spare time, use it to add more to earlier consults.

Here's how the timing works."

Timing explanation

Describe and demonstrate the timing method you have chosen.

"When your time is up, please start right away with the next person at your table; otherwise they'll lose out on their consulting time.

If there are less than [number of chairs at each table] people at your table, the extra time at the end can be used for additional consulting. However, please stick to the timing schedule for each person until everyone has had a turn."

Regular table sharing format

If time is short, or you have more than 50 participants, I suggest you use the regular table sharing format. Say:

"When it's your turn, you have three jobs to do:

1. Read the challenge that is in front of you out loud.

2. Start asking questions of the person whose challenge it is to clarify the issue.

3. Take notes of the ensuing discussion on the paper in front of you. When The Solution Room is over, each of you can tear off and take away with you the paper that contains your challenge and the notes made about it, or take a photograph.

Everyone at the table should join in to ask clarifying questions and give advice and support."

Alternative question/suggestion/discussion table sharing format

If you can allow at least 15 minutes per person and have fewer than 50 participants, you may decide to use this longer, more structured sharing format. Here's how it works. Say:

> *"When it's your turn, you have three jobs to do.*
>
> *1. Read the challenge that is in front of you out loud.*
>
> *2. Start asking questions of the person whose problem it was to clarify the challenge in front of you. Take about a minute to get started. When the minute is up there will be a question round, then a suggestion round, and then a discussion.*
>
> *3. Take notes of the ensuing discussion on the paper in front of you. When The Solution Room is over, each of you can tear off and take away with you the paper that contains your challenge and the notes made about it.*
>
> *In the question round, each of your peers in turn will ask you a question about your challenge. Answer it succinctly, but don't get into a discussion of your answer. Those of you who are listening, ask for clarification, if needed, and then do what you can to help your colleague.*
>
> *In the suggestion round, each of your peers in turn will make a suggestion about dealing with your challenge. Listen and make notes of the suggestions, but don't respond during this round.*
>
> *Finally, use the remainder of your* [previously calculated number of] *consultation minutes to discuss your challenge. I'll let you know when a minute remains. Please use all your time; don't go on to the next person early. If you have any spare time, use it to add more to earlier consults. When the time is up, please start right away with the next person at your table; otherwise they'll lose out."*

Start the sharing

Now say:

> *"A reminder: what is shared here remains confidential, for your table's ears only.*
>
> *If you or your group would like help working on a challenge, raise your hand and* [I and any other available facilitators] *will come and help as many of you as we can.*
>
> *I'd like someone to volunteer to start at each table."*

Check that a hand is raised at every table, and prompt if necessary.

> *"First person, begin!"*

For each table member's sharing:

> *One minute before sharing time is over, say, "You have a minute remaining."*
>
> *When sharing time is up, say, "Please bring your sharing to a close."*

CHAPTER 34: The Solution Room

Wait a few seconds and then ask the next person at the table to begin. It saves time if the first person who shares chooses the direction of sharing around the table. If there's plenty of time for the exercise, you can ask for someone at each table to volunteer to be the next person to share.

While sharing is going on, monitor the table conversations to ensure a single conversation at each table. If you notice cross-conversations, politely ask what's going on, and this will usually bring the participants back on task.

When everyone has shared at the tables that have one empty seat, say:

> "If everyone has shared at your table, please use this final sharing time for additional consulting."

When all sharing is complete, say:

> "Remember, you can continue these conversations after the session!"

Running the comparison comfort level spectrogram

Now say:

> "Now we're going to see how comfortable you feel about working on your challenge, compared to how you felt before. Please take any notes on your table you wish to keep, or photograph them, and move back to the spectrogram space. [Point to the spectrogram corridor and wait until people are moving there.]
>
> Remember where you stood at the beginning of The Solution Room to indicate your comfort level on how you felt about working on solving your challenge? Go and stand there! [Wait until people have moved to where they stood before.]
>
> OK, don't move yet; listen to the instructions!
>
> We're going to assess how comfortable you feel now about working on solving this challenge.
>
> Reminder [point to Wall A]—Think: a wonderful evening around a campfire with friends and guitar music—if you have a high comfort level now about working on solving this challenge. [point to Wall B] You're in the middle of the jungle, you can hear wild animals around you and it's very, very dark. That would be a low comfort level about working on solving this challenge now. Now, I'm going to invite you to decide where to place yourself between these two walls to represent your comfort level about working on solving your challenge. High comfort [point to Wall A]; low comfort [point to Wall B].
>
> Don't move yet! Decide where you're going to move to indicate your new comfort level. If you're more comfortable now, move toward the campfire [point to Wall A]. If you're less comfortable now, move toward the jungle [point to Wall B]. Any questions?
>
> When I say go, move to your new spot, and watch what's happening with the group.
>
> Go!"

Summarize the trend you see (e.g., "Most of you seem much more comfortable about working on solving your challenge, though the comfort level for a few is unchanged, and a few people are less comfortable about working on solving their challenge than they were.")

Running the final spectrogram (optional)

If you are projecting the campfire and jungle images turn them off now. Then say:

> *"Finally we're going to map the likelihood that you will work to overcome the challenge you've just shared.*
>
> *If you are definitely going to work to overcome the challenge you've just shared then you should stand next to this wall* [point to Wall A]. *Perhaps you've been convinced by your peers that you shouldn't work on this challenge? If so, stand next to this wall* [point to Wall B]. *Now, place yourself between these two walls to represent the likelihood that you will work to overcome the challenge you've just shared. Will definitely work* [point to Wall A]; *will definitely not work* [point to Wall B]."

Summarize the trend you see (e.g., "It looks like most of you have some productive work ahead of you, while a few of you have second thoughts.")

Ending The Solution Room

A brief closing is best. Say something like:

> *"You've all been great! Thank the people who gave you advice!* [Pause] *Remember to continue these conversations later. You all made this session possible, so a warm round of applause from everybody for everybody else!* [Pause for applause] *The Solution Room is over! Thank you very much!"*

CHAPTER 35
Post It!

Description

Post It! is a simple technique for uncovering topics and issues that a group wants to discuss. It is a simpler version of Affinity Grouping, described later in this book. Post It! can be used at various event levels for:

- All the attendees at an event.
- Breakout groups discussing a specialty set of topics.
- A single conference session.

If you're a conference presenter with an audience of less than 50 people, you can use Post It! to rapidly discover audience interests and help decide what those present would like to hear about.

Alternatively, Post It! provides an effective and efficient way for a group to learn and reflect on its members' interests. If you need to process in more detail the topics uncovered, consider using the Affinity Grouping technique.

When?

Run Post It! at the opening of an event, breakout group, or a single session.

Resources

It is surely no surprise that you'll need one or more sticky notes (e.g., Post-it® brand) for each participant. If you're using Post It! for a presenter tool at a single session, supply a single 2″ × 3″ note to each attendee. For a group display of topics, supply one to four 6″ × 8″ (preferred size) notes, or 3″ × 5″ notes if posting space is limited.

Have sufficient pens available.

Finally, you'll need clear, accessible wall or noticeboard space for posting. Walls should be smooth and clean, as sticky notes don't adhere well to rough or dirty surfaces. Test any wall you're planning to use beforehand as some surfaces will not hold sticky notes reliably, in which case you'll need to tape up some large sheets of paper to hold the notes. If you're using Post It! as a presenter tool, the posting area should be close to where you are standing in the room so you can easily refer to it.

How?

How a presenter can use Post It! to shape the content of a session

Before the session begins, give each participant a single sticky note and a pen. Ask the audience to write down the one topic they would like explored or question they would like answered during the session. Give everyone a couple of minutes to write their response and collect the notes as they are completed. As you collect the notes, browse their contents and mentally categorize them into broad themes. For example, some attendees ask specific questions, some may want an overview of your topic, and some may want you to cover one particular aspect. Once all the notes have been collected, briefly read each note out loud and add it to a cluster of similar notes on the wall next to you. You may find a note that is unique and needs to be placed by itself.

Once all the notes have been stuck on the wall, it should be clear to both you and your audience what the group is interested in. Don't feel obliged to cover everything mentioned. Instead, use the notes to make a plan of how you will spend your time with the group. Describe your plan briefly, and apologize for topics that you're not able to cover in the time available. Even if you don't cover everything requested, your audience will have the information to understand why you made the choices you did. If you're going to be available after the session is over, you can invite attendees to meet with you to talk more.

As you continue with your audience-customized session, you can refer to the note clusters to confirm that you're covering your plan.

Using Post It! to make public the interests and questions of a group

Before the session begins, decide on the number of sticky notes to give participants. This is determined by the size of the group and the time available for any resulting sessions. See Table 35.1 for recommended number of notes by group size.

TABLE 35.1 • *Suggested number of notes provided to each person for group Post It! exercise*

SIZE OF GROUP	SUGGESTED NUMBER OF NOTES FOR EACH PARTICIPANT
20–30	2–4
30–50	2–3
50–100	1–2
100+	1

Hand out the sticky notes and a pen to attendees. Ask them to write down one or more topics they would like explored or questions they would like answered during the session, one per note. Tell them they do not need to use all their notes. Indicate the wall area where notes can be posted, and ask them, once they have finished, to post their notes on the wall. Give participants a few minutes to write their responses. As the notes are posted it is natural for people to hang around the wall and read what others have written. Let them do this, but ask people to allow late posters to get to the wall.

Once all the notes have been posted, provide some time for everyone to take in the topics and questions. This group sharing can then be used as a starting point for Open Space, fishbowls, Plus/Delta, and so on.

CHAPTER 36
Middles

THIS SECTION OF THE BOOK covers participation techniques that can be profitably used during the "middle" of a group's time together. These techniques focus on improving *learning*, *engagement*, and *connection* during the sessions that fill most conventional events: that is, sessions that inform attendees about what the event program designers consider to be core content.

I've divided these techniques into three groups:

Techniques that facilitate productive small group discussions

As I explained in the first part of this book, learning, engagement, and connection are more effective and more likely to occur when people work in small groups. The techniques in this section cover a wide variety of ways to appropriately integrate small group work into sessions.

Techniques that support effective voting

Voting is often just seen as a quick method for a group of people to make choices between alternatives: whatever gets the most votes "wins." But voting can do much more than this. In this section I describe voting techniques that can be used to:

- Explore preferences
- Discover and share aggregated group information
- Determine the flow of group conversation and action
- Share information about individual participants and their choices

- Test degrees of consensus
- Uncover group resources and commitment

Techniques that create learning opportunities

This section offers powerful participation techniques that provide effective learning via carefully prepared scenarios, allowing participants to experience and interact in realistic environments that are rich in learning potential.

CHAPTER 37
Small group discussions

IT SHOULD BE CLEAR from the first part of this book that small group discussions are key to improving learning and connections at events. One-to-one conversations allow individuals to meet and get to know another person, and direct the resulting discussion along mutually beneficial paths that inform subsequent discovery and learning.

Perhaps the most valuable aspect of the group discussion processes described in the following chapters is that they allow us to both access and create a collective wisdom that is unavailable to us when we work alone.

The benefits and pitfalls of small group discussions

When we scale up conversations to groups of more than two people, we create a more complex discussion environment that encompasses new factors, some beneficial, and some potentially detrimental.

Some favorable aspects of including more people in a discussion

- Greater knowledge base. The more people present, the more experience and expertise potentially available.
- More diverse opinions. When two people agree on something there's not much more to talk about. A larger group increases the likelihood of different points of view that compel further discussion and learning.
- Increased synergy. Significant change and learning often requires a critical mass of contrasting viewpoints, expertise, and experience—an environment more likely to be found in a larger group.

Some negative aspects of including more people in a discussion

- Some people may dominate, while others may be uncomfortable speaking up. Two-person "conversations" in which one person does all the talking are not, thankfully, particularly sustainable, but larger group conversations in which some monopolize and others never say a word can, all too often, continue interminably.
- Groupthink. While groupthink can occur in a group of any size, larger groups may feel more confident in conclusions that ignore alternative viewpoints.
- Valuable ideas and points of view may not be expressed. Unstructured large group discussions are usually poor formats for introducing and considering creative or novel ideas.

One purpose of this section then is to introduce methods for small group discussion that maximize the positive benefits and minimize the pitfalls.

The purpose of small group discussions

To choose an appropriate technique for small group discussion, first consider the desired outcome, which might include any or all of the following:

- Facilitating learning of new concepts and information
- Solving problems
- Uncovering existing ideas
- Creating new ideas
- Reviewing ideas
- Clustering ideas
- Prioritizing ideas
- Reporting back to a larger group

Each of the small group techniques described in the following chapters focuses on a different mix of these outcomes. Allow sufficient time to choose the tool that best matches your specific needs.

CHAPTER 38
Pair share

Description

Pair share, sometimes called think-pair-share, is a fundamental participative technique that develops and reinforces learning via discussion of a topic or question with a partner during a session. Unlike many of the techniques described in this compendium, pair share works in a fixed seating environment, such as an auditorium or theater seating, and is an excellent technique to maintain learning and alertness under such circumstances. The technique is simple: A short period for individual thinking about a presented topic is followed by discussion with a nearby partner.

Pair share is effective because it requires participants to think about a topic or question, rather than passively receiving information from a presenter. During pair share, half of those present are actively talking while the other half listens and processes. Formulating ideas and discussing them with a partner provides further active learning opportunities as participants reflect on their own and their partner's ideas.

Pair share can also be used prior to group discussion or idea generation, with the goal of providing a modest amount of partner feedback before ideas are shared with the group.

A bonus of the technique is that it provides a (frequently welcome!) short break for a presenter/facilitator while participants are thinking and discussing.

Once a pair share is over it can be followed by small group or whole room discussion or, if appropriate, some form of vote. The initial sharing with a partner helps to reduce the barriers to participation in a larger group.

Pair share is also an effective strategy for people to get to know each other, as described later in this chapter.

When?

Pair share is one of the simplest and most effective ways to improve learning and retention during a conference session. Use it with a prepared question after every 10 to 20 (maximum) minutes of presenter content. *This requires planning!* Content must be chunked appropriately, with pair share questions crafted around what has just been covered and what is to come.

Resources

The only room set requirement for pair share is that participants are seated or standing where they can easily talk to one other person. If your audience is in fixed auditorium-style seating, participants will have to turn to face each other, which is uncomfortable in the long term. If you are running multiple pair shares in this situation, switch alternate pairings so that everyone turns to a new partner on their opposite side.

A timer or watch with a second hand is helpful to keep track of thinking and discussion times.

How?

Choosing partners

Fixed seating

In a fixed seating environment, participants should work with one of the people on either side of them, or immediately in front or behind them. The latter may not be practical if people are seated in high-back chairs or in a steeply banked auditorium. In practice, people at the ends of rows may have to move to find a partner. If several rounds of pair share are desired you may want to schedule a brief break after every couple of pair shares, at which point participants can get up, stretch, and move to a different place in the room.

Flexible seating

With movable or open-plan seating, simply ask participants to find a partner sitting near them to work with. Once most people are paired, ask people without partners to raise a hand so that the unpartnered can find each other. If the seating is easily movable, encourage participant pairs to face each other as much as possible while they work together.

Standing

If participants are standing, ask everyone to quickly pair up with someone nearby. Establish a meeting area in the room where people without partners can find one. Have people form pairs standing face-to-face during pair share. If you wish to run a second pair share immediately after the first, ask the pairs to stand back-to-back. Ask (or repeat) the pair share question and then invite everyone to find a different partner and begin the new pair share.

Pre-planning pair share

Pre-planning for pair share is important, though the technique can also be used to explore impromptu topics or questions that arise during a session. Donald Bligh, in *What's The Use of Lectures*,[133] lists possible objectives for pair share activities as *information acquisition* (clarification, feedback, consolidation of understanding, and using concepts and terminology), *promotion of thought* (practicing specific types of thought, and teaching relevance), and *cultivating attitudes and feelings* (releasing tensions, respite for anxious lecturers(!), confidence for reticent students, and building supportive relationships).

If you are incorporating participation into a presentation to keep attention high, plan to run pair share or another brief participative technique at least every 20 minutes. Consider which of Bligh's objectives are relevant for each one, and craft questions that illustrate the points you wish to cover.

Although pair share can be used to improve retention of presented information—e.g., "describe the three ways that . . ."—adult learners are usually best served by open-ended questions, which promote creativity, encourage discussion, and tend to better engage participants.

Running pair share

To run a pair share for the first time, start by briefly summarizing the exercise. As an example, you might say:

> *"We're now going to discuss the barriers to implementing new membership models in your associations. To do this you're going to work in pairs. Once you're paired up, I'll give you a question to think about, and then ask you to discuss your answers with your partner for a couple of minutes. We'll then poll your answers and discuss them as a group."*

Give the necessary instructions to pair up.

Next, pose a relevant question and ask participants to think about their response for 30–60 seconds.

> *"OK, here's the question for you to think about. What are, in your view, the three most important barriers in your association to implementing a new membership model? I'm going to give you a little under a minute to think about your answer."*

Wait 45 seconds.

> *"Now you have a couple of minutes to discuss your answers with your partner. Begin!"*

Provide a 30-second warning before the end of partner discussion. If some pairs finish before others, you can have them compare answers with their neighbors.

> *"Let's find out what the most common barriers are . . ."* [Ask for specific answers and use hand voting to tabulate their frequency.]

Pair share for introductions

I frequently use a modified pair share as a break during sessions. Simply ask participants to stand up and spend a few minutes introducing themselves to someone they don't know. This exercise can be repeated every twenty minutes or so, and serves as an excellent way to facilitate meeting new people and raise attendee alertness and attention. I sometimes hand out The Three Questions on cards, briefly explain them, and use these as the basis for the introductions.

CHAPTER 39
Guided discussions

Description

Impromptu discussions occur all the time in our daily lives. We are continually meeting people and having unscripted conversations, whether they are salespeople at a store, former acquaintances met unexpectedly, a group of folks at a party, or peers who turn up at the same conference presentation we've chosen.

Many presenters, knowing that they "should" involve the audience in some way, try to encourage some kind of conversations around a session topic. Unfortunately, many attempts to facilitate audience interaction are unsuccessful, because it's quite challenging to hold a successful and productive controlled discussion among a large group.

Traditionally, a presenter attempts to incorporate participation into their sessions by regularly asking for audience questions and comments. As Donald Bligh points out in his comprehensive book *What's The Use of Lectures,*[134] this *controlled discussion* technique often fails to meet its worthy objective for the following reasons:

- Most attendees won't contribute unless the audience is very small.
- Those who are lost or confused are the least likely to take part.
- Extroverts are more likely to contribute than introverts.
- There's no guarantee that important presenter points will be reviewed in a balanced way.
- It's often hard to get discussion started.

These issues can be largely overcome *by dividing an audience into small discussion groups regularly during a presentation*. Bligh uses the terms *buzz groups* and *horseshoe groups* to label variants of this

CHAPTER 39: Guided discussions

approach. I call this technique *guided discussion* and incorporate appropriate participant seating into the process.

The power of guided discussion is that different answers, viewpoints, and levels of understanding are exposed during the small group discussions, creating multiple simultaneous rich customized learning environments in the room. Guided discussion supports participant learning by providing support for:

- Consolidating understanding
- Problem solving
- Feedback for participants and presenters
- Brainstorming and divergent thinking
- Evaluating alternatives
- Making useful connections with others

By using a personalized and active format, guided discussion provides a much better learning environment than the traditional lecture with a brief question and answer period tacked on at the end. Having said that, using guided discussion in conjunction with some of the other techniques described in this book will lead to even better learning outcomes!

A good resource for learning more about guided discussion is *The Art of Focused Conversation*.[135]

When?

In the absence of any of the other participatory techniques described in this book, guided discussion, like pair share, should be scheduled frequently during a presentation. Ideally, this means every 10 to 20 minutes. Remember that after 10 minutes of lecturing, audience attention and retention decline. After 20 minutes of lecturing, relatively little will be absorbed or retained.

Don't restrict yourself to using guided discussion after a period of lecturing. It's perfectly possible to begin a presentation with guided discussion, perhaps to explore participants' knowledge and interest in the topic. By doing this you model right at the start that your session will incorporate participation and sharing, making it easier to people to become involved in what follows.

Resources

Room setup

Sadly, small group discussion just doesn't work in a fixed seating environment, such as a theater. Guided discussion requires movable chairs.

Plan your room setup in advance. The best room setups for a pure presentation—those where each audience chair directly faces the presenter—are not conducive to small group work, where group members face each other. This leads to two options:

- Moving between two chair arrangements whenever a shift is made between presentation and group work.
- Using a compromise room setup that supports small group work but necessitates participants turning their chairs when listening to the presenter.

The first option is most appropriate in a classroom situation in which attendees sit at rectangular tables facing the front of the room. When it's time for small groups, have some participants form groups by moving their chairs to sit at the other sides of already populated tables.

The best room setup for the second option depends on whether tables are in the room. While small groups are most effective without tables, they are often a fact of life; for example, in a classroom, or at a meeting where they are needed for the next activity.

In the absence of tables, consider using a chair layout similar to Figure 39.1. By rotating their chairs, participants can either face the presentation area or the other members of their small group. If the presentation doesn't require visual aids, you can place the presentation area in the center of the room and have the small groups surround it.

FIGURE 39.1 • *Suggested room set for switching between presenter and small groups.*

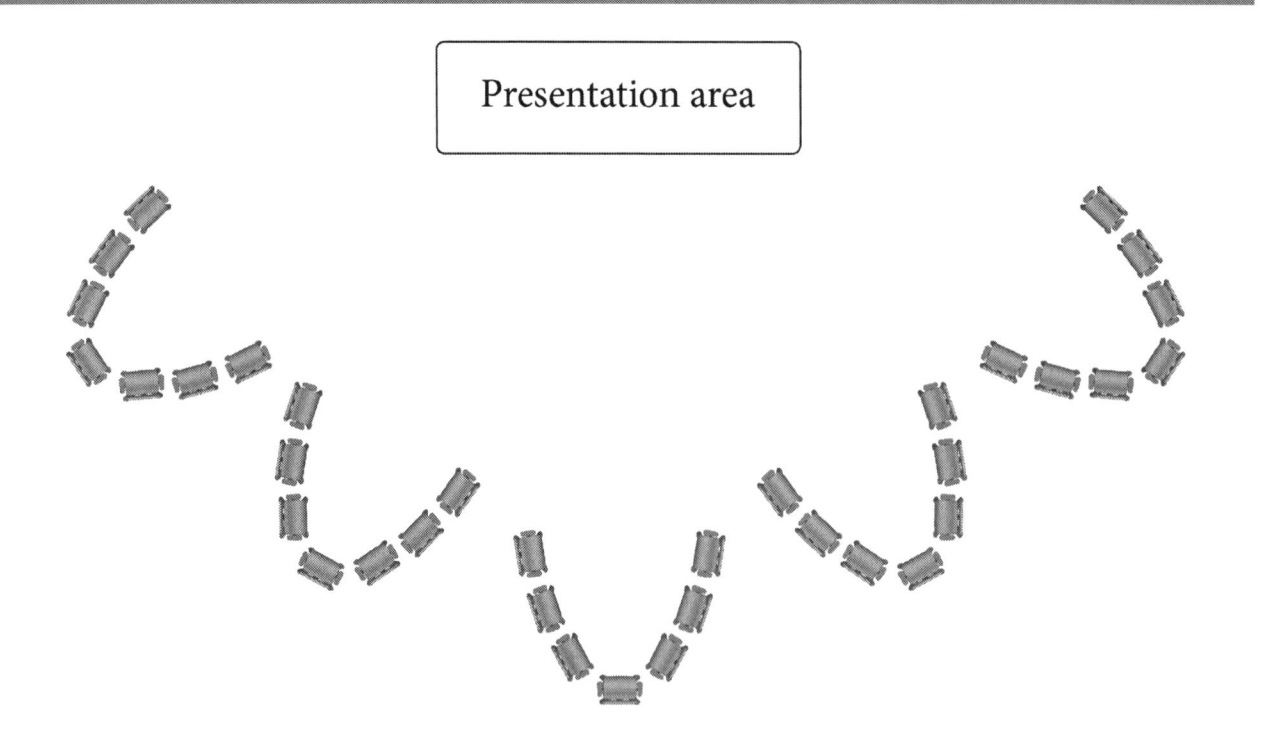

When tables cannot be avoided, set up small group seating around them. Use small rounds or rectangular tables—any setup that will allow the group members to sit close to and easily hear each other. With rectangular tables, arrange them so their long sides point toward the presentation area, omitting chairs on the short side closest to the presenter, and limit the number of people sitting on each long side to three (because four or more people will not be able to see everyone on their side).

Small group size

Small groups should contain three to eight people. All groups should be the same size as far as possible. Determine group size by considering the following factors:

- Task chunking. Will the presenter be breaking the topic into small, quickly discussed pieces? Or will discussion revolve around complex issues? Larger groups can handle simple discussion quickly, but may bog down on complex topics.
- Time available. Use smaller groups in shorter sessions, so that discussion can be carried out more quickly.
- Group purpose. Will the small group be discussing issues or problems? Consolidating understanding? Solving problems? Brainstorming ideas? Larger groups contain more resources for achieving the latter two goals.
- Intergroup discussions. Will the presenter spend time exploring results between groups? If so, smaller groups may lead to a greater variety of conclusions for public discussion.

As groups form for the first time, be prepared to check that they each have the same number of people. Without supervision, groups frequently end up too large or small. If there's more than one extra person, groups should be redistributed to other groups to even up numbers.

Tracking topics

A flip chart, whiteboard, or projected word processing document provide a visible session memory of topics for both presenter and participants. Also, consider having a dedicated scribe who can document topics as they arise and express them accurately and concisely in large and legible writing.

If topics arise that need to be stored and returned to later in the discussion, create a *parking lot* for them. This can simply be a space labeled "Parking Lot" on a flip chart or whiteboard where these ideas can be written down for future recall. Storing topics here reassures the people who suggest them that their ideas will not be forgotten.

How?

Unlike many of the techniques in this book, guided discussion is not reducible to a simple formula or set of instructions, so you won't find a recipe here. Rather, how to best use guided discussion is determined by the topic and goals of your session. Be clear about your goals, and carefully plan how this technique will support them.

Here are some general guidelines:

Have small group members work individually first. If a small group jumps straight into responding collectively, some members can avoid participating. Initial go-arounds, while better, are more effective if everyone is given a short amount of time to first write their thoughts. This solo work at the start increases subsequent participation when discussion starts.

Guided discussion needn't take much time. Giving participants a time limit can rouse them to action and active learning. For example, give them a minute to write down their opinion or most important point about the material just covered, and then have them each briefly share their answers with their small group.

Use guided discussion to obtain feedback. Rather than asking the whole group whether there are any questions, give a short exercise that tests understanding. As the groups work, the presenter can circulate and listen in to the group discussions. This may be sufficient to provide feedback on the level of understanding. Alternatively, small groups can report out briefly once discussion is over.

Include opportunities for divergent thinking; not just solving problems with well-defined solutions. Problem solving is an important tool for developing and demonstrating mastery of a topic, which is why it's used both for teaching children and for adult training. When you bring adults together to learn, consider leveraging the combined expertise and experience of small groups to explore divergent solutions to loosely defined problems—e.g., ways to work with disruptive fifth-graders in class, or strategies for increasing association membership—rather than those with neat clear answers. Doing this provides valuable experience tackling messy "real world" issues in a group setting.

Monitor groups as they carry out their work. While listening to a group, sit on an extra chair or crouch at their level so you don't dominate the flow of conversation. Look for quiet attendees, group members monopolizing the discussion, misunderstanding of the exercise, drifting off topic, etcetera. When you observe any of these behaviors, gently correct them.

Mix up groups. When appropriate and possible, change the composition of the small groups. This will provide some fresh faces and perspectives during the session, allowing people to meet and get to know more of their peers.

Here are some ways to use guided discussion:

Consolidating understanding

We've all thought we've understood something presented to us, only to discover later that our "understanding" has evaporated. To reduce the likelihood of this, use a short period of guided discussion of material that has been covered. A good way to do this is to ask participants to connect what has just been presented to earlier session material or to their personal experience. If new terminology or concepts have been introduced, design the discussion so that group members use them—this will help them become familiar.

Problem solving

Ask participants to solve problems that revolve around the presentation material. ("Now you've been introduced to pivot tables, pick one of the data sets you brought and explore together what you can discover from it.") As described above, decide on your preferred outcome—mastery, exploration, or both—and design your problem appropriately. Good problems provide openings for participants to form and defend judgments, encouraging group discussion and debate.

Feedback for participants and presenters

Individual or group-developed points of view offer valuable feedback to participants and presenter alike. Consider asking groups to briefly report out their conclusions to all participants. This uncovers agreements and differences in perspective that can form the basis for further discussion or illumination by a presenter. While groups are engaged in discussion, presenters can obtain valuable feedback by moving around and listening to individual groups for ideas expressed, levels of understanding, arguments used, and so on. This kind of informational feedback is far more useful and effective than that gained by asking "Are there any questions?" every now and again.

Brainstorming and divergent thinking

During a presentation, I'll often use small group guided discussion to tackle a problem for which I don't have "the answer." The outcome is invariably a host of new ideas, fresh perspectives, and unexpected agreements (and disagreements). Take a look at affinity grouping process described in Chapter 43 for ideas on using guided discussion to brainstorm tough questions and issues.

Evaluation of alternatives

Guided discussion provides a couple of approaches for evaluating alternatives. ("To solve our transportation infrastructure funding problems, we've discovered that some of you support increasing the gasoline tax, others propose issuing tax-exempt bonds, and a third group prefers introducing tolls on interstates. Let's explore these alternatives.") You can assign each alternative to one or two small groups and have them discuss and report on the relevant pros and cons. Alternatively, assign all alternatives to each group, have them rank or pick their favorite, and then report out.

Making useful connections with others

Working with others in small groups enables participants to meet and get to know each other. You can maximize this attractive aspect of guided discussion by mixing up groups from time to time during the session.

CHAPTER 40
Open Space

Description

Open Space, dreamed up by Harrison Owen in the late 1980s and described in his book *Open Space Technology: A User's Guide*,[136] is a simple technique that allows participants to create their own conference sessions. Probably its biggest advantage when compared to other participant-led formats is that it can be run in a short amount of time; as little as a few hours. While other approaches, such as the *Conferences That Work* design described in my previous book, provide more structure, they also require a significantly longer time commitment.

Over the years, "Open Space" has become a somewhat elastic format. The version I describe here is modified slightly from Owen's original formulation, stripped down to process—an opening explanation of the format, a short period for people to offer sessions, and the sessions themselves—that can be used during the morning or afternoon of an event.

The rules of Open Space

Harrison Owen's original formulation of Open Space has Four Principles and One Law. The principles are: *Whoever comes are the right people; Whatever happens is the only thing that could have; Whenever it starts is the right time; When it's over, it's over.* The Law is *The Law of Two Feet*.

These principles, which are explained later in this chapter, create an environment in which people are asked to convene around topics and issues they have suggested with the belief they can work on them productively and fluidly in the time available to them. The Law gives attendees the freedom to leave a session if they feel they are not in the right place—unable to learn or contribute further—and move elsewhere.

CHAPTER 40: Open Space

> ### Why I don't like unconferences
>
> If you've read my first book, *Conferences That Work: Creating Events That People Love*, you're probably scratching your head at the above title.
>
> "Adrian," you're thinking, "unconferences are what you do! How can you not like unconferences?"
>
> It's the word *unconference* I object to, not what it represents. Unfortunately, *unconference* has come to mean any kind of conference or conference session that isn't a traditional format. Originally the word was coined to describe a participant-driven meeting, but in recent years—rather like the encroachments on *counterculture* and *green*—it has started to be used to imply that a conference is cutting edge, even if it still employs the programmed speaker-centric event designs that we've suffered for hundreds of years.
>
> It's unfortunate that the meaning of the word *conference* has been corrupted to virtually the opposite of its original intent. As I describe in *Conferences That Work*, conference was first used around the mid-16th century to describe the act of conferring with others in conversation. Over time, the word's meaning shifted to denoting the meeting itself.
>
> Regrettably few of today's "conferences" provide substantive opportunities for conferring—consultation or discussion. They are instead primarily conduits for the one-to-many transfer of information on the conference topic.
>
> I believe that participant-driven and participation-rich event process is a response to this drift of meeting process that has occurred over the years. In a sense, these events are the true conferences: events where conferring is supported and encouraged.
>
> To be accurate, we should be calling *traditional* conferences "unconferences," reserving the word *conference* for the participant-driven and participation-rich event designs that are gradually gaining popularity.
>
> Sadly, that's unlikely to happen, so I talk about "participant-driven and participation-rich events" and generally avoid using the term *unconference*.
>
> In the end, I know my thoughts on the meaning and use of a word carry little weight. With rare exceptions, our culture, not the pronouncements of an individual, determines the meaning and usage of words. But if you agree with me, feel free to follow my example and spurn unconferences—but just the word, not the concept!

Despite its simplicity, Open Space sometimes gets a bad reputation via those who have suffered through sloppy process masquerading as Open Space. With a little care to emphasize the cardinal rules of Open Space, especially the Law of Two Feet, you'll be able to avoid a poor experience.

Warning: Introverts can be poorly served by Open Space!

I am an Open Space enthusiast, but many who are familiar with Open Space see it as *the* single alternative to traditional broadcast-style conference sessions. Thus I'm taking the unusual step of explaining why, in my view, it is not the only participant-led session format you should consider using.

Open Space session topics are determined by individuals who stand up in front of the entire group and announce their chosen topic. Generally, this is easier for extroverts, who don't mind speaking to a group extemporaneously, than for introverts, who tend to shun such opportunities. The end result, in my experience, is that introverts are usually silent during the opening process, and the subsequent Open Space session topics are biased toward those proposed and often dominated by a comfortably vocal minority.

Given that introverts are reckoned to make up 25–50% of the population (higher in some industries, such as information technology), this is not good.

We know that introverts can bring much to the table. Using participant-led process that favors extrovert participation is a disservice to everyone present, not just the introverts. In my opinion, it's a significant shortcoming of Open Space. But, when time is limited, Open Space can provide a credible alternative to traditional broadcast-style sessions.

When?

If you plan to dedicate a portion of your conference to Open Space, I recommend you schedule it toward the end of your event. Because participant-led sessions are uniquely invigorating, it's mildly disconcerting and anticlimatic to go back to pre-scheduled sessions afterwards. Consider scheduling Open Space before a traditional closing session, personal introspective, or group spective, as described in the "consolidating learning" section later in this book.

Do not schedule Open Space simultaneously with other conference sessions. This is a mistake I've seen made many times. The invariable result is that most people, not knowing what Open Space is, choose the safety of a conventional conference session. Making Open Space a plenary session ensures that the majority of people will attend.

I recommend at least 150 minutes for Open Space. Although it's possible to run the initial opening and an hour-long time slot in 90 minutes, I find that giving people only one opportunity to sample Open Space sessions is somewhat disappointing. Scheduling two or three hourly time slots over a morning or afternoon allows participants to have more of the Open Space experience and generally increases participant satisfaction.

Resources

For the Open Space opening you'll need a room large enough to easily hold everyone, with enough movable chairs for everyone to have a seat.

The traditional Open Space room setup uses one or more large concentric circles of chairs. I like this setup, especially if Open Space is going to be run for a day or more, when a more formal opening becomes appropriate, but the short Open Space sessions described here work just as well with curved theater seating.

CHAPTER 40: Open Space

You will need a large blank wall or notice board on which to post sheets of paper. This is where a grid of potential session locations (columns) and session time slots (rows) is made before the Open Space starts. Open Space time slots are usually an hour long. Create the grid divisions with masking tape. The posting area should have enough clear space in front so that the entire group can easily gather round and view the posted sessions. Label the locations and time slots along the top and side of the grid. If some of the locations can hold more than others, order locations in order of size of the rooms and write down the number of people that each location can hold.

Make sure you have sufficient fine tip markers, sheets of paper, and masking tape to create and post the session schedule. For small groups, large sticky notes can be used instead of sheets of paper.

If your group is large, provide a couple of microphones to allow people to hear the opening facilitation and participants' session descriptions. It's also a good idea to have a timekeeper to gently cut off any long-winded descriptions of proposed sessions during the opening.

Traditionally, the Four Principles and One Law of Open Space are individually posted on large pieces of paper around the main meeting room so they can be referred to during the opening. However, in my experience, this is not essential.

If you decide to harvest the group's Open Space experience, as described in the next section, plan how you'll do this before you run the session.

Finally, you'll need separate breakout spaces for each simultaneous session. While it's possible, and sometimes necessary, to hold multiple sessions in the same room, try to avoid this. The more spaces available the better, but you can estimate a minimum target number by dividing the number of people present by your desired average size of each session. Breakout spaces can be anywhere that works (e.g., outside in fair weather), but are most effective if they are all close to each other and the main room. As in the main room, provide chairs and omit tables.

How?

The following process works well for a half day dedicated to Open Space sessions. If you decide to allocate a day or more to Open Space, review *www.openspaceworld.org* to learn about options for more structured opening and closing session process.

Opening Open Space

With your attendees seated, either in curved theater seating (stand facing them) or a few large concentric circles of chairs (stand in the center), briefly introduce them to the rules of Open Space by saying something like this:

> *"This is Open Space, an opportunity for you to create the agenda for the next few hours. You'll be able to suggest any topic or issue and hold a session on it. You should have some passion for what you choose, and a desire to make it happen here today.*

> *Open Space has a few helpful rules to guide what happens: four principles and one law. The principles are:*
>
> *Whoever comes are the right people. The people who show up at a session are the right people to be there. Don't worry about the people who aren't there, or who you think should be there.*
>
> *Whatever happens is the only thing that could have. Stay positive. Let go of the could haves, might haves, and should haves. You will have a great experience when you do.*
>
> *Whenever it starts is the right time. We will give you a framework to schedule what happens here today. But great ideas can occur at any time; feel free during the entire Open Space to adjust or completely alter what we're going to put together during the next few minutes if it seems like the right thing to do.*
>
> *When it's over, it's over. It's possible that a session will accomplish everything that those who are there need it to do in 15 minutes. Don't feel you have to fill a given time slot!*
>
> *These principles are ultimately about having a positive and flexible attitude about what happens during Open Space. If you come with doubt, criticism, or rigidity, the results will likely be disappointing. But if you come with good energy, interesting, useful, and amazing things will happen. Pay attention, work hard, and prepare to be surprised!*
>
> *The one law of Open Space is The Law of Two Feet and you need to pay special attention to it because it's about changing a behavior we're all used to. We have all learned at conferences that once you're attending a session you shouldn't leave it. Open Space is different. During Open Space you have the right and responsibility to use your two feet to go to the session where you can learn and contribute the most. So if at any time today, you find you're not making best use of your time here, move somewhere else!"*

Ask for questions. Answer them, and continue like this:

> *"OK, it's time to get started! I have one question for you.*
>
> *What are the issues and topics around* [theme of conference or session] *for which you have passion and for which you will take responsibility for convening time with others today?*
>
> *You do not have to be an expert in what you propose; just be willing to make the session happen.*
>
> *When you come up with your answer to the question, come to* [the front of the room/center of the circle] *and share your name, the title of your session, and a 30-second or less description, if needed. Then, write your session title and name on the* [paper/sticky notes] *provided. Finally, over here* [point to the session grid] *is a place to post the sessions you decide to hold; the columns represent locations and the rows possible time slots.* [If appropriate add: The estimated number of people each location can hold is shown too.] *Feel free to adjust locations and times as necessary.*
>
> *Any questions?"*

CHAPTER 40: Open Space

Answer any questions and ask participants to start to share their sessions. This may take a little time to get going—be prepared to stand silently for a while and wait for people to step forward. If necessary, encourage more people to propose sessions. You might say:

> *"If you have something in mind, just step forward and share it now; you can work out the details later.*
>
> *Some of the best sessions can be two or three people. Don't worry how popular your session might be."*

If you have more proposals than scheduled space, look for additional places to meet (hallways, outside, etc.). And be prepared to swap allocated locations to different sessions if some prove more or less popular than estimated.

Once it's clear that no more sessions are forthcoming, say:

> *"From here on out—you're on your own! We'll see you all back here at* [appropriate time]."

Supervising Open Space

At this point your work in opening Open Space is largely over. While the sessions are under way, wander around and check that everything seems to be going well. Rooms and the session grid may benefit from occasional tidying up. Occasionally, people may ask for advice on what to do—feel free to pass the responsibility for choosing back to them. Occasionally someone may try to control a session or start lecturing. Should this occur, diplomatically remind those present of the Law of Two Feet.

Harvesting Open Space

When the group reconvenes at the end of the Open Space session, you may want to *harvest* the learning that has occurred, though this is often not necessary, especially if the sessions have turned out to be around a variety of disparate topics. Harvesting is process that summarizes/explores the learning that has taken place for the whole group. If you decide that whole group harvesting is of value, you can use a group spective, described in Chapter 58. Alternatively, you may want to explore the harvesting techniques—such as reports, recordings, stories, making metaphors, and graphic renderings—used by the Art of Hosting community.[137]

CHAPTER 41
World Café

Description

> "The World Café reintroduces us to a world we have forgotten. This is a world where people naturally congregate because we want to be together. A world where we enjoy the ages-old process of good conversation, where we're not afraid to talk about things that matter most to us. A world where we're not separated, classified, or stereotyped. A world of simple greeting, free from techniques, technology, or artificiality. A world which constantly surprises us with the wisdom that exists not in any one of us, but in all of us. And a world where we learn that the wisdom we need to solve our problems is available when we talk together." —*Margaret Wheatley*[138]

World Café was developed in 1995 by Juanita Brown and others[139] as a format for dialogue in small groups around questions that have been determined in advance. Typically, World Café is run with between 20 to 100 participants. Variants of the process have risen over the years, but its core components are:

- One or more pre-meetings to decide on the questions that the World Café will address.
- A comfortable, cozy "café" setting, with many small round tables (often sporting a floral centerpiece and each seating four to six people) that are covered with flip chart paper and a supply of colored pens.
- A friendly welcome and explanation by a host facilitator of how World Café works.
- Several short, typically 20- to 30-minute rounds of conversation at each table, either about a common question for the whole group or about a question specific to each table. At the end of

every round, participants each move to a different table, so that new people are met at each round. A *table host* stays at each table to provide continuity for discussions between rounds.
- A concluding *harvest* during which participants can share their learnings and observations with the entire group.

World Café is useful whenever a group wants to explore an issue, topic, or possible directions. While it can be used for traditional organizational needs such as strategic planning, perhaps its greatest strength is its ability to foster creative and open discussion and dialogue between group members who may enter the process with very different perspectives on the questions to be discussed.

A variant of World Café, suitable for small groups, uses a distinct fixed question at each table with enough rounds of conversation for every attendee to discuss most or all of the questions with different peers at each table. This is a good way to get an entire group's input via unique small group discussions on a number of topics.

When?

While World Café can be used as the sole process for a short meeting, you'll often want to embed it in a longer event. When to schedule World Café depends on your reasons for using it. If you want to use World Café to investigate a specific issue during your conference, simply schedule the session at an appropriate time. If your event's theme needs definition, and attendees could benefit from getting to know each other better, run the session at or close to the start of the event. World Café can even be used as a harvesting tool toward the end of an event (see the Pro Action Café chapter if you're interested in doing this) to draw together disparate threads of meeting activity and discover consensus for future actions.

The questions that are asked during the rounds of conversation are key to creating a successful World Café, so it's critical that you carefully select them in advance. Once you've figured out the questions, deciding when to schedule your World Café should become fairly obvious.

Resources

Staffing

Unlike many of the techniques covered in this book, World Café requires significant planning. You'll need to organize an appropriate team to meet in advance to develop the right discussion questions. One of these team members can then facilitate the World Café session. Other team members, or suitable participants, will serve as table hosts during the session. Staffing World Café adequately, therefore, requires one person for each table, plus a facilitator.

If you will be holding a harvest at the end of your World Café, consider including a *graphic recorder*: someone who can capture people's ideas and expressions using pictures and words in a large format that all can see while the harvest is taking place. The resulting record of the proceedings is a great way to document and make visible what has transpired.

Planning and questions

> "Good questions—ones that we care about and that we want to answer—call us outward and to each other. They are an invitation to explore, to venture out, to risk, to listen, to abandon our positions. Good questions help us become both curious and uncertain, which is always the road that opens us to the surprise of new insight."
> —Margaret Wheatley[140]

Your planning team first needs to decide on the goal(s) and scope of the World Café session. Once the goals and scope of the World Café have been established, it's important to take the time to create the right questions that will be asked during the rounds of conversation. Determine whether you will pose one group-wide question (which may stay the same from one round to the next) per round of conversation or whether you will assign each table a fixed specific question throughout the conversation rounds.

Perhaps the most important criteria to use in determining the questions are (1) *the questions are clear* and (2) *the answers matter to the participants*. Here are some suggested questions[141] that can be posed for a group-wide round. Use them as a guide to generate your own, and don't feel like you need to provide an exhaustive list.

Questions for focusing collective attention:

- What question, if answered, could make the greatest difference to the future of the situation we're exploring here?
- What inspires you about [topic or issue], and why do you care?
- What's important to you about this situation and why do you care?
- What draws you/us to this inquiry?
- What most attracted you to the idea of participating in this Café?
- Who called you to this Café? What role did this person play in your expectations?
- What's our intention here? What's the deeper purpose—the "big why"—that is worthy of our best effort?
- What opportunities can we see in this situation?
- What do we know so far/still need to learn about this situation?
- What are the dilemmas/opportunities in this situation?
- What assumptions do we need to test or challenge in thinking about this situation?
- What would someone who had a very different set of beliefs than we do say about this situation?

Questions for connecting ideas and finding deeper insight:

- What's taking shape here? What are we hearing underneath the variety of opinions being expressed? What is in the center of our listening?
- If there is a deeper reason for us to be here, what is it?
- What's emerging that is new for you? What connections are you making?
- What have you heard that had real meaning for you? What surprised you? What puzzled or challenged you? What question would you like to ask now?
- What is missing from the picture so far? What are we not seeing? Where do we need more clarity?
- What has been unsaid that needs to be said?
- What gives you courage to continue even in the face of uncertainty and setback?
- What has been your major learning or insight so far?
- What's the next level of thinking we need to address?
- What stands in the way of each of us being fully present in this gathering?
- If there was one thing that hasn't yet been said but is needed in order to reach a deeper level of understanding/clarity, what would that be?

Questions that create forward movement:

- What would it take to create change on this issue?
- What could happen that would enable you/us to feel fully engaged and energized in this situation?
- How can we offer hope?
- What do I still need to learn?
- Collectively, what could we let go of?
- What's possible here and who cares about it?
- What needs our immediate attention going forward?
- How can we stay connected?
- How could this work be more fun?
- What would be one small yet powerful step you could take that would impact what you care most about?
- If our success was completely guaranteed, what bold steps might we choose?
- How can we support each other in taking the next steps? What unique contribution can we each make?
- What images, symbols, key phrases (e.g., "I have a dream") might cause a shift?
- What challenges might come our way and how might we meet them?
- What would engage more people in working toward change?

- What conversation, if begun today, could ripple out in a way that created new possibilities for the future of [our situation . .]?
- What seed might we plant together today that could make the most difference to the future of [our situation . .]?

If you are using different questions for each round, have later questions build on earlier questions to focus the conversation appropriately. For example, a World Café session might start with a question like *What inspires you about* [topic or issue]*, and why do you care?*, followed by *What gives you courage to continue even in the face of uncertainty and setback?*, and then move to *What would be one small yet powerful step you could take that would impact what you care most about?*

Finally, decide on the number and length of conversation rounds. If you're using a single question per round, you might have three or four 20- to 25-minute rounds. If you're assigning questions to specific tables, you may want to have a larger number of shorter rounds. The final round is often held with people back in their original first round seats.

Pre-session training

A brief pre-session meeting with the table hosts is recommended to explain their duties, which are:

- Remain at your table for all rounds
- Facilitate discussion, keeping it on topic
- Introduce information and relevant points of view from previous rounds

Materials and room set

Hold World Café in a room that is large enough to provide *at least* 17 square feet per participant.

Strive to create a comfortable and inviting environment, ideally with the decor and ambiance of a café. Playing music quietly as people arrive can help. Provide enough 36- (for four chairs) or 48-inch (for five or six chairs) round tables to seat everyone. Don't use larger tables because people will be too far apart to talk intimately. If possible, cover the tables with attractive draped table linens. Then cover tabletops with enough layers of flip chart paper to prevent bleed-through from the pens that participants will use. Supply each table with fine tip markers in a variety of bright colors, with at least two pens available for each seated participant. A small floral arrangement at the center of each table adds a welcoming touch.

To emphasize the café theme, have a refreshment table in the room that participants can visit during the session.

As for any group session, if you'll have more than around fifty people, provide a couple of wireless microphones for the session facilitator and audience input.

If you plan to harvest the discussion, supply any needed materials, such as flip charts, pens, large sticky notes, masking tape, and wall paper for group summaries.

The host should have a watch or other timing device to keep track of the time for each round of discussion.

You may want to post the following Café Guidelines (often called Café Etiquette) on walls around the room before the session starts:

- Focus on what matters
- Contribute your thinking and experience
- Speak with your mind and heart
- Link and connect ideas
- Listen together for deeper themes, insights, and questions
- Facilitate yourself and others
- Slow down, so you have time to think and reflect
- Play, Doodle, Draw—writing on the table coverings is encouraged
- Have fun!

How?

Design principles

Before describing how to hold a World Café, it's helpful to review the design principles that the Café community has developed. Bearing them in mind will help you stay true to the spirit of World Café. Here's a slightly modified version, taken from The World Café website.[142]

1. Clarify the purpose

Pay attention early on to the reason you are bringing people together. Knowing the purpose of your meeting enables you to consider which participants need to be there and what parameters are important to achieve your purpose.

2. Create a hospitable space

Café hosts around the world emphasize the power and importance of creating a hospitable space— one that feels safe and inviting and nurtures mutual respect. When people feel comfortable to be themselves, they do their most creative thinking, speaking, and listening. In particular, consider how your invitation and the physical setup contribute to creating a welcoming atmosphere.

3. Explore questions that matter

Finding and framing questions that matter to those who are participating in your Café is an area where thought and attention can produce profound results. Your Café may explore a single question, or several questions that support a logical progression of discovery throughout several rounds of dialogue. In many cases, Café conversations are as much about discovering and exploring powerful questions as they are about finding effective solutions.

4. Encourage each person's contribution

Most people don't simply want to participate; they want to actively contribute to making a difference. It is important to encourage everyone in your meeting to contribute their ideas and perspectives, while also allowing anyone who wants to participate by simply listening to do so.

5. Connect diverse perspectives

The opportunity to move between tables, meet new people, actively contribute your thinking, and link the essence of your discoveries to ever-widening circles of thought is one of the distinguishing characteristics of the Café. As participants carry key ideas or themes to new tables, they exchange perspectives, greatly enriching the possibility for surprising new insights.

6. Listen together for insights

Through practicing shared listening and paying attention to themes, patterns, and insights, we begin to sense a connection to the larger whole.

7. Share discoveries

After several rounds of conversation, it is helpful to engage in a whole group conversation. This offers the group an opportunity to connect the overall themes or questions that have emerged, and perhaps begin to create a collective action plan. Make the resulting collective knowledge and insight visible and actionable.

Welcome

As participants arrive, welcome them, offer refreshments, and ask them to sit at tables. Don't worry if people tend to sit with people they already know, since they will be moving to different tables for later rounds.

Once everyone is seated, welcome them and introduce the context and reasons for the World Café. Next, go through the café etiquette guidelines listed in the previous section by saying something like this:

> *"I'd like to introduce you to some guidelines for our time together.* [If relevant, point to where they're publicly posted.] *First, we ask everyone to focus on what matters. In other words, stay close to* [the context and theme just described] *during our discussions.*
>
> *Next, we invite you to contribute your thinking and experience. All of us have something to offer today, and World Café works best when we all participate.*
>
> *We ask you to speak with your mind and heart. We want not only your thoughts and ideas, but also your feelings. Passion and emotions are fine to express here.*
>
> *As we discuss and share, please work to link and connect ideas and listen together for deeper themes, insights, and questions. When we create together we are capable of building many things that would not have come into being if we were working alone.*

Also, facilitate yourself and others. We have provided table hosts at each table who will stay and provide connections between the rounds of our discussions. More about them in a moment. But we rely on all of you to help us create a respectful space where everyone has time to share and be heard.

A reminder that it's fine to slow down, so you have time to think and reflect. Sometimes it's those moments of silence that allow a new idea to form.

Those table coverings in front of you are there for a reason! Play, Doodle, Draw—writing on the paper is encouraged. Document your thoughts and ideas there, so that you create a record for the next people to sit at your table.

And finally—Have fun! As we dive into our work today we'll build a community, one that relishes joyful, playful discovery. Have fun during this journey; it's a wonderful way to become energized, inspired, excited, and creative.

[Pause]

Before I explain how World Café works, are there any questions?"

Answer any questions.

Explain World Café process

Here's how you might now explain what happens next. You'll need, of course, to adapt this transcript to your specific situation.

If your World Café uses a single question for each round of discussions:

"Here's what we're going to do. Our World Café will consist of [number of rounds] of discussions. During each [number of minutes] round you'll discuss a question at your table and use the paper on it to record your ideas, in words or drawings. At the end of each round, everyone except your table hosts moves to a different table to sit with new people for the next round of discussion."

If your World Café uses a single question for each table:

"Here's what we're going to do. Our World Café will consist of [number of rounds] of discussions. Each table has a question associated with it. During each [number of minutes] round you'll discuss the question for your table and use the paper on it to record your ideas, in words or drawings. At the end of each round, everyone except your table hosts moves to a different table to sit with new people for the next round of discussion."

Then continue:

"Each table has a table host. Table hosts, identify yourselves please! [Wait for table hosts to identify themselves.] Your table host's job is to supply a brief summary to the new table group and share, as needed, any previous discussion that has occurred.

Any questions?"

Answer any questions. If you've decided to use a single question for each round of discussions, introduce the first question and let the group begin. If your World Café uses a single question for each table, ask the table hosts to introduce the question for their table.

At the end of the first round of conversation, invite people to move to a different table—one at which they have not sat before—and remind the table host to stay behind and provide a brief summary of what was said to the new group. Encourage people to try and sit with new people at each round.

Repeat the above process for each round.

For the final round you can optionally ask participants to return to their first table. This allows everyone to see how much has been added to their initial contributions.

Harvesting

At the end of your rounds of questions, the table paper will be covered with ideas, comments, and pictures. It's common in World Café to have the group *harvest* these learnings through some kind of communal process. Here are some forms of harvest that are commonly used.

Gallery Stroll

During a gallery stroll, the table papers are gathered at a central location—a set of tables pushed together or a wall—and participants browse the resulting gallery. Once everything has been viewed, you can hold a facilitated discussion (see below) about what people noticed and want to share.

Or, you can post a large sheet of paper and invite people to write key ideas, common themes, and so on. The resulting summary, which can be photographed and distributed, provides a permanent record of the group's time together.

Facilitated discussion

Another option is a facilitated discussion. If the group is small, people can stay at their tables and summarize the conversations and sharing there, assisted by the table paper record and the table hosts. Using a fishbowl, as described in the next section, can be helpful to structure discussions with a large group.

After the facilitator draws out the ideas uncovered during the World Café, the next step, if appropriate, is to create plans and action items, assigning people and resources. Use dot voting or another appropriate voting technique if you need to prioritize group choices. Don't forget to plan for follow-up meetings and future group communications.

World Café Lite

If you realize during an event that a stripped down version of World Café might be appropriate, consider using what facilitator Viv McWaters calls World Café Lite[143]. Omit the tables, paper, and pens, and run three rounds of World Café with participants sitting in small groups of four. But don't skimp on spending enough time to craft good questions that explore the theme of the event and move from the general toward the specific.

Using World Café when strong differences of opinion are present

Here's a creative approach, described by Chris Corrigan, to use World Café with groups that include people with strong disagreements.[144]

"At the outset of the café as I was introducing the process I gave the following instructions:

> That paper in the middle is for all of you to use, as are the markers. We want you each to record thoughts and insights that other need to hear about. So before we begin I invite you to pick up a marker and write your name in front of you. <People write their names.> Now I want to invite you to answer this question: What is one thing you can do to make sure that this meeting is different? Write your answer beneath your name.

People took a moment to write their names and their commitments. And they shared them with each other at the table. That is how we began.

The first round of conversation proceeded as usual, but I noticed something very powerful in the second round. When everyone got up and moved around they took a seat in someone else's place, and often the first thing they did was to read the name and the commitment that was in front of them. Can you imagine coming across the name of someone who you have a disagreement with only to see that they have written 'I won't fight anymore' beneath their name? The core team is now going through all of the tablecloths and making a list of the commitments that people made. Taken on their own, they form a powerful declaration of willingness.

People reported that this was the best meeting the community had in a long time. And it had a lot to do with this tiny intervention of public ownership for the outcomes."

CHAPTER 42
Fishbowls

Description

The term *fishbowl* can refer to a couple of different techniques for focused group discussion.

In the more common *standard fishbowl* design, the format assures that the conversation at any moment is restricted to a few clearly defined people, while allowing attendees to join the discussion in a controlled manner if they have something to say.

A second variant, which I'll call the *two sides fishbowl*, allows representatives of a point of view to listen to and question representatives of an opposing viewpoint for a period of time, after which the two sides switch roles. For example, a two sides fishbowl can explore introverts' experience of extroverts and vice versa, examine two alternative proposals for solving a business problem, or go deeper into divergent views on a social issue.

Most of us have had to suffer through a "discussion" in the presence of a large number of people, most of whom never get an opportunity to speak. Standard fishbowls provide a simple, ingenious process that readily enables anyone who wants to speak to have a turn. Two sides fishbowls work a little differently; they avoid monopolization of a discussion by allowing people with similar viewpoints an uninterrupted period of time to question and better understand those on the other side on an issue.

The advantage of a focused discussion over informal discussion is that it greatly reduces the cross-conversations that frequently occur when many people want to respond or comment on something that's been said. And it manages this feat without limiting discussion to a few voluble people, as it provides all attendees an equal opportunity to contribute.

Both kinds of fishbowls can be used with up to around a hundred people, making them one of the best ways to work effectively with groups that are too large for effective informal discussion.

When?

You can use a standard fishbowl any time group discussion is appropriate and you want to ensure that an orderly conversation occurs. Typically you'll use the technique with a group of more than about twenty people, but if you discover that a smaller group includes strongly held points of view, a standard fishbowl provides a good way to maintain order during a discussion.

Use a two sides fishbowl when a group includes representatives of two contrasting or conflicting viewpoints and you need a structured method to deepen each side's understanding of the opposing point of view in a constructive way.

Resources

Provide chairs for all participants for both styles of fishbowl. Include four or five more chairs than the number of participants for a standard fishbowl. The chair layout used depends on the circumstances, as described below.

Standard fishbowl

For a standard fishbowl, chairs can be set in one of two layouts, horseshoe or circle, as shown in Figures 42.1 and 42.2. Either layout will work, with the circle version preferred for square rooms, and the horseshoe layout for rooms that are significantly longer than wide. I like the circle version for general discussions, and the horseshoe version when decisions may be made or if you are scribing discussion points onto flip charts, which can then be placed next to the small row of chairs for all in the horseshoe to see.

The number of chairs in the "mouth" of the horseshoe or the center of the circle is typically four or five. The fishbowl facilitator sits in one of these chairs for the duration of the fishbowl.

If necessary, provide one microphone for the fishbowl facilitator, and, optionally, a second microphone for the other people in the mouth or center of the fishbowl.

PART 3: Compendium of Participation Techniques

MIDDLES

FIGURE 42.1 • *Fishbowl seating layout (horseshoe version)*

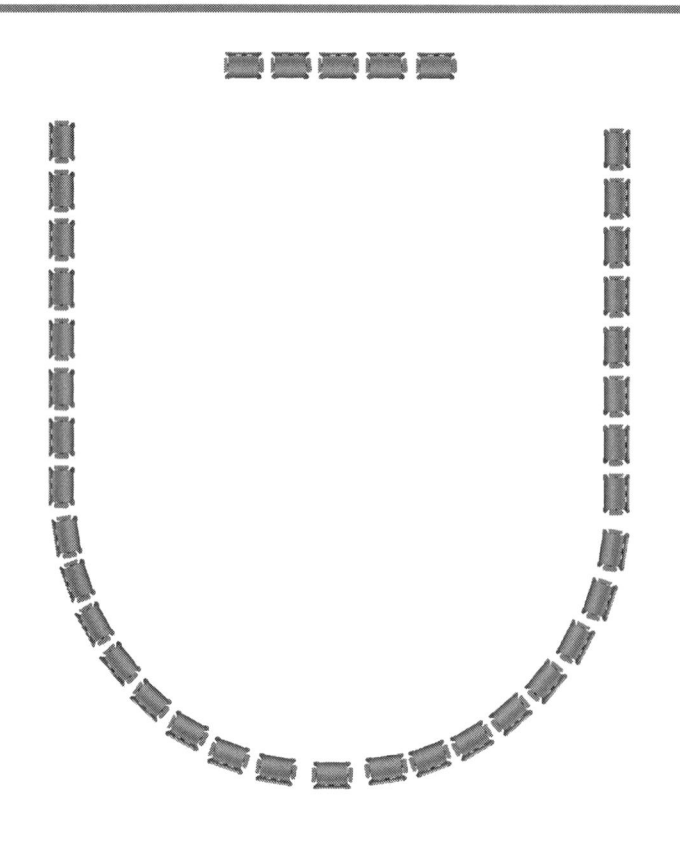

FIGURE 42.2 • *Fishbowl seating layout (circle version)*

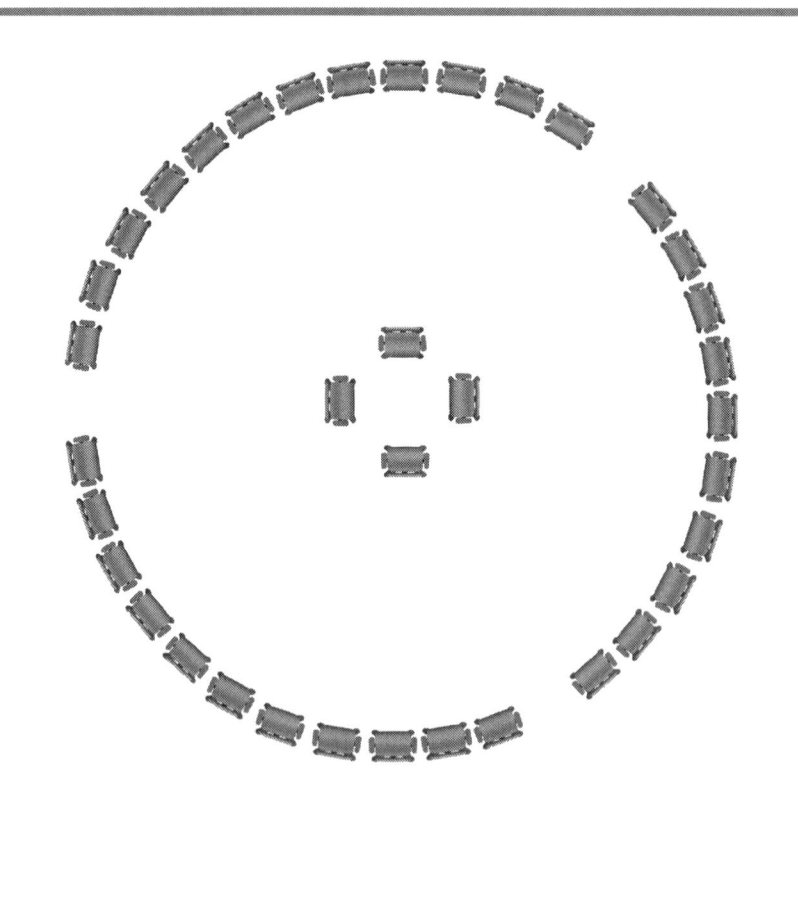

232

Two sides fishbowl

A two sides fishbowl uses a chair layout of two concentric circles as shown in Figure 42.3. Since, in general, the number of people on each side will not be known in advance, this layout will need to be set up on the fly once the sizes of the two groups are known. If the groups are not approximately the same size, participants will need to reposition chairs appropriately when the two sides swap places.

Use either a single facilitator for both sides, or choose a facilitator from each group to lead the inner circle discussion. If the circles are large, one or more runners with wireless microphones may be needed.

FIGURE 42.3 • *Two sides fishbowl seating layout*

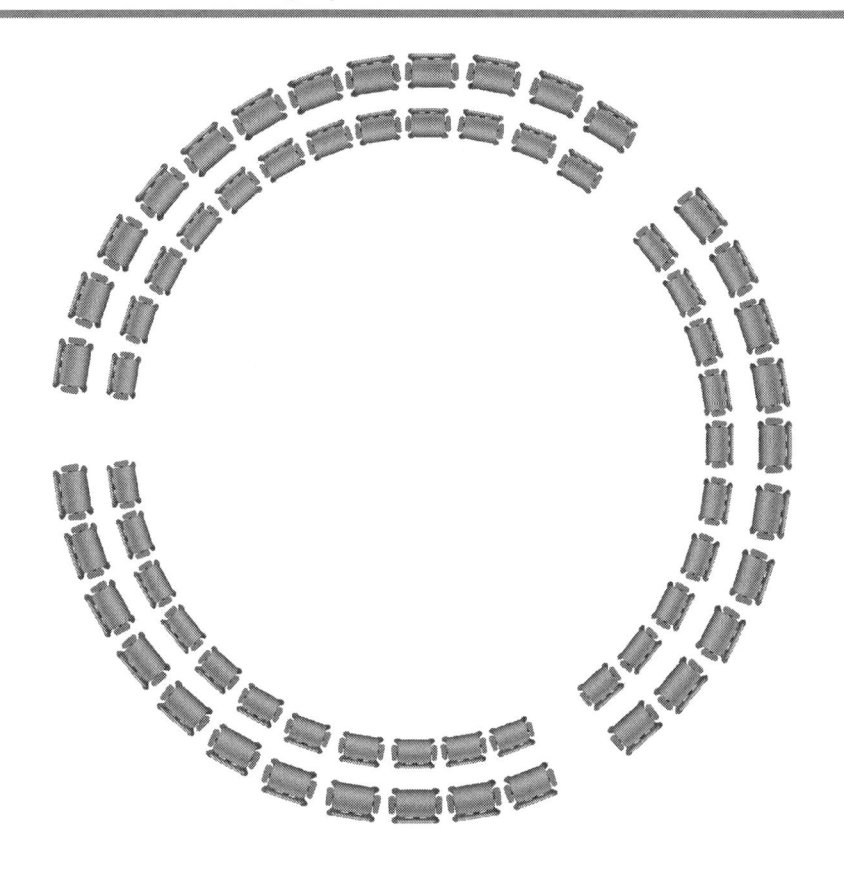

How?

Running a standard fishbowl

At the start of the fishbowl, the facilitator sits alone in the small group of chairs. She explains how the fishbowl works by saying something like this:

> *"We're about to start a focused discussion using a fishbowl. A fishbowl is a facilitated informal discussion, with the difference that, if you want to talk, you must come and sit in one of these chairs next to me. If all these chairs are full and no one has yet spoken, wait a little—*

otherwise, when you come up, someone sitting here must go back to a chair in the [horseshoe/outer circle]. *Also, if you're sitting up here and have finished what you have to say, go back to a* [horseshoe/outer circle] *chair. When you're up here, you can address your comments to someone else in these chairs or to the whole group—the choice is yours.*

Any questions?

[Pause for questions.]

The discussion is now open. Who would like to start?"

You'll probably find that some attendees will want to talk from their chair in the horseshoe or outer circle. When this happens, gently interrupt and gesture for them to come up and sit next to you. If they've interrupted someone in the conversation chairs, steer the conversation back to the folks up front.

Once people get the hang of the focused discussion, they are generally pleasantly surprised by how well it works. Participants appreciate how the small group format focuses the discussion, how the contributors change as needed, how simply the front row or inner circle shows who may talk, and how it's clear when the conversation on a topic has run its course.

Running a two sides fishbowl

Once the groups for the two sides fishbowl have been established (a one-dimensional human spectrogram can be used for this) decide which group will go first and have them sit in the inner circle of chairs. The other group sits in the outer circle.

The rules for a two sides fishbowl are simple. The inner circle does most of the talking. Inner circle members, guided by a facilitator, discuss, explain, or champion their viewpoint for the benefit of the outer circle group. At the start, the facilitator should clarify and/or obtain agreement on the goals of the fishbowl (e.g., for the two sides to better understand each other's point of view, or to obtain information for later work on next steps or consensus). Outer circle members are not allowed to respond to what they hear, except to ask questions that clarify the inner circle discussion.

After a useful discussion has been held, the groups change places and an approximately equal amount of time is given to the new inner group to repeat the above process. After both sides have had their turn, it may be appropriate to follow up with a standard fishbowl or other guided discussion technique to build on what has been shared.

CHAPTER 43
Affinity grouping

Description

Affinity grouping, sometimes called "cards on the wall," is a way to discover and share ideas that arise at a session or conference and group them into categories, so they can be organized and then discussed. It's a process that allows and encourages every attendee to participate, sparks creativity as people listen to others' ideas, generates a substantial list of ideas, and provides a way to consensually categorize the idea list.

Use affinity grouping when it's clear there's the desire and energy for future activities. This is because the technique works best when there's a clear question to be explored. To help decide whether affinity grouping is appropriate, ask yourself whether the focus question, *"What do we want to do in the future?"* seems likely to be a key starting point.

This technique can require significant time to run satisfactorily. While a simple topic with a group of five or six people can be usefully covered in 30 minutes, many affinity group sessions may require several hours to generate the specific clusters of ideas. Schedule additional time to discuss next steps and implementation.

A word about brainstorming

Most people have experienced brainstorming, a group technique for gathering ideas that was popularized in *Your Creative Power* by Alex Osborn in 1948. The concept of soliciting ideas from a group is sound; it's just that brainstorming is usually not the best way to get them. (Exception: if you're in a big hurry.) As education professor Keith Sawyer explains, "Decades of research have consistently shown that brainstorming groups think of far fewer ideas than the same number of people who work alone and later pool their ideas."[145]

Affinity grouping has been around since the 1960s, and offers a more nuanced and effective way to discover and share ideas. It starts with private, individual generation of ideas (individual brainstorming, if you will), moves next to discussing the ideas in small groups, and finally transitions to whole group posting and clustering of those ideas that dominate the process.

The multiple stages of affinity grouping support both the safe initial generation of ideas, and the subsequent discussion and critique that the group needs in order to come up with a viable consensus.

When?

Run affinity grouping when a group needs to make plans for the future. Sometimes an entire meeting can be devoted to this task, but usually you'll use the technique toward the end of a meeting once potential issues to be explored and resolved have surfaced.

Resources

For affinity grouping, you'll need a room with enough space for participants to comfortably split into small groups, flexible seating, cards (and the means to post them on a wall), pens, and wall space.

Cards

Bring enough 5″ × 8″ or similar sized cards to give three or four to each participant. These cards won't be posted on the wall. Also have on hand at least ten 5″ × 8″ cards or large sticky notes for each small group (see Table 43.1 for the number of groups to be formed). These group cards will be posted on the wall, so you'll need a method, approved by the venue, to post them securely (e.g., masking tape, repositionable spray adhesive). See Chapter 14 for a comprehensive list of posting methods.

Pens

Supply a regular pen to any participant who needs one, and provide enough fine tip pens for the small groups to write on the cards/notes that will be posted on the wall.

Wall space

At least 8 feet of flat blank wall or whiteboard with enough empty space for the entire group to congregate in front of it will be needed. Make sure that the card mounting method you are planning to use will work and is sanctioned by the venue. Large sticky notes are a great option, since they can't damage any wall surface, but check beforehand that they'll stay stuck to the wall surface for the duration of the exercise.

How?

Many of the ideas in this section are derived from *The Workshop Book*.[146]

Affinity grouping involves the following steps, which are covered in more detail below:

CHAPTER 43: Affinity grouping

- Describe the affinity grouping focus question, process, and working assumptions
- Ask attendees to individually brainstorm ideas
- Divide attendees into groups
- Discuss ideas in groups and put distinct ideas on cards
- Post clearest and different ideas on wall for entire group to view
- Sort ideas into clusters
- Create names for clusters
- Discuss next steps and implementation

I have not included precise timings for the later parts of this technique because they vary so widely depending on the complexity of the topic, the depth to which it is explored, and the size of the group. In general, expect to take at least thirty minutes for a small group working on a simple topic, and at least one to two hours to develop idea clusters for more complex affinity groupings. Include additional time to discuss next steps and implementation.

Describe the affinity grouping focus question, process, and working assumptions

Start your affinity grouping exercise by supplying a focus question, which will normally be of the form *"What do we want to do in the future?"* If your question's scope is limited by time or other considerations, you may want to make it more specific. Write the focus question on a flip chart sheet or whiteboard so everyone can see it.

Next, briefly describe the affinity grouping process, saying something like this:

> *"Here's an outline of how affinity grouping works. First, we'll brainstorm responses to the focus question individually, and write them onto cards. Next, we'll work in small groups to share our ideas with others. Then we'll share our work with the entire group, putting our idea cards up on the wall, and consensually categorizing them. Finally, we'll reflect on what we've created and discuss next steps and implementation. Any questions?"*

Answer questions, and then go over the working assumptions for the session:

> *"There are three working assumptions I'd like us all to keep in mind for this exercise. One: There are no wrong answers. Two: We all have something to contribute. Three: Everyone will have the opportunity to hear and be heard."*

Have attendees brainstorm ideas individually

Give each attendee a few 5″ × 8″ or similar sized cards, and say:

> *"Please take a few minutes to write down your responses to the focus question. Aim for between five and ten responses. Concentrate on capturing your ideas; don't worry about precisely expressing them."*

Give a minute's warning when most people have finished writing. Then, ask them to add a star to their three best ideas, however they define "best."

Form attendees into groups

Divide attendees into random, diverse groups. My suggestions for group number and size are given in Table 43.1. Ask participants from the same organization to join different groups, and have each group sit separately, so its members can talk without disturbing other groups. If you create groups of eight or more people, consider choosing a facilitator for each group.

TABLE 43.1 • *Affinity Grouping Suggested Number and Size of Groups, and Ideas Per Group*

NUMBER OF ATTENDEES	NUMBER OF GROUPS	SIZE OF EACH GROUP	IDEAS (CARDS) PER GROUP
20	6	3–4	4–6
40	7	5–6	5–7
60	8	7–8	5–7
80	8	10	5–7
100	8	12–13	6–8

Discuss ideas in groups and put distinct ideas on cards

Once the groups are settled, hand out 10 cards or large sticky notes to each group and say:

> *"For the next 15 minutes or so, I'd like your group to discuss all the ideas you've come up with. Go around the group in turn, sharing one idea at a time. Start with your starred ideas, and use the rest as needed. We'd like to get [number from Table 43.1] distinct ideas from each group. As you decide on each idea, express it in a short, specific phrase of three to six words and write it in large, clear, bold letters on a new card. When we've finished, your ideas will be shared with the entire group."*

Monitor the groups as they discuss their ideas, checking that everyone is participating and that groups don't get stuck discussing one idea. Periodically remind them how much time they have left. Then do the following:

Post clearest ideas on wall for entire group to view

When the discussions subside, ask each group to select two or three of their "clearest" ideas. Give the groups a minute or two to make their selection. Have the groups congregate around the wall or whiteboard that will be used to display and categorize the ideas chosen. Ask for the "clearest" cards, shuffle them, read them aloud, and place them randomly on the wall.

When the cards have been posted, give the entire group an opportunity to ask questions that *clarify* what a card's contents mean. If needed, have the card writer explain the idea on the card. Avoid discussion on the *merit* of any idea.

Post different ideas on wall for entire group to view

Now ask each group to briefly discuss and select one or two of their cards that contain a different idea from those that have been posted. Shuffle the cards, read them out, and add them to the wall. Again, give attendees a chance to ask questions to clarify the ideas on these cards.

Sort ideas into clusters

To start clustering the displayed ideas into categories, say:

> *"Now it's time to group these ideas into categories. We'll do this by first looking for pairs of ideas that have something in common. If you don't agree with this pairing, say so and we'll talk about it.*
>
> *Who wants to pick a pair?"*

As each pair is chosen, place the named cards next to each other and draw a common symbol (square, circle, triangle, cross, check mark, star, etc.) on both cards. Ask for more pairs, group the chosen cards together, and add a unique symbol to each new cluster. In what follows, encourage people to refer to a set by its symbol, rather than by an idea in the cluster. This helps prevent premature naming of idea clusters.

After several sets of ideas have been paired, say:

> *"If you see other cards that can be added to the existing clusters, feel free to suggest them from now on."*

Continue to create idea clusters with the cards on the wall, until each of the cards is in a set. If an idea is significantly different from the rest, put it in its own cluster.

Once all the cards on the wall are in sets, ask the groups to give you their remaining cards that don't fit the existing clusters. Read these cards out, one at a time, discuss them and either create a new cluster or add it to an existing one. Usually, at this point, you'll have between six and a dozen clusters identified.

Finally, ask the groups to mark their remaining cards with the symbol of the cluster they should be in. Add these cards to the appropriate sets on the wall.

Rearrange the clusters into adjacent columns, one column for each cluster.

Create names for clusters

Don't be in a hurry to name each set of idea cards. You're looking for a group consensus that captures what the cluster is about, with the cluster name providing, in three to six words, a direction or answer to the focus question.

First, read aloud all of the cards in the largest cluster. Ask attendees to pick key words to describe the cluster. Then, ask for name suggestions. Cluster names are typically a few words, for example, "develop website" or "plan follow-up meeting." Look and ask for group agreement. When you've got it, write the cluster name on a card placed at the top of the cluster column.

Repeat this procedure for all clusters. If you have many or time is short, you can assign the job of naming a cluster to each small group. When a group finishes, give them another one to name until all the clusters have names. If you use this approach, when all clusters have been named, check each name for clarity with the entire group of attendees. If you don't find overall consensus for a cluster's name, repeat the process for the cluster with everyone's involvement.

Once all the clusters are named, document your work. A clear photograph of the completed, named clusters is the fastest way to do this. If a camera isn't available, have a volunteer scribe the columns of ideas. Make copies, and distribute them to attendees as quickly as possible.

Discuss next steps and implementation

When is the best time to discuss action on the ideas that have flowered during this session? Right away, after a short break! The ideas are fresh, with attendees maximally invested in what they have co-created. It's time to discuss next steps, and build and staff a framework for action. Have a scribe document the ideas and commitments generated during this final step.

You might say something like this:

> *"We've done some great work here! There's one more vital step. Let's discuss possible next steps and implementation of these ideas. First, I'm going to read them all out."*

Read out all the cluster names, with a pause between each idea. Next, say:

> *"Now, let's have a discussion that concentrates on three aspects of these ideas:*
> - *Priorities: Which ideas are most and least important?*
> - *Ease of implementation: What kind of effort is needed for implementation?*
> - *Next steps: What next steps could we take?"*

Facilitate a short discussion on these topics. Besides helping to make attendees' opinions explicit, this discussion will also provide information on the energy available for work on the ideas expressed as well as identifying those attendees willing to work on next steps.

As direction and energy on particular ideas emerge from the discussion, look for a consensus on next steps to be taken, and ask for volunteers to staff a small committee to work on them. Agree on what will be accomplished, and a basic timeframe for the work. Don't over-recruit volunteers—it's likely that one or more ideas may reflect longer term goals that attendees are either unwilling or unable to work on at this time.

CHAPTER 44
Participatory voting

Look up "voting" on Google and the top search results are dominated by links about *electoral* voting. Making decisions (about elected leaders, opposing choices, and action plans, etc.) is the first function of voting that comes to mind for most people.

In a participatory environment, however, rather than simply a means to make a decision, *voting is most useful as a way to obtain information early in the process*; a "straw poll" that provides public information about viewpoints in the room and paves the way for further discussion—a process I call *participatory voting*. The following six chapters detail a variety of useful participatory voting techniques.

Ways to use participatory voting

Perhaps surprisingly, voting is not a simple, well-defined process. The International Society on Multiple Criteria Decision Making[147] lists more than four thousand articles on decision theory in its bibliography. Voting, it turns out, can be a complex and subtle business.

For most of us, "group voting" brings up the concept of voting as decision-making. But voting can be used to test learning, and to elicit and share information. To guide your choice of participatory voting techniques, here are short descriptions of various ways to use voting.

Using voting to determine consensus

It's often unclear whether a group has formed a consensus around a specific viewpoint or proposed action. Consensual participatory voting can quickly show whether a group has reached or is close to consensus, or wants to continue discussion. It can also pinpoint those who have significant objections to a majority position and give them the opportunity to clarify their reasons for opposition.

Using voting to make decisions

How people use voting techniques depends a lot on their presentation/facilitation/management style. If you are focusing on making a decision, voting is a tempting method to obtain an outcome. But if a vote is held prematurely, before adequate exploration of alternatives and associated discussion, the "decision" may have poor buy-in from those who voted in the minority or who feel they weren't heard. People will rightly feel ambushed if they are asked to vote on a decision without adequate warning and opportunities for discussion.

Thus, if you plan to use voting for decision-making, explain up front the processes and time constraints you will be using prior to the vote. Unless the vote is purely advisory, give participants the chance to determine what they will be voting on, and how it will be framed. Such preparation lets people know their opportunities to shape discussion, and minimizes the likelihood that unexpected premature voting will cut off exploration of important creative or minority options.

Using voting to test learning

Polling an audience is a time-tested technique, as old as teaching itself, for teachers to obtain feedback on student understanding. "Pop" quizzes, multiple-choice tests, and modern Audience Response Systems can be useful ways to test audience learning. But they have their limitations.[148] As meeting designer Jeff Hurt explains:

> "[Audience Response Systems] *are good for immediate feedback. They are good for 'knowledge learning.' Studies show they increase engagement and let someone know whether their answer is right or wrong. In short, they are good for surface knowledge. They however do not promote deep learning . . . which leads to higher level thinking skills such as estimation, judgement, application, assessment and evaluation of topics.*"[149]

The participatory learning philosophy espoused in this book concentrates on these deeper learning skills. From this perspective, traditional voting supplies limited information when used as a testing tool.

Using voting to set context

We've seen that small group discussion is key to effective learning during an event. But how do we set an initial context for discussion? Participatory voting techniques supply important information about the views, preferences, and experiences of participants, both as a group and as individuals. This information can then be used to set up appropriate discussions.

Using voting to elicit information

Perhaps the most important benefit of the voting techniques described in this book is their ability to elicit important information about the people, needs, and ideas in a group and make it available to the entire group. Although some of the techniques can be used to provide anonymous or semi-anonymous information, I believe that sharing information provided by group members to group members is one of the most powerful ways to strengthen connection, openness, and a sense of community in a group. Allowing participants to discover those who agree or disagree with them or share their experience efficiently facilitates valuable connections between participants in ways unlikely to occur during traditional meetings. Giving group members opportunities to harness these techniques for their own discoveries about the group can further increase engagement in the group's purpose.

Using voting to determine the flow of group conversation and action

Participatory voting techniques such as card voting provide large groups the real-time feedback required to productively steer a complex conversation to best meet the needs of the group.

Using voting to plan action

Finally, we can use participatory voting to uncover group resources, interest, and commitment on specific action items from individual participants.

Before voting

If you're using voting to test understanding of a concept or explore a group's knowledge of a topic, include time for small group discussion before the vote. Pair share, described in the previous section, is a great technique for this. Provide enough time for each participant to think about their answer and then have them pair share their understanding. After the vote, you can facilitate a discussion with the entire group about the differences uncovered.

Some concluding observations about voting

To avoid making premature decisions, use *consensual* voting to uncover significant alternative viewpoints and test the depth of agreement *before* confirming that you have substantial agreement through decision-oriented voting.

Think about when and how you use voting. Voting on alternatives that have been inadequately explored or discussed is counterproductive.

Use public voting methods whenever appropriate—which is, in my experience, most of the time.

If people wish to "sit out" their vote when using participatory voting, support their right to do so unless you are testing for consensus, in which case it's reasonable to ask for their feedback. Consider using anonymous voting if people seem reluctant to express an opinion.

Low-tech versus high-tech voting solutions

There is no shortage of high-tech systems that can poll an audience. Commonly known as ARSs, Student Response Systems (SRSs), or "clickers," these systems combine an audience voting method—a custom handheld device, personal cell phone/smartphone, personal computer, etc.—with a matched receiver and software that processes and displays responses.

There are a number of reasons why high-tech ARSs may not be the best choice for participatory voting:

- ARSs necessitate expense and/or time to set up for a group. The techniques described in this section are low or no cost and require little or no preparation.
- Most ARS votes are anonymous; no one knows who has voted for what. When you are using voting to acquire information about participant preferences and opinions, as opposed to deciding between conflicting alternatives, anonymous voting is rarely necessary. (An exception is if people are being asked potentially embarrassing questions.) When a group of people can see who is voting for what (and, with some techniques, even the extent of individual agreement/disagreement), it's easy to go deeper into an issue via discussion or debate.
- All the participatory voting techniques described in this section involve more movement than pushing a button on an ARS device. As we saw in Chapter 4, physical movement improves learning. Some of the techniques include participant interaction, which also improves learning.

For these reasons, this section of the book describes no-tech and low-tech techniques for participatory voting. The former require only the attendees themselves, while the latter use readily available materials such as paper and pens.

This is as good a place as any to emphasize that *human spectrograms* are an excellent participatory voting technique that could have just as well been included here, rather than in the *Openers* section.

CHAPTER 45
Hand/stand voting

Description

> "In small assemblies the vote is often taken by 'show of hands,' or by 'raising the right hand' as it is also called."
> —Roberts Rules of Order Revised - VIII

Hand voting is the classic method for audience members to indicate responses to a question posed during a session. "Raise your hand if you are/think/prefer/choose X" has been used in all sorts of group gatherings since time immemorial. Other useful hand voting variants are card and Roman Voting, described in the next two chapters. Alternative ways to use hands to vote aren't covered in this book because they are chiefly useful for consensus decision-making in small groups—the interested reader can learn more from the notes.[150]

A variant of hand voting, *stand voting*, is good for yes-no votes, especially those that carry a little more weight than normal or when you're looking for unanimity. I use it for cementing agreement on maintaining confidentiality at my participant-driven events. If you need a more sophisticated method of assessing agreement, consider using Roman Voting.

When?

Use hand/stand voting when you need to quickly poll an audience on a clear public choice between two or more answers or options. You should be familiar with the other voting techniques described in the next five chapters, since they (and human spectrograms) may better fit your voting needs.

Resources

None.

How?

Hand voting

What could be simpler than hand voting? Well, there are plenty of ways you can go wrong with this simple technique.

Before you poll, make sure you list *all* the possible choices. If you're asking an only-one-of-these-answers-is-right question, providing all options in advance helps to reduce the natural hesitation to pick the early "correct" answer when you haven't heard all the alternatives.

Then, ask whether the alternatives are clear and complete, and give the audience a chance to clarify the choices you've provided, or incorporate additional potential answers you've overlooked.

Now it's time to ask for a show of hands. Present each answer in turn and give people time to respond. After each answer, estimate the proportion of the audience that has hands raised and *give that feedback to the audience*. "About half of you prefer Y." Remember that because you're at the front of the room you can see how many hands are raised better than anyone in the audience except perhaps the people in the back row. It's frustrating for audience members to take the trouble to vote and not be informed of the group's response.

Stand voting

Stand voting is even simpler than hand voting, and is appropriate when a yes-no vote is required with abstaining not an option. Ask everyone in favor/agreement to stand. (If any audience member is unable to stand, have them raise their hand.) Then say "Everyone standing sit, everyone sitting stand." If anyone is now standing, ask them to explain what they feel they can't commit to, and, if necessary, work on an agreement as to how to proceed.

CHAPTER 46
Roman voting

Description

How should groups make decisions? Common answers to this question include "by voting" or "by discussion and then the boss gets to decide." But what if we want a decision method that provides consensus, or as near consensus as we can get?

An individual making a decision may agonize over it, but when more than one person is involved, the decision-making process can turn into an argument. Groups need a way to test their agreement, discuss concerns, and arrive at a decision that all can support.

When people are forced to make a yes/no vote about a proposal, the degree of support for the resulting vote is hidden. If the level of enthusiasm for a decision is tepid, or a minority of those voting are adamantly opposed, serious problems can surface later when it's time for implementation.

A better approach is to publicly discover the degree of consensus at the time the proposal is made. If doubts or opposition are uncovered, then they can be addressed before a final decision is adopted.

My favorite solution for gauging the strength of consensus is Roman Voting, as described by Esther Derby in *Self-facilitation Skills for Teams* © 2004–2005, Esther Derby.[151]

The description of this technique is excerpted, slightly modified, with permission from Derby's article.

When?

Roman Voting can be used whenever a group wants to gauge the strength of support for a proposal or option.

Resources

No resources are needed if the group is small. With a group of 30 or more, use card voting with three cards to make it easier to view the vote.

How?

The Romans indicated their will in the gladiator's arena with a thumbs-up or a thumbs-down. A modern modification of Roman Voting helps groups arrive at a decision.

>Thumbs-up = "I support this proposal."
>
>Thumbs-sideways = "I'll go along with the will of the group."
>
>Thumbs-down = "I do not support this proposal and wish to speak."

If all thumbs are down, eliminate the option. On a mixed vote, listen to what the thumbs-down people have to say, and recheck agreement. Be cautious about choosing an option if the majority are thumbs-sideways: This option has only lukewarm support.

This technique generates consensus. Consensus doesn't necessarily mean complete unanimity. Consensus means that everyone must be willing to support the idea, even if it's not his personal first choice.

Sooner or later, you'll have a situation in which one person withholds support for any option. Manage this situation before it happens. At the start of the consensus process, set a time limit:

"We'll work really hard to reach consensus until the end of this meeting. If we don't have agreement by that time, we will turn the decision over to _____, or take a vote, or _____ (a technical expert, coach, manager) will decide."

Most people don't hold out to be obstinate; they are responding to a deeply held value or belief. Often the lone holdout will move on, but not at the cost of relinquishing an important belief. Respect the belief, use your fallback decision-making method, and move forward. However, when a group seldom reaches consensus, but instead relies on voting or deferring to authority, it's a sign there are deeper issues at play.

CHAPTER 47
Card voting

Description

Card voting is a highly flexible way to poll an audience. It's a voting strategy that deserves wider recognition, with its use limited only by your imagination. The technique is essentially an extension of hand/stand voting that provides more than two options for a participant's response to a question.

Card voting is perhaps most useful during large group discussions, where it can help maintain an orderly process despite a complex flow where people wish to speak, provide supporting information, or indicate that discussion be refocused. But, once facilitators and participants are comfortable with the technique, it can be used in many helpful ways.

The basic premise of card voting is simple. Each participant is given a set of different colored cards, typically three or four. Voting is conducted by assigning a meaning to each color and having people raise the appropriate card to indicate their voting choice.

A specific colored card can represent (in increasing order of sophistication):

- The participant's answer to a posed multiple-choice question (testing knowledge or comprehension): *"If you believe the right answer is G raise your green card, if Y show your yellow card, or if R hold up your red card."*
- A vote for a particular course of action (how should we proceed?): *"If you would do G in this situation raise your green card, if R show your red card, if Y hold up your yellow card."*
- The degree of interest in or agreement with a proposal (e.g., Roman Voting for large groups): *"If you support this proposal raise your green card, if you'll go along with the will of the group show your yellow card, or if you do not support the proposal and wish to speak hold up your red card."*

- The category of a contribution to a discussion (aka comment threading): *"Hold up your green card if you wish to speak, yellow card to indicate you can clarify the point being discussed or answer a question that is being raised, or red card if you believe the current discussion is off-topic."*

I don't recommend using more than four colored cards. With more, participants tend to drop or misplace cards during the voting process. Occasional votes for more than four options can be handled by holding two rounds of votes with the cards representing four options during the first round, and another four during the second. If you plan to routinely have more than four choices during a session, consider using dot voting (Chapter 49) or electronic voting systems.

I suggest supplying card sets to attendees when they arrive. Once they are in participants' hands you will likely find multiple situations during an event when card voting can be extremely useful, provided event facilitators and presenters are adequately briefed on the technique beforehand.

In this chapter I'll cover using card sets for the following three activities:

Classroom voting

Classroom voting actively involves participants in their learning. When a vote is held, participants have to process the question, form an opinion, and share it by voting for one of a set of possible answers predetermined by a presenter. The presenter and class obtain feedback, and the vote supplies an entry point for discussion. The supplied answers might be different proposed solutions to a challenge the group has to tackle, choices from a set of upcoming participant tasks, feedback on how well participants think they understand information just presented, or any other set of choices that furthers the learning goals of the session.

Consensus voting

Card consensus voting allows you to use Roman Voting, described in the previous chapter, with larger audiences than is feasible for hand voting.

Discussion guidance

Holding a discussion among a large group is difficult but sometimes necessary—for example, when decisions about group governance must be made, or when a facilitated question and answer period is desired at the end of a presentation. Card voting can help guide a large group discussion by allowing participants to vote to shift topic, express an urgent comment, or indicate that discussion is off-point.

When?

Use card voting when you need to poll an audience on any of the activities described in the previous section. Because you need to supply and distribute cards and clearly explain the technique up front, card voting is most appropriate when a complex discussion is needed or there are many questions to be answered during the meeting session.

For example, suppose the leaders of an organization are making a proposal about future activities to a large group, followed by participant discussion. Participants can use card voting to indicate they wish to speak, have an urgent comment, think the discussion has moved off-topic, indicate that discussion on the current topic should be brought to a close, and so on. If voting on multiple options is needed, the cards can also be used to display participant preferences.

Resources

Once you've decided how to use card voting, you'll need to supply each participant with an identical set of colored cards, one color for each possible answer needed. Using 3″ × 5″ cards is fine for up to around a hundred people; bigger cards should be used for larger groups.

Use brightly colored cards that can easily be distinguished from each other, and make sure you're in a well-lighted space.

For consensus voting, use red, yellow, and green cards. For discussion guidance, use these three colors plus another distinctive color.

If you are using cards for classroom voting on multiple-choice questions you'll need a whiteboard, flip chart, projected image, or other appropriate method to display the questions and multiple-choice answers to the group. You'll also need to prepare in advance the questions and associated answer choices for your display.

How?

However you use card voting, be sure to share the vote out loud after you've seen the cards displayed. Remember that, as the person standing in the front of the room, you're the only one who can see how people vote!

Classroom voting

You can use card voting as a low-cost SRS during a presentation. Prepare in advance your questions and up to four associated possible answers, which might be different proposed solutions to a challenge the group has to tackle, choices about which part of a task each participant wants to help with, or answers that test how well participants understand the information just presented. As with any voting process, learning will be best when you allow time for reflection and discussion before the vote.

Pose a question and display up to four possible answers to the audience, each coded with a color corresponding to one of the colored cards in the hands of each audience member. Give audience members individual time to consider their answer, and then have them discuss their answers using pair share or small group discussion. Finally, have them vote with their cards. Announce the result and continue the session appropriately. For example, you might ask those who voted one way to explain their votes to the whole group.

Consensus voting

Consensus card voting is a form of the Roman Voting described in the previous chapter, with hand voting replaced with colored cards. Because the cards are easier to view, it can be used with larger groups than hand voting (though obtaining consensus with large groups is often not an easy task). Here's the "How" of Roman Voting, adapted for card voting:

- Green card = "I support this proposal."
- Yellow card = "I'll go along with the will of the group."
- Red card = "I do not support this proposal and wish to speak."

If most cards are red, eliminate the option. On a mixed vote, listen to what the red people have to say, and recheck agreement. Be cautious about choosing an option if the majority of cards are yellow: This option has only lukewarm support.

This technique generates consensus. Consensus doesn't necessarily mean complete unanimity. Consensus means that everyone must be willing to support the idea, even if it's not his personal first choice.

Sooner or later, you'll have a situation in which one person withholds support for any option. Manage this situation before it happens. At the start of the consensus process, set a time limit:

"We'll work really hard to reach consensus until the end of this meeting. If we don't have agreement by that time, we will turn the decision over to _____, or take a vote, or _____ (a technical expert, coach, manager) will decide."

Most people don't hold out to be obstinate; they are responding to a deeply held value or belief. Often the lone holdout will move on, but not at the cost of relinquishing an important belief. Respect the belief, use your fallback decision-making method, and move forward. However, when a group seldom reaches consensus, but instead relies on voting or deferring to authority, it's a sign there are deeper issues at play.

During pre-vote conversation, cards can also be used to influence the course of the discussion, as described below.

Discussion guidance

Here are two ways that a group's members can use colored cards to guide a discussion. Whichever protocol you use, be sure to clearly explain the process before the discussion starts. It's a good idea to have a definition of each card's meaning displayed to the audience while discussion is underway. As the discussion progresses, audience members raise the appropriate card to express their opinions, while a facilitator uses this group feedback to guide the discussion.

Consensus discussion guidance

This technique concentrates on supporting a search for consensus. It's especially helpful if there's a concern that a few strong voices will override others, as it ensures that everyone who wants to gets to speak. You will need three cards: red, yellow, and green—the same cards required for card consensus voting described above.

- Green card = "I wish to speak."
- Yellow card = "I can clarify the point being discussed or answer a question that is being raised."
- Red card = "The current discussion is off-topic, or we are not adhering to the process we agreed to."

General discussion guidance

This technique supports audience members who are engaged in a general discussion, usually on agenda items or a question and answer session after a presentation. You will need four cards: red, yellow, green, and another color (suggest blue or orange).

- Green card = "I think we should move to the next/another topic."
- Yellow card = "I have something to say on the current topic."
- Red card = "I have an urgent comment."
- Blue card = "The current discussion is off-topic, or we are not adhering to the process we agreed to."

The facilitator calls on those who raise their yellow card in the order raised. You can add rules for using these cards depending on your specific circumstances such as time constraints, whether the discussion is preliminary or binding, and so on. For example, you may want to restrict each participant to a single use of a red card, or ask people not to use their yellow card a second time until at least three other people have spoken.

An additional color card can be used for general discussion guidance: a card that indicates when shown "I agree with what the speaker is saying." This gives useful real-time feedback to the discussion facilitator and the group.

CHAPTER 48
Table voting

Description

Table voting is a technique used for polling attendees on their choice from predetermined answers to a multiple-choice question, and/or for dividing participants into preference groups for further discussions or activities.

The technique is simple: A table is set up for each response and participants are asked to gather by the table displaying their preferred option. Using this method, participants can, for example, quickly decide on a preferred activity for an entire group, or create separate groups for each available activity.

With some preparation, table voting can be used to obtain responses to multiple questions.

A variant of table voting is *poster voting*, with posters replacing the tables.

When?

Use table voting to conduct an out-of-one's-seat vote on a predetermined question for attendees, or when you need to divide participants into subsequent activity or discussion groups. Questions used for table voting should have clear, unambiguous answers that form a complete set and do not overlap. For example:

"Which is the primary model organism your medical lab uses for research: Cell culture, Rodents, Fish, Frogs, Primates, Worms, or Other?"

"Would you classify yourself primarily as a practitioner, vendor/supplier, independent consultant, or other?"

Unless you have prepared volunteers stationed at each table, I suggest using this technique for a single question rather than multiple questions asked one after the other.

Resources

Before holding a table vote, arrange tables in clear areas around the room, providing one for each possible answer to the predetermined question. You may want to also include tables for "Other" and/or "Can't decide."

Place on each table a sheet of paper listing one of the answers. If you wish to use table voting for a number of questions, create sheets of paper displaying the sets of answers and station someone at each table who will change the answer displayed as needed.

How?

Table voting requires preparation before the session in which it is used.

When it's time for the table vote, clearly state the question and, if possible, display it on a screen or poster in the room. You can either point out the table for each of the answers, or ask people to circulate among tables and read the set of answers. Invite participants to stand by the table that contains their preferred option. Once everyone is at a table, process the voting appropriately (e.g., count votes, split into associated groups, etc.). If you have "Other" or "Can't decide" votes, you may want to ask these respondents to explain their choice.

If you are asking multiple questions, once a question has been answered, ask event staff or volunteers to replace the table answers with a new set, and continue with the next question.

CHAPTER 49
Dot voting

Description

Dot voting is a flexible technique for public *semi-anonymous* voting (semi-anonymous because it's hard to determine how individuals vote without watching them during the process). Participants are given identical sets of one or more colored paper dots, one dot per vote, which they stick onto paper sheets, each listing one of the available choices. Dots can be of equal value, or different dot colors can represent ranked choices (e.g., red for your favorite option, yellow for your second favorite) or other voting preferences (e.g., a green dot means "I'd like to work on an issue").

Dot voting can be used either with *predetermined options*, or as part of a *two-step* process in which options are first generated by a technique such as *Post It!* or *affinity grouping* and then voted on.

Dot voting can be more than a decision-making strategy. Think of it also as a powerful method for both investigating support for ideas and options as well as informing fruitful discussions that follow a vote.

If you require a more deliberative voting technique, check out Idea Rating Sheets.[152] This is a paper-form-based approach, particularly suitable for large groups working on decision-making, in which ideas are written on special paper forms and participants fill in dots to record their degrees of agreement. If ideas to be voted on are generated prior to the session, Idea Rating Sheets can be used to uncover their popularity and the amount of agreement existing in the group. The forms can be downloaded from the Idea Rating Sheets website for free.

When?

Use dot voting when you need a tool to explore and prioritize ideas, rather than a means to choose a specific action or outcome. When participants come up with multiple proposals and the time available is too short to give them all adequate attention, dot voting provides a useful instrument to help a group focus on what it sees as most important, and, optionally, determine an order to discuss the ideas.

Resources

Dot voting requires:

- Colored sticky paper dots, which are sold adhered to a backing sheet.
- Paper sheets onto which participants stick the dots.
- Markers to list choices for dot voting on each piece of paper.
- Alternatively, sufficient colored markers (if dots are not available—see below).

Sticky dots general requirements

Determine dot requirements before voting, using the information supplied in the remainder of this section. Decide whether dot color will indicate significant information, and, if so, assign an appropriate color to each desired choice.

Use dots that are at least half an inch in diameter, as smaller dots are hard to remove from their backing and stick in position. Pick colors that contrast.

Prepare sets of dots, still attached to their backing, to hand out to participants when the vote occurs. Buying sheets of dots with multiple colors on each sheet can reduce the cutting necessary to create multiple identical sets of dots. If only one dot is needed for each person it's possible to distribute dots as needed, peeling them off the backing as they're handed over, but in general it's better to let voters remove the dots from the backing themselves. Provide somewhere to dispose of the backing paper.

Dot paper

Use flip chart or other large sheets of paper for dots, as sticky dots are too hard to remove from permanent surfaces like walls and tables.

If you're using predetermined issue voting you'll need a sheet of paper for each idea. Label each sheet so people know where to attach their dot.

If you're using two-step voting, be sure you have enough paper area for the quantity of ideas expected. Draw a regular grid on each piece of paper with each grid square large enough to hold a sticky note with the written idea plus space for dots around it.

Dot substitutes

If no paper dots are available and participants are trustworthy, people can make their own dots with colored markers. In this case it's a good idea to clearly display on a poster or screen the number of color dots to be made, along with their significance.

How many dots to use?

While there are no widely accepted metrics on how many dots to provide each participant, here are some rules of thumb suggested by facilitators who have experience in dot voting:[153]

If you are looking for the top X of N ideas (where X is predetermined in advance)

- Give each participant X+1 dots. (X+1 should be less than N!)
- Or use weighted voting. For example, give each participant six dots: three for top choice, two for second, and one for third. Participants cannot use all their dots for one option.

To rank a set of N ideas

- Give each participant between N/2 and N/5 dots. This will usually allow you to categorize ideas into 3–5 bands of similar importance.

To discover importance/influence/commitment/vetoes/must dos

- Give each participant one or more colored dots for each factor you are exploring: for example, green dots to mark what's important, red dots to indicate options on which the voter has influence or control, and blue dots for issues to which the voter will commit time and energy. You can also assign colors for "vetoes"—options that a participant feels should not be pursued—and "must-do" issues.
- If you are exploring other issues besides importance or ranking, optionally have additional dots available on demand so that people can dot as many influence/commitment/veto/must-do items as desired.

Dot coding and usage

It's crucial that participants completely understand the voting process. Determine the following:

- How multiple dots can be used: only one vote per item; multiple votes per item; three for the highest priority, two for the second highest, etc.
- What each color signifies: importance, must do, veto, commitment, influence, and so on. Although some schemes use different colors to indicate first choice, second choice, and so on, I find it harder to evaluate the resulting votes and prefer to provide weighted voting either by allowing multiple dots on a single choice or the weighted voting scheme described above.

Unless the voting description is very simple (e.g., "Please place your dot on the issue that's most important to you."), post the voting instructions next to the voting sheets or project them on a screen for all to see.

How?

Dot voting preparation

All but the simplest dot voting requires preparation. Determine the following, with reference to the previous section and the additional information below:

- What will be voted on? For ideas/options generated by participants in the session, use *two step dot voting*. For specific predetermined options/ideas use *predetermined options dot voting*.
- How many colors to use.
- How many dots to use.
- The voting rules (see below).

Here are some additional rules you may want to incorporate into your voting process.

Pre-voting and/or voting silently

Voting may be influenced by participants' perceptions of how others vote—for example, people may be reluctant to be the first to vote for an option. One way to minimize this is by pre-voting. To do this, give every option a letter or number and allow time for everyone to survey the available options without placing their dots. Have participants write their options' letter/number on their dots without discussion and then vote.

Dot meanings

Give each color dot used a specific meaning and share with participants. Possible meanings include:

- This item is essential (must do). This item is one of my most important/highest rankings.
- I have influence or control over this option (optional: add participant name).
- I am willing to personally devote time and energy to this issue (optional: add participant name).
- This option should not be considered/acted upon (veto).

Multiple dot application

If you are distributing more than one dot of a given color, decide how dots may be applied:

- Only add one dot to each desired option.
- Dots may be distributed in any way—for example, all given to one idea.
- Give x dots to your first choice, y to your second, etc.—for example, 3 dots for top choice, 2 for second, 1 for third.
- Use x dots with the pre-voting procedure described above. Remaining dots are added as desired in a second round of voting. This provides a combination of uninfluenced and influenced voting.

You can also require everyone to commit to one of the ideas (see above) in a first round of voting before they are allowed to vote in a second round on the importance of the ideas themselves.

Two step dot voting

Two step dot voting precedes the voting with idea/topic generation, using *Post It!*, *affinity grouping*, or any other appropriate idea generation technique. The resulting options should be written on sticky notes, each of which is placed in the center of one of the grid squares on the voting sheet. If you are planning to dot vote on topics generated by affinity grouping, build the affinity grouping on a large paper sheet so dots can be applied close to the relevant sticky notes.

Predetermined options dot voting

Once voting choices have been developed and displayed, it's time to dot vote. Here are the steps:

Clarify what is to be voted on

Clearly explain the available voting options. Ask whether it's clear what people are voting on and resolve any questions before the vote begins.

Hand out dots and describe how to vote

Distribute an identical set of dots to each participant. Explain how to vote. Cover:

- The purpose of the voting. Examples: Find the top three options; rank these ideas by importance to you/highest priority/your commitment to them; register a veto on options we should not pursue.
- What each color dot represents.
- How multiple dots can be distributed.
- Voting round details. Examples: one round for all the dots; one round for each color dot; mixed rounds of pre-voting and free voting.
- Any other voting rules, such as a commitment voting requirement.

Ask whether there are questions, and answer them.

Vote!

Give people enough time to vote. When most people have voted, announce that voting will close in 30–60 seconds. Announce when voting is closed.

Review the vote

Once voting is closed, give people time to review the voting for themselves. Then review what you see and check that the group shares your understanding.

Unless you are using dot voting to make a quick decision on priorities ("After voting we will work on the three highest ranked issues"), you should allocate time to discuss the outcomes and consequences of the vote. Do the results make sense? If not, the questions asked should be rethought or reframed. Have clear priorities emerged? Are some options ranked as high priority but there is little commitment to making them happen? Perhaps there are items that have weak support; should they be put aside for now? Exploring what the vote means to the group is an important component of this technique.

CHAPTER 50
Anonymous voting

Description

Although one of the big advantages of participatory voting is that you learn specific opinions, preferences, and information about other participants, there are situations in which anonymous input is appropriate. Discovering how the members of a team are feeling about working together, finding out what proportion of an audience is divorced, or obtaining ideas on how management can supervise better are some examples. This is traditionally done via anonymous paper ballot or ARS voting—methods that avoid voter engagement with the generated ideas. In this chapter I'll cover two simple anonymous sharing techniques that involve participants: *Idea Swap* and *Thirty-Five*.

Idea Swap is not a pure voting technique, but rather a simple and quick way to anonymously share ideas or opinions in a group of ten or more. If desired, the results can then be voted on using any of the techniques in this section. Idea Swap ensures that the group hears each idea, leaving discussion for later. Because ideas are shared one at a time, the technique is best used with fewer than a hundred people.

Devised by the Thiagi Group's self-styled "Resident Mad Scientist" Sivasailam Thiagarajan, universally known as Thiagi, Thirty-Five is an interactive technique for group rating of anonymously submitted ideas. It cleverly incorporates discussion of the ideas while the rating is constructed and can be used by any number of participants.

When?

Use anonymous voting techniques whenever you need to obtain ideas or opinions anonymously and don't have an ARS available. The techniques I describe also have a learning advantage in that they actively involve participants in sharing or evaluating the topics being discussed.

Resources

Idea Swap

Provide a piece of paper and pen for each participant and a clear space in the room large enough for participants to throw their crumpled piece of paper. You may want to arrange a scribe to record ideas and opinions. Idea Swap takes a few minutes for people to write their ideas or opinions plus enough time for each idea to be read aloud.

Thirty-Five

Provide an index card, 3″ × 5″ or larger, a pen for each participant, and, if appropriate, a scribe to record the top ideas. An attention-getting device such as a chime or whistle is useful for large groups. You'll also need enough clear room space for participants to mingle easily. Thirty-Five typically takes between 20 and 40 minutes to run.

How?

Idea Swap

Want to know what your employees *really* think about the new incentive plan? Should association supplier members pay higher dues than practitioner members, and if so, how much? Use Idea Swap to obtain ideas or opinions on a topic about which participants are unlikely to be frank without anonymity. Distribute a piece of paper and pen to participants. State the topic and check that it's clear, answering any questions. Ask all gathered to write their response in private on their piece of paper. Explain that no one will know who has written what, and that, because someone else will be reading their paper, it's important to write legibly. Give people a time limit to write, typically a couple of minutes.

When time is up, ask participants to crumple up their paper with the writing inside and throw the resulting ball into the clear space in the room. Jumble up the pile if necessary. Tell people to pick up a ball of paper, and uncrumple it. Note that it's okay if you pick up your own paper again. Then go around the room asking each person to read what's on their paper.

If desired, scribe responses for follow-up discussion. Do not post the papers, as people may recognize handwriting; instead, trash them after they've been shared.

Thirty-Five

Thirty-Five is shared by kind permission of Thiagi (Sivasailam Thiagarajan).[154]

Present an open-ended question to participants and make sure it's clear, answering any questions. Hand a card to participants, asking them to write a short, clear, and legible response. Explain that no one will know who has written what, and that, because others will be reading their card, it's important to write legibly. Give people a time limit to write, typically a couple of minutes.

Explain that responses will be evaluated in comparison with others, and warn participants that it's no big deal if their response receives low scores.

Ask everyone to stand and walk briskly around the room, holding their card with the written side down. Tell them to exchange cards with each person they meet, without reading the cards.

Once several swaps have occurred, get everyone's attention, tell them to stop moving and pair up with whoever's nearby.

Ask each pair of participants to review the responses on each of the cards they now have. Tell them to distribute 7 points between these two responses to reflect their relative usefulness. Give examples of 7-point distributions: 4 and 3, 5 and 2, 6 and 1, or 7 and 0. Tell participants to avoid using fractions or negative numbers. When ready, ask participants to write the score points on the back of each card.

Once everyone has written the score points on the backs of their card, ask participants to once again walk around and exchange cards. After 20 seconds or so, ask participants to find a new partner, compare the two responses on their cards, and distribute 7 points. Have them write the new score points on the back of the card, below the previous number.

Announce that you will be conducting three more rounds of the activity. (If time is really short, reduce this to one or two more rounds.) Ask participants to maintain high levels of objectivity even if they end up with their own card, and by disregarding earlier score points on the backs of the cards.

At the end of the fifth round, ask participants to return to their seats with the card they currently have. Ask them to add the five score points and write the total.

After pausing for the totals to be computed, explain that you are going to count down from 35. When a participant hears the total on the card, she should stand up and read the response from the card. Begin counting down to identify the card with the highest score. After the participant reads the response from the card, lead a round of applause. Repeat the countdown process until you have identified the top five to ten responses.

If appropriate, ask participants to select a few responses for further discussion and/or implementation. Your scribe could also record all responses sorted by their scores and distribute a copy to each participant.

CHAPTER 51
Creating learning opportunities

Are there other formats that support learning besides traditional lectures and the variety of small group discussions I've described?

Yes!

We can productively mix short presentations with group discussion using two short form presentation formats that have become popular in the last decade: *Pecha Kucha* and *Ignite*. And we can offer a lively learning environment for participants by immersing them in *case studies* and *simulations*. Read the next two chapters to find out more.

CHAPTER 52
Short form presentations: Pecha Kucha & Ignite

Description

Pecha Kucha (the Japanese for *chit-chat*, often written as PechaKucha) and Ignite are dynamic short-form presentation formats that have spread globally since their invention in Japan in 2003 (Pecha Kucha) and Seattle in 2006 (Ignite). In this chapter I'll refer to them as *PK-I*. The only difference between these two formats is their length—both limit presenters to 20 slides automatically advanced, each shown for 20 seconds (Pecha Kucha) or 15 seconds (Ignite), while the presenter shares his or her passion about a topic. Because each presentation lasts just 6 minutes and 40 seconds (Pecha Kucha) or 5 minutes (Ignite), presenters are challenged to be concise, targeted, and creative—and you can pack four Pecha Kucha or five Ignite presentations into 30 minutes.

The PK-I format, with slides advancing automatically whether the presenter is ready or not, adds entertainment and a somewhat dramatic impact to presentations. Presenters may use their audience time in any way they choose: straightforward information sharing, a humorous commentary, or a passionate plea about a cause are common. For example, I've seen PK-I that incorporate (not all at the same time) musical performance, irony (the presenter says one thing while the slides tell a different story), poetry, and the seemingly mundane.

Although not the focus of this book, PK-I are frequently used as social events by scheduling the presentations during an evening social, with accompanying food and drink. This is the format used at Pecha Kucha and Ignite Nights, held in hundreds of cities[155] all over the world. A typical PK-I session at such an event consists of around an hour or more of back-to-back presentations. There's no time allocated for questions during the presentations, and (unless people start throwing stuff) no participation during each presenter's time on stage.

At this point you might be thinking, "If Adrian is such a fan of event session participation, why is he including techniques in this book that aren't participatory in nature?"

One reason is brevity. All PK-I presentations are purposefully short, shorter than the time that 99% of presenters speak uninterrupted during a session. You can think of PK-I as speed dating for ideas. Although the PK-I design explicitly excludes formal questions and answers during the session, the expectation is that presentations will spark dialogue outside the session.

A single Pecha Kucha or Ignite presentation provides a rapid introduction to a topic, an idea, or an experience that acts as a jumping-off place for stimulated viewers to start learning more through post-presentation engagement. Thus, PK-I presentations should be immediately followed by small group discussions with the presenters. Incorporating participative process is key to making PK-I a valuable and effective tool for group sharing and learning.

When?

PK-I can be used at almost any point during an event when it makes sense to briefly introduce interesting and/or provocative ideas or points of view. The poetic format of PK-I can offer a welcome contrast to more serious sessions, so consider scheduling PK-I as an entertaining yet informative break between more traditional session formats.

Although it's perfectly possible to run a single PK-I, it's generally most effective and interesting to hold a number of PK-I sessions back-to-back, followed by small group discussions hosted by the presenters. Typically, an hour-long session might incorporate six Pecha Kucha or seven Ignite sessions, immediately followed by 20 minutes of small group presenter discussions.

Resources

While it's fairly easy to *host* PK-I presentations, most of the work required for a successful session must be done before the event, as described in the next section. You'll need to decide on which format to use, promote the session, solicit presenters, and send them appropriate presentation templates. Have presenters send their complete 20-slide presentations to you several days before the session—you'll need sufficient time to review them and incorporate them all into one master presentation.

On PK-I day, you'll need an appropriately sized room with presentation-friendly lighting, a wireless mike and sound system, a screen, a projector, and a laptop running PowerPoint or Keynote. Add an emcee with the schedule and a staffer for the projector's laptop and you're ready to go!

How?

PK-I presentations require significantly more pre-session preparation than most of the other techniques described in this book. For guidance and examples, refer to the official Pecha Kucha and Ignite

CHAPTER 52: Short form presentations: Pecha Kucha & Ignite

websites listed in these resources.[156] In this section I've included additional important information that will help ensure a successful PK-I session.

Pecha Kucha or Ignite?

The first question any PK-I organizer has to decide is whether to use the Pecha Kucha (20 seconds per slide) or Ignite (15 seconds per slide) format. Look at the time you have available along with the potential number of presentations you'd like to fit in to decide which works better. Personally, I prefer the slightly longer time available in the Pecha Kucha format, but don't lose any sleep over this decision; it's not critical.

PowerPoint or Keynote or both?

The second question for any PK-I organizer is which presentation software to use. There are two considerations here: the platform that each presenter uses to create and practice her presentation, and the platform used for the final session presentation that combines all the individual presentations into a single long slideshow. The Wintel/Apple debate may have lost some of its fervor over the last few years, but in the world of presentation software it's alive and well, as shown by the popularity of both PowerPoint and Keynote. Unless you're running a session at a school or organization where all the presenters have access to the same software, it's unfair in my view to restrict presenters to only one of these products. In my experience, while PowerPoint has greater market-share, Keynote is more likely to be used by the creative types who often tend to populate PK-I presentations.

This means, of course, that you'll need access to both software packages, which means you'll have to use a Macintosh, since that's the only platform that runs Keynote. If that's the case, I recommend you build the final session presentation in Keynote, which I consider the superior software for PK-I–style presentations.

Permissions for Pecha Kucha

1In order to avoid confusion with the Pecha Kucha Nights held all over the world, one-off Pecha Kucha events should comply with the following rules (current as of June 2011):

- "Pecha Kucha" (or any derivative) should not be used in the title of the event.
- Organizers should obtain the Pecha Kucha graphic badge[157] that indicates that the event is "Powered by PechaKucha," which they will need to include on any material used to publicize the event.
- In the case of events that are "for profit," the Pecha Kucha organization asks that a minimum donation of $200 be made, to help support the Pecha Kucha network.

Selection criteria for presenters

If your presentations are to reflect the interests and variety of a community, I suggest you provide relaxed criteria for selecting presenters. Creating and practicing a PK-I presentation is a significant amount of work, and I am reluctant to impose selection criteria on what people offer to do. If you receive many more offers of presentations than you can accommodate, then consider scheduling multiple sessions and populate each one with a somewhat consistent set of presenters.

PK-I templates

To create a uniform look, provide all presenters with templates for your session. These typically will include an opening slide containing presenter and/or topic information (and, if appropriate, an event logo), 20 "blank" slides, and a closing slide with presenter contact information: 22 slides in all.

I like to provide a visual indicator of time passing on each of the slides, and use a translucent circle that moves from left to right in 20 (Pecha Kucha) or 15 (Ignite) seconds along the bottom of the screen. I don't recall from whom I stole this technique, but it works well and is appreciated by presenters. The notes include links to sample Keynote and PowerPoint templates and instructions for Pecha Kucha[158] that use this technique. Make similar templates for Ignite by adjusting the template timings.

Make these templates available to presenters several weeks before the event. Creating good PK-I takes time and the quality of your session will suffer if presenters must rush to create and practice their presentations. Since the templates are large, upload them, together with a set of instructions, to a file-sharing site and send your presenters the link.

Some presenters may ask whether movies can be used in their presentations. "Pure" PK-I presentations do not allow embedded movies, but you may choose to permit, say, a single movie to replace one of the 20 slides. Clearly communicate whatever you decide to your presenters in the instructions you include with the presentation templates.

A word about fonts

Tell presenters not to use obscure fonts in their presentations, as this may cause ugly font substitution effects if the computer on which the master presentation file is created does not have that font.

Before the session

Before the PK-I session, round up all the individual presentations, convert them (if necessary) into the chosen software format, check them, and merge them into a single large presentation. Don't underestimate the time required to perform these steps, as it's easy to be stymied by a late presenter, omit a slide component when converting, or delete one of the many slide auto-transitions. For a set of six presenters, I'd allow several hours to do a careful, accurate job. I tell presenters that their presentation is due 10 days before the session, send reminders a few days before the due date, and follow up immediately with those who don't respond. Invariably, one or two presentations will be late, but at least the rest can be converted, checked, and merged into the master file while inveigling the tardy.

How to merge multiple PK-I presentations into one master

To merge multiple PK-I presentations into one master Keynote file, start with an appropriately renamed master copy of your Keynote template. Next, decide on the order that the individual sessions will be run. How you merge each individual presentation into the master Keynote file depends on whether it's Keynote or PowerPoint.

Keynote merge

It's easy to merge an individual Keynote presentation into the master file:

- Switch to Navigator View of the individual presentation, and click on one of the slides in the slide view.
- Select all (Command-A) the slides and copy (Command-C) them.
- Switch to the master presentation and click on the slide right before where you want to insert.
- Paste (Command-V) to insert the entire individual presentation into the master file.

PowerPoint merge

As you might expect, merging a PowerPoint presentation into the master Keynote file is more complicated, and there are more opportunities to make mistakes:

- Begin by adding a blank copy of your presentation Keynote template into the master Keynote file, using the technique described in the previous section.
- Copy the presenter-supplied text on the opening title slide and paste it into the corresponding slide in the master Keynote presentation.
- Click on the first of the 20 PowerPoint presenter slides and carefully select all the elements on the slide, *except* the animated timing circle.
- Copy your selection, switch to Keynote and paste into the corresponding Keynote slide in the master file.
- Click on the animated Keynote circle and choose Bring to Front from the Arrange menu. If you omit this step, the moving circle may not be visible when the slide is shown.
- Repeat the above three steps for each of the 20 presentation slides.
- Finally, copy the presenter-supplied text on the closing title slide and paste it into the corresponding closing slide in the master Keynote presentation.

Final steps

Word to the wise: As the above processes may take several hours, frequently save your work! You may want to add a title slide for the entire PK-I session to the front of the completed master file. I also like to add a black slide at the end for the production crew to display once the final presentation is over.

Testing the master presentation

Once you've created the master presentation it's time to test it. *To avoid font and hardware problems, use the computer that you will be using at the event.*

Testing the master presentation requires closely attending to the entire presentation. Check that:

- The presentation pauses on each presenter's opening and closing slides.
- All slide elements have been copied correctly from each of the 20 slides in the individual presentations.
- The presentation auto-advances every 15 (Ignite) or 20 (Pecha Kucha) seconds on each of the 20 presentation slides.
- You have only one animated circle moving on each slide.
- The animated moving circle is visible on each slide.

Presenter tips

In your instructions to presenters, emphasize the importance of practicing their session. Even if the presenter knows her content well, discovering what can be said in the 15 or 20 seconds before each slide advances takes practice, and multiple run-throughs will help presenters learn to recover from the inevitable minor slips that occur. Explain that it's an art to match what you say with the brief time each slide is on the screen, and, like most art, one's skill improves with practice.

Sound concerns

As with every presentation, your PK-I session can be severely impacted by poor sound. If any of your presenters have included sound in their presentations (yes, it happens) you will need to arrange to mix the sound output of the presentation computer into the sound system for the event. Presenters should use a wireless lavalier (preferred) or wireless handheld mike so they are free to move about during their presentation. Ideally, three microphones should be used (one for the emcee, one for the current presenter, and one for the upcoming presenter) but you can get away with a single handheld microphone if that's all that's available.

Presenter introductions

Think about how you will introduce each presenter. The approach I like, much appreciated by audiences so far, is to ask each presenter to write a short poem about herself. I've employed the haiku (4 line) or cinquain (5 line) forms—you can obtain a description of these online. I encourage presenters to be creative and/or amusing with their poems, and not to worry about following the precise formal poem structure. At the event, the emcee slowly reads each presenter's poem out loud before she starts.

Recording the session

If possible, video the entire session and arrange for someone to take photographs too. The movie can be uploaded to a video-sharing site, and photographs provide a great memento for presenters and good content for marketing a subsequent event.

Room setup

Plan your room setup to handle the PK-I presentations and the subsequent discussions. Use curved theater-style seating for the presentations. If your presentation space is large enough, the discussions can be held in small groups around the room; otherwise, have nearby breakout space available and a plan for who will go where.

On the day

Once the presentations are done, ask presenters to lead small group discussions of their content. Typically, allow 20 to 30 minutes for this, and suggest that audience members can move between groups as they wish.

CHAPTER 53
Case studies and simulations

Description

Unlike the other techniques described in this book, comprehensive coverage of developing and using case studies and simulations would demand a book of its own. So in this chapter you will have to content yourself with a mere introduction to these two robust vehicles for learning. But worry not—I've included references that will allow you to explore them further.

I've combined case studies and simulations in one chapter because both start from the central premise that learning can be powerfully stimulated when you transform a classroom or conference environment into an engrossing story-world: a place where participants can create and explore in a semi-realistic way alternative roles, points of view, puzzles, and positions. Case studies take a more cerebral approach—they can be thought of as virtual events—while simulations plunge participants into an experiential situation, but the immersive treatment of participant perspective and involvement is common to both techniques.

> "A good case is the vehicle by which a chunk of reality is brought into the classroom to be worked over by the class and the instructor." —Paul Lawrence[159]

Case studies

Case studies are a powerful technique for providing a rich learning experience based on narrative of an actual or fictional situation set in an environment appropriate to the learner's interests and needs. A well crafted case study:

- Offers excellent opportunities to evaluate, synthesize, and apply presentation content.
- Presents one or more critical problems or conflicts that participants must resolve.
- Brings concepts to life by embedding them in a context of a carefully chosen story about realistic characters in a contemporary setting that has relevance to the participants' lives.
- Provides enough concrete details for participants to make meaningful judgments.
- Evokes empathy for the main characters.
- Allows participants to practice taking a position and making complex decisions about real-life situations.

> "... a good case presents an interest provoking issue and promotes empathy with the central characters. It delineates their individual perspectives and personal circumstances well enough to enable students to understand the characters' experience of the issue. The importance of the compelling issue and the empathetic character reflects the fact that cases typically focus on the intersection between organizational or situational dynamics and individual perception, judgment, and action." —John Boehrer and Marty Linsky, *Teaching with Cases: Learning to Question*[160]

Terminology

The various fields that have adopted case studies as components of education have spawned a variety of nomenclature. Legal education has long used the *case method* or *casebook method*, medical education *grand rounds* (more recently *clinical problem solving*), and the Harvard Business School the *case method* for business education for over a hundred years. In this century, the *case study method* has been used for teaching a widening variety of sciences.[161]

Case studies can be *closed* or *open* cases. Closed cases, common in medical education, have a right/wrong answer reached through a teachable process. Open cases evoke multiple plausible solutions that concentrate on the process of synthesis, analysis, and evaluation rather than finding the "correct" answer.

Approaches

The structure of specific case studies depends considerably on the scope and type of learning goals. Case study *narratives* can be as brief as a few paragraphs or contain pages of detail, tell a true or fictional story, and focus on one or multiple issues. Case study *formats* can involve the whole class, small group discussions, or a combination of the two. The case study design may supply all the necessary information at the start or offer it in stages (an *interrupted* case). Case study *outcomes*—besides the learning engendered by the process—can be a single "best" solution or alternative options and their accompanying rationale. Obviously it's crucial that the designer select clear participant learning outcomes before creating a case study.

An interesting case study variant is for participants to create individual *dialogue cases*. These are short written dialogues between two fictional people about a controversial topic (e.g., an ethical issue), followed by the participant's opinion and any appropriate references. This can be done as a pair exercise, with each participant contributing one side of the dialogue.

Simulations

> "Good simulations tend to adapt themselves to the needs of each participant. Simulations have no 'correct' answers. To get the most out of a simulation, you wrestle with the situation and try to do the best you can in the particular situation. You will not always be aware of what the simulation is simulating, but that's okay." —Jerry Weinberg[162]

If you've ever played a childhood game, you have experienced one kind of simulation. Checkers simulates a battle between two players, "mommy and daddy" explores children's view of adulthood, and Monopoly™ imitates the cutthroat world of real estate.

Unlike case studies, in which participants spend time reading and analyzing the case, simulations immerse participants in a simulated situation in which they must respond in real time as it develops. Simulations have been used for educational purposes since the 1960s and, before the development of the personal computer, involved one or more participants interacting in a physical space. Such simulations have been used for many years in situations in which real life experiential learning opportunities are expensive, dangerous, or rare, such as health care, military training, and emergency response.

Of the participative techniques described in this book, simulations offer the widest range of formats and scenarios. At one extreme, in a few minutes we can simulate what mild chaos feels like (try this on someone!):

> Have people clasp their hands in front of their bodies. Ask them to describe what that feels like. Then have them notice which thumb is on top. Ask them to re-clasp their hands with the other thumb on top. Ask them to describe what that feels like.

At the other extreme we can run an elaborate business simulation that provides an engrossing story told via professionally produced video segments with supporting written materials involving multiple-choice points. Small groups decide what should be done at each juncture, and this determines what happens next. In the debrief, participants learn about the consequences of their choices. To create simulations like these requires a significant investment of time and money.

Although simulations can be surprisingly effective in imparting knowledge about factual information, they are most useful for experiential learning about key system relationships. Business simulations provide feedback about the effects of raising or lowering employment or wages, historical simulations

CHAPTER 53: Case studies and simulations

provide a vivid experience of the clash of geopolitical forces in a bygone era, and ecological simulations bring home the impacts of decisions about wetlands conservation and development.

Today our culture is awash in electronic simulations. Designers attempt to make computers easy to use via *skeuomorphism*—simulating a familiar physical reality like turning the pages of a paper desk calendar—while video games simulate a million different worlds, some realistic, some fantastical. Since computers can provide programmed responses to user input, one-person simulations like single-user video games have become common. As this book is about face-to-face participation techniques, I limit this chapter to *situational simulations*: multiperson live simulations that can be experienced in physical rather than electronic realities. However, the boundary between electronic and physical simulations is becoming ever more blurred with the advent and adoption of technologies such as Google Glass™.

Simulations provide valuable learning because they supply immediate feedback to participants regarding their actions. Adding some form of competition or scoring in a simulation helps raise participants' emotional involvement as they play.

Well-designed simulations simplify a real-world system, maintaining the fidelity of central aspects while heightening awareness of system complexity. Participants learn about crucial aspects of the real system without having to invest the time to undergo this experience in the real world. This helps them master the application of concepts to real situations. *Debriefings*, held during and/or after the simulation, complement the learning experience.

When?

Both case studies and simulations can be run at any time that's appropriate for the learning opportunities they supply. When they are scheduled, however, is often constrained by the amount of time they require. This is determined entirely by the specific design employed.

Case studies

An hour or two is sufficient for a simple case study, while a complex case study requires significantly more time, often spread over several days. Participants typically study complicated case study materials in advance, and concluding debriefs may be reserved for a later session.

Simulations

Simulations are normally scheduled for a single time-period. A simple simulation, like the Harvest example described below, can take as little as 30 minutes. At the other end of the spectrum, Jerry Weinberg's Verseworks simulation of a fictional organization typically runs 4 to 5 hours (but once lasted an entire day and night).[163] Unlike case studies, which generally build in time for adequate reflection and discussion, simulations may incorporate deliberate time pressure into their design.

Resources

The resources required to run case studies and simulations depend entirely on the details and format of the proposed case or simulation. For example, the room layout for a case study will reflect whether whole class discussion, small group discussion, or some combination is used. Some simulations can be carried out with few or no additional resources, while others require weeks of preparation at significant cost.

Case studies

Sufficient time allocated for preparation is probably the most important resource required for a successful case study. When a case study is complex, assign sufficient time for participants to review the case study materials, which should include a set of questions for them to consider. Also be sure to allow enough time for an adequate discussion of the case study.

Simulations

Resources required for simulations vary widely. Simple simulations, such as the Harvest example described in the next section, may require easily available low-cost objects such as cards, pens, whiteboards, dress-up clothes, and other props, while high-end simulations can entail producing multiple realistic video segments involving actors, sets, and production staff.

How?

Providing comprehensive explanations on how to create and facilitate case studies and simulations is a massive task—one that would warrant its own book. Instead, this section contains some introductory information plus resources for additional research.

Case studies

Development

> "It is possible to write your own case studies, although it is not a simple task. The material for a case study can be drawn from your own professional experiences (e.g., negotiating a labor dispute at a local corporation or navigating the rocky shoals of a political campaign), from current events (e.g., a high-profile medical ethics case or a diplomatic conundrum), from historical sources (e.g., a legal debate or military predicament), etc. It is also possible to find published cases from books and on-line case study collections."
>
> —*Case Studies-Teaching Excellence & Educational Innovation-Carnegie Mellon University*[164]

A good way to explore and gain experience with case studies is to use one that someone else has developed. When you're ready to develop your own, probably the most important prerequisite is that you have a well-defined vision of your desired learning outcomes and the specific audience with whom you plan to work. Once these are clear, you can start building your case study, usually through modifying an actual situation you've experienced/heard/read about. Typically, your case study will be cast as a story with a protagonist, supporting characters, a realistic physical context, and just the right amount of pertinent detail.

Structure

Although there is no standard structure for case studies, most share certain common elements:

- *Title*: A catchy title helps to provoke interest in the case study.
- *Introduction*: A short introduction generally introduces a protagonist, the decision that must be made, and the context (who, what, why, where, and when).
- *The case problem*: The case study story, including crucial details and frequently presented in chronological order, is told here; often from the point of view of the protagonist.
- *Supporting materials*: Information and resources needed to understand and analyze issues and options. These are elements that would be distracting if included in the body of the case study.
- *Teaching note*: If you are creating a case study for others to use, a teaching note provides advice for conducting the case study.

Implementation

Successfully implementing case studies requires competent facilitation rather than traditional teaching. This can be challenging for subject matter experts who are used to providing participants with content and direction. After introducing the case study and describing the format and goals of the session, you become a guide to the participants who take lead roles in exploring and discussing the case study.

> "Regardless of the format in which you employ case studies, it is important that you, as the instructor, know all the issues involved in the case, prepare questions and prompts in advance, and anticipate where students might run into problems. Finally, consider who your students are and how you might productively draw on their backgrounds, experiences, personalities, etc., to enhance the discussion."
> —*Case Studies - Teaching Excellence & Educational Innovation - Carnegie Mellon University*[165]

Here are typical steps for running a case study:

- Provide sufficient time for participants to prepare. Give them the case study with the instruction to review it in advance, together with the questions to be addressed and an idea of the depth of response expected.

- At the session, introduce the case, describe the format you will be using, and share guidelines on how to proceed. This may include a set of ordered steps you ask participants to perform.
- If you are using group discussion, form groups and monitor subsequent discussions to ensure that everyone contributes and that the discussions do not wander off track. Groups can be assigned different perspectives (e.g., different stakeholders in the case) or have perspectives reflected by specific individuals in each group. Group roles such as facilitator and recorder can also be assigned at this point.
- Guide participants toward achieving the goals of the case study. These can include: solving a problem or recommending a course of action on the basis of the information available, determining and expressing the pros and cons of different approaches, obtaining the best compromise solution, etc.
- Debrief the experience with the group, including sharing what has been learned about process as well as the learning about the case study's topic.

Case study resources

- Teaching and the Case Method[166]
- Using Case Studies to Teach Science[167]
- How to Write a Business Case Study[168]
- Case Studies - Teaching Excellence & Educational Innovation - Carnegie Mellon University[169]
- A peer-reviewed collection of 500+ case studies in all areas of science and engineering[170]
- Progress in Practice: Teaching and Learning with Case Studies[171]
- Writing Case Studies: A Manual[172]
- Ethical Dilemmas, Cases, and Case Studies[173]

Simulations

Creating a useful simulation, even a simple one, is a difficult task. Although there are many short articles on the topic, I've been unable to find comprehensive written resources on how to construct simulations. So if you desire to build your own simulation from scratch you may want to learn experientially by taking a course on the topic. A couple of appropriate workshop and conference resources are the Center For Medical Simulation[174] and the Society for Modeling & Simulation International.[175]

As with case studies, developing a simulation starts with a well-defined vision. What do you want the simulation to accomplish, and for whom?

Resist the tendency to incorporate too much in a simulation. Your experience with the concept or topic can lead you to underestimate the difficulty for a less-experienced participant to absorb everything you include.

It's essential to thoroughly debrief a simulation, as this is when significant learning occurs. Debriefing allows participants to make sense of their experiences through sharing ideas and discussions with their peers. Without a debrief, a simulation may be viewed as little more than a game.

CHAPTER 53: Case studies and simulations

Take care when considering designing or running simulations that address issues of power, race, and ethnic identity. Simulations can evoke uncomfortable feelings in participants who play powerless or minority roles, and insensitivity to such outcomes may lead to undesired consequences. This is not to say that simulations should avoid these topics; however, they should be run by experienced facilitators, preferably with participants experiencing both powerful and powerless roles in conjunction with extensive debriefs.

Simulation resources

- Simulation in the classroom[176]
- Experiential Learning 3: Simulation[177]
- Effective Use of Simulations in the Classroom[178]
- Barnga: A Simulation Game on Cultural Clashes[179]

A simulation example: Harvest by Dennis Meadows[180]

This is one of several versions of Harvest, which Dennis Meadows originally designed as a computer-assisted role-playing game. This is an in-person version. Harvest is in the public domain and may be adapted and used by anyone. Meadows adds that "a slightly more complex version of Harvest, based on teams, is described in the *Systems Thinking Playbook*."[181]

Supplies
One medium-sized bowl, a whistle or bell, and 150–200 pieces of candy.

Participants
The game may be run for groups of from 3 to 15.

Player Instructions
Here is a bowl with 50 pieces of candy in it.

In just a moment I will blow my whistle to start the first round. Then all of you will have 5 seconds to take from the bowl as many pieces of candy as you wish to or are able to grab.

After 5 seconds I will blow my whistle again, and you must stop.

After you stop, I'll count how many pieces of candy are left in the bowl, and will double them or bring the total up to 50, whichever requires fewer pieces of candy. So, for example, if you left 35 pieces in the bowl, I'd add 15, making the total for the next round 50. If you left 20 pieces in the bowl, I would add 20.

After I've added the required number of pieces of candy, I'll give you a few moments to consider your strategy, and then I'll blow the whistle again to start the second round. In that round each of you will once again have 5 seconds to take as many pieces as you wish to or are able to grab.

After 5 seconds, I'll stop the round, count the candy, add the necessary pieces, and give you few moments to consider your strategy. Then I'll blow the whistle for the third round.

We will continue in this way for several cycles.

Your goal is to get as much candy for yourself as you can.

continued on following page

Facilitator Notes

I usually try to blow the whistle for the first round before they have a chance to talk about a common strategy. But after that, if they ask about the possibility of talking together, I say they should do whatever they feel will let them maximize the amount of candy they can get. If they ask how many rounds will be played, just say, "We'll do this for awhile, until I decide to stop."

Debrief

A key issue in the game is the choice between collaboration and competition. Collaboration requires joint decision-making, coordination, and trust. It is useful to get the participants to share their thoughts, observations, and strategies on this choice and to discuss where and how this choice confronts them in real life.

The game introduces a concept analogous to "Maximum Sustainable Yield" in a renewable resource system. If the participants take the candy to zero, you do not add any more for the subsequent rounds. But blow the whistle anyway for several more rounds, so they can experience intensely the frustration of going to an empty bowl. If they do not take any candy, leaving it at 50, you also do not add any. By taking enough candy in each round that the bowl is left with 25 pieces, the participants can maximize the amount that you must add each round.

Of course, over the long term, they cannot take out on a sustainable basis more than you put in. You can draw a graph to make this clearer. On the horizontal axis is "Number of pieces at the end of the round" ranging from 0 to 50. On the vertical axis is "Number of pieces added" ranging from 0 to 25. The data curve has the shape of an equilateral triangle with its peak at the point (25,25). Engage them in discussions about where this kind of regeneration confronts them in real life. The relation to fisheries, forests, and ground water is obvious. The game also makes points about softer resources, like faith in government.

CHAPTER 54
Endings—consolidating learning and moving to outcomes

EFFECTIVE LEARNING REQUIRES SUCCESSFUL FOCUS on the meaning of presented information and experience. I've covered many ways to provide rich, just-in-time, personal learning experiences during conferences, using the power of participation to uncover and explore the learning that participants seek and need.

Though they are a vast improvement over traditional lectures, these methods are insufficient on their own. For truly effective learning, participants must recap, reflect, and reexamine what they have learned, consider how their specific learning can be applied in the future, determine resulting priorities, and plan how to act on them.

That's not all. Besides providing a platform for individual learning, conferences provide a unique environment for participants *as a group* to share and celebrate learning, discover commonalities, create and develop new ideas, and move to action. Through devoting appropriate attention to event closings, powerful new group initiatives often emerge that have widespread, grassroots support. Options for group futures can be generated, evaluated, and adopted. Events that use these techniques can be fertile ground not only for individual development and growth but also for successful organizational planning and meaningful community building.

Sadly, most events completely bypass these opportunities, typically closing with a motivational speaker or final banquet. In so doing, the event planners waste a tremendous opportunity for leveraging the learning, connections, and community building that has occurred.

Four powerful participation-rich techniques that provide effective closings for an event are described in this section: *Pro Action Cafés*, *Plus/Deltas*, *Personal Introspectives*, and *Group Spectives*. The *Solution Room*, described in the Openers section, can also be used to supply additional learning and connections at the end of an event.

CHAPTER 55
Pro Action Café

Description

> "Pro Action Café, used at the end of a conference to generate and develop concrete actions, is so far the best process in my practice for getting good ideas out of the room with passion, precision and participation."
> —Chris Corrigan, Practice Notes: Cafés for taking a conference to action[182]

A Pro Action Café is a blend of Open Space (Chapter 40) and World Café (Chapter 41) that facilitates reflection, discussion, consolidation of ideas, and moving to action. The process starts with discussion questions proposed by participants via Open Space. Next, participant questions are assigned to Café tables, and three table rounds of conversation focus on the following questions:

- What is the quest behind the table question?
- What is missing?
- What next steps will I take? What help do I need? What did I learn?

When?

Pro Action Café can be the sole activity for a short community organizing meeting, but is most often used as a closing session for a longer event.

CHAPTER 55: Pro Action Café

Resources

The ideal setup for Pro Action Café combines those needed for Open Space and World Café in a single room—a large circle or set of concentric circles of chairs in one part of the room, and a set of small round tables with chairs in another part. If space is tight, have participants help reconfigure the room as needed.

Review the resource sections of the World Café and Open Space chapters. Because the whole session takes place in a single room, you won't need the separate breakout spaces usually required for Open Space.

Allow 2 to 3 hours to hold a Pro Action Café.

How?

Because Pro Action Café combines Open Space and World Café process, I've supplied only a general overview of the process here. Refer to the chapters on Open Space and World Café for technique-specific details.

Get started

Begin in Open Space format with everyone sitting in a large circle or concentric circles of chairs. Ask participants whether they have a question, project, or issue on which they would like discussion, advice, or support.

Create the table topics

Explain that each question, project, or issue will be assigned a separate table for discussion using a technique called World Café. Ask those with a table topic to announce it, move to a free table, and write the topic on the table paper. Once all tables have been assigned to topics or there are no more issues raised, ask the remaining participants to choose the table they would like to join for the first World Café round and go there.

Each table should have a table host who remains at the table for all three question rounds. The table host can be the person who proposed the table's topic, or a volunteer. Explain the table host's duties and obtain one for each table.

Explain World Café

Introduce World Café etiquette, as described in Chapter 41. Then announce the following three questions that will be used, one for each round of discussion, and say you'll explain them in more detail at the start of each round.

- What is the quest behind the table question?
- What is missing?
- What next steps will I take? What help do I need? What did I learn?

Run the World Café

Allow 20 to 30 minutes for each question round. Be flexible about the time allocated, depending on the energy level in the room. When conversation starts to dry up or turn to other topics, bring that round to a close. Provide a short break, 5 to 10 minutes, between rounds. After each of the first two rounds, ask participants to move to new tables, with the table hosts staying put.

Round 1: What is the quest behind the question?

Explain that the purpose of this round is for table participants to explore the question in more detail. This round is not for providing advice but discovering deeper meaning(s) behind the question and clarifying to the table host what the question means.

Round 2: What is missing?

The purpose of this round is to flesh out aspects of the question, project, or issue that have not yet been addressed. Ask table hosts to quickly brief new table participants, who will then explore perspectives and options that haven't yet been considered.

Round 3: What next steps will I take? What help do I need? What did I learn?

If the table host is not the topic owner, owners should return to their original table for this final round. Once the table host has quickly briefed participants, have the topic owner reflect on what has been uncovered and harvest insights with the table members' help. Provide time for all table members to share what they have learned during the Pro Action Café, whether it's related to action on an issue or learning about process. Encourage all participants to take away an action from this round for themselves.

Concluding circle

Have all participants move back to an Open Space circle of chairs and facilitate sharing insights with the whole group. At a minimum, ensure that table hosts or topic originators share their insights and takeaways.

CHAPTER 56
Plus/Delta

Description

Plus/Delta is a simple but highly effective review tool that allows participants to quickly identify what went well and what could be improved. Plus/Delta delivers a fast evaluation of a session or conference while also providing an opportunity to share and compare experiences. It is useful even if evaluation is not a high priority.

In my experience, Plus/Delta is one of the best ways to launch a closing review because it efficiently provides everyone present with a fresh, collective picture of participants' responses to their experiences. Following Plus/Delta with discussion is important because the technique is more qualitative than quantitative—it does not evaluate in detail the relative strengths of the views expressed. The Plus/Delta quickly uncovers potential discussion topics that can then be explored using a fishbowl or other appropriate discussion techniques.

An *Action Plus/Delta* is a variant of this technique that uncovers actionable items that participants want to work on, as well as issues they currently don't know how to address.

A sample Plus/Delta is shown in Figure 56.1.

FIGURE 56.1 • *Plus/Delta example (Google Doc version)*

2011

Plus	Delta
• good integration of new attendees • broad spread of people with overlapping interests • good mix of vendors • Peddie did great job • increased number of peer sessions • more energy this year • good mix of IT and academic sessions • flexibility of session discussions • exchange of ideas • sharing beer • dinner in Princeton • demo showcase format • different computing devices • organization and time management • like the bigger name tags • schedule on back of badges • av equipment worked well • comfortable dorms • discussion on site visits • school tour • keynote speaker and having the speaker facilitate a peer session • xbox • softball game • social time • online calendar	• vendor map needs description at site • vendor presentation started too close to lunch • put city on badge • big campus map at registration • not enough peer sessions on Tuesday • let's try one non peer session on Tuesday • need large peer session • Wiki is confusing to some • more colleges • need clearer session descriptions • more paperless • maybe do first half of session creation immediately after round table • confusion on how to answer three questions in the beginning • buddy system? • no hangout at registration area • when is the end of the session? • non-school affiliated attendees • some sessions seemed focused on particular aged students • recall this list • better mattresses

Discussion

- smaller regional gatherings as a webinar?
    - organize on the listserv
    - Alex will post to listserv about the probability of webinars
- Joel's idea on consortium purchasing
    - we aren't all that large a group to be attractive to vendors?
    - maybe let's just do team purchasing - organized over listserv

When?

Use Plus/Delta to begin group review at the end of a session or conference. The technique can be carried out in as little as a few minutes for a one-session evaluation and may require 30–40 minutes for an evaluation of a multiday event. Be sure to include enough time in your schedule after the Plus/Delta to discuss the topics, issues, and ideas it uncovers.

Resources

If necessary, supply a microphone for the facilitator and a handheld or stand microphone for contributors.

Although not strictly necessary, I like to provide two distinct areas in the room for contributors to the Plus/Delta to line up with their plus or delta comments. This is easily done by re-creating the Plus/Delta design shown in Figure 56.2 on the floor of the room, using masking tape or (my preference) fabric straps. Adding a sheet of paper with a large "+" and "Δ" at the top of each floor column makes it clear where people should line up. If you're using a stand microphone it can be placed at the intersection of the Plus/Delta floor lines.

If you are running Plus/Delta for a very large group, consider providing two microphones on stands, placed at the head of each Plus/Delta column.

Low-tech resources

For up to 50 people, a single flip chart, markers, a scribe, and a place to display (plus materials to mount) completed flip chart sheets are all you need.

High-tech resources

With more than 50 participants, I suggest a projected Plus/Delta document. If you only have a single computer, you'll be restricted to using a single scribe who types directly into the word processing document that's displayed on the projected computer. A better solution uses two or more internet-connected computers, one of which is projecting a shared Google Doc that mimics the Plus/Delta diagram.[183] This allows multiple scribes, which makes it easier to keep up with documenting the ideas expressed. For this to work, be sure to make the Plus/Delta Google Doc visible to and editable by the scribes.[184]

How?

To do a Plus/Delta evaluation and sharing, create two columns on a flip chart, whiteboard, or electronic projected word processor document headed with the symbols "+" and "Δ" as shown in Figure 56.2.

FIGURE 56.2 • *Plus/Delta Chart*

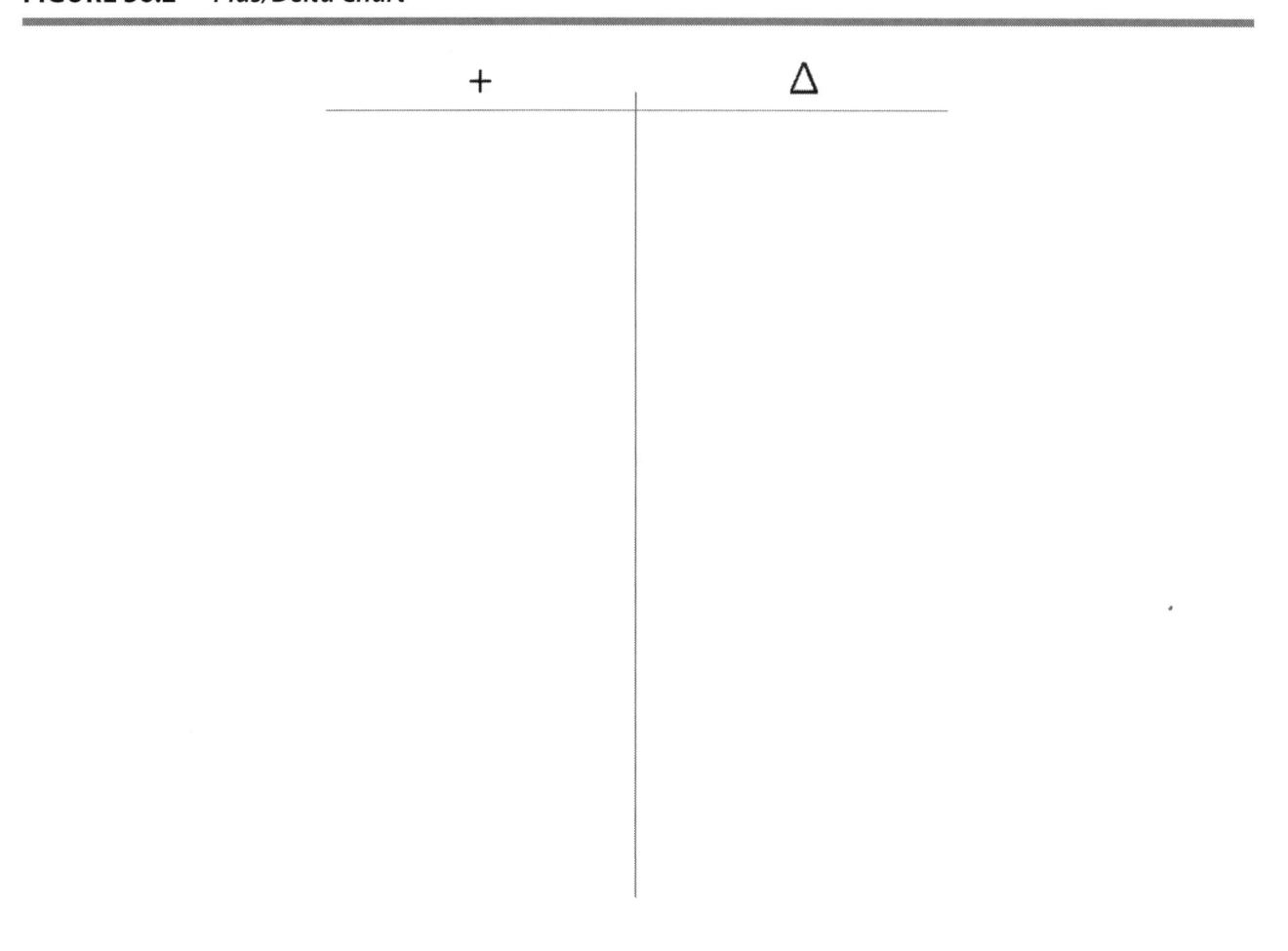

+	Δ

Explain to the group that Plus/Delta is a quick way to identify and share what went well at the session or conference and what could be improved. Ask participants to provide *brief* items for the list. Make it clear that after the Plus/Delta has been created it will be used as a basis for discussion of the points and ideas raised.

Introduce the session scribe(s).

Next, ask participants for positive comments *only*. If you have set up the Plus/Delta design on the floor, ask commenters to line up in the plus column. When necessary, direct the next person to speak. People may be hesitant to start the exercise, so give them time to volunteer their thoughts. Once comments have started, encourage people to step forward and line up without waiting for the previous commenters to finish.

If people start to share improvements (deltas) at this stage, gently ask them to remember their comments and keep them until the delta part begins.

When positive comments start to trail off, encourage the group to keep sharing. Once there are no more positive comments forthcoming, announce that it's time to move to the delta phase.

Now, ask for ways in which the session or conference could be improved and list them in the delta column. Explain that sometimes an *improvement* for one person may be considered an overlooked *plus* for another, and that it's okay to add more pluses to the list if they arise at this stage. This is when the two Plus/Delta columns floor areas are helpful to organize commenters who step up. If you have people waiting to share in both columns, alternate contributions from each.

If participants start to discuss the details or pros and cons of a list item, politely interrupt and bring them back to the task of creating the Plus/Delta lists.

When comments start to trail off, ask for more, and leave time for people to respond.

The "curious" variation

An addition to Plus/Delta that can be useful in some circumstances is to add a third column titled "Curious." A Curious column provides a place for listing new ideas, or questions to be explored. Have attendees make suggestions for this column once the pluses and deltas have been listed. Alternatively, this column can be used to hold issues that arise as the Plus/Delta is taking place and that people want to discuss later in more detail.

The "action" variation

To transform Plus/Delta into a tool for action, redefine the two columns as follows:

> Plus ⇒ actions I/we want to work on
>
> Delta ⇒ issues that concern me but that I don't know how to address

When used in conjunction with a personal introspective, described in the following chapter, this Plus/Delta variant allows participants to move from the personal decisions made at the introspective into sharing, discussion, and support of initiatives to which individuals have committed (the plus column). The Delta column then offers the group a place to list other, unresolved, ideas and who might be able to work on them.

Follow up

Once comments are exhausted, the resulting lists can be used as a basis for discussion and comments about the group's session or conference experience.

CHAPTER 57
Personal introspective

Description

A personal introspective is a two-part closing conference session that guides participants through a review of what they have learned and a determination of what they want to consequently change in their lives.

First, attendees privately reflect on their answers to five questions they are given at the start of the session. Then, participants are invited to share their answers with a small group of peers. (They can opt out of this, though few do.) The personal introspective reinforces attendees' learning while it is still fresh, and increases the likelihood of personal and professional change and growth. Interestingly and importantly, the group sharing invariably creates a heightened sense of connection and intimacy among the group members. The session typically takes between 45 and 60 minutes, though it can be easily extended to give more time for individual reflection and sharing.

Each attendee is free to respond at whatever level he finds appropriate and comfortable. Some people come up with ideas for small changes in their lives, while others come to profound realizations with significant consequences. If this benefit were all that a personal introspective provided, then, in the words of the Jewish Passover song "Dayenu"—*It would have been enough*. But the subsequent sharing by attendees adds more to the personal introspective, creating a heightened sense of connection and intimacy among group members. It can feel risky to share with others what are often personal aspects of the changes one wishes to make, and to then share the decisions one has made to start work on such changes. Taking such risks is an integral step on the path of building intimacy—not only the increased intimacy that the sharer feels, but also the group's connectedness as more and more people share. In a safe environment, the outcome is increased trust, which further builds safety.

CHAPTER 57: Personal introspective

I continue to be surprised by the power of a personal introspective. At every session I have run, a number of people have emotionally announced how important the exercise was for them. In peer conference evaluations, typically about 60% of attendees rate personal introspectives "high," 35% "moderate," and 5% "low." Giving people the opportunity to come together, process, and then share their experiences and realizations generates a sense of connection and intimacy among attendees that has to be experienced to be believed.

When?

I like to hold a personal introspective as the first session on the last day of a multiday (3+ days) conference, despite the obvious drawback that the rest of the day's sessions can't be included in the introspective. There are two reasons for this scheduling choice. First, sharing attendees' answers to the introspective questions builds a surprisingly intimate atmosphere during the session, creating a wonderful launch for the final conference day. The second reason is practical—invariably some people leave before the end of the conference, and would miss the personal introspective if it was held as the last session. Participants who haven't experienced a personal introspective tend to underestimate its value until they go through the process themselves. Scheduling the session at the start of the last day can reduce the number of attendees who, not understanding the value of personal introspectives, decide to leave early.

If you want to hold a short personal introspective at the end of a shorter conference, it should be scheduled just before the final closing session, which at my events is always a group spective.

Resources

A personal introspective requires enough open space for participants to sit in small circles of six to eight chairs. The circles should be far enough apart so that their members can converse with others in their circle without being overly distracted by the conversation from neighboring circles.

Before the introspective starts, prepare some examples of vague versus measurable goals and actions that connect with your conference's subject, guided by the examples given in Table 57.1. Print a personal introspective questions card—5″ × 8″ is a good size (Appendix 2)—for each participant, and have pens available for those who need one.

I used to hold personal introspectives in a single large circle, as described in *Conferences That Work: Creating Events That People Love*. I've since found that the session works better in small groups. If your personal introspective is going to immediately follow a session in which the entire group is seated theater-style you can provide the session instructions right away and then ask participants to move their chairs into the small sharing circles described next. Otherwise, prepare the personal introspective meeting space by setting up small, equally sized circles of six to eight chairs per circle. Use the smaller number if time for the session is at a premium. So that each circle's chairs are filled, set out as many chairs as there are participants.

Calculate the average time for each attendee to share by subtracting 15 minutes from the time allocated for the introspective, dividing the result by the number of attendees in each small group, and rounding down to the nearest minute or half-minute.

Use one of the timing methods described in Chapter 15 to provide an audible reminder to end each participant's group sharing. I recommend you also provide a preliminary 30-seconds-to-go warning sound during sharing.

When describing the introspective in advance, emphasize that it's important that everyone is present when the exercise starts.

How?

Populating the small circles of chairs

If participants are in theater-style seating when the personal introspective starts, skip the rest of this section and implement it when indicated in the next section.

Right before the session starts, adjust the number of chair circles available to accurately reflect the number of participants. To facilitate getting circles completely filled, you can initially provide slightly fewer chairs than there are participants and add more chairs for one or two circles once the existing circles are full.

If you are starting an introspective with small circle seating already in place, ask participants to choose and sit in a circle of chairs that does not contain other people from their organization (or division if this is a corporate event), and, as much as practical, a circle with people they don't know. Explain that you need full circles for the exercise.

As people take their seats, monitor the circles and encourage people to fill each circle completely. Invariably some small groups will have fewer people than others and you'll usually have to direct those people in sparsely filled circles to abandon their circle and join partially filled circles. *It's OK for some circles to have one chair vacant, but keep moving people and do not start the introspective while any circle has two or more chairs empty. Also, do not let people add themselves to a circle that is already full. (Yes, they will try this.)*

To check whether the seating distribution is satisfactory, ask circle members to raise hands if they have more than one empty chair. Keep checking until *all* the circles are an acceptable size.

Once all hands are down, ask whether anyone is sitting with someone else from their organization or division and have them swap with someone from another circle.

If latecomers appear, assign them to partially filled circles. If all circles are full, they will have to join an existing circle; make it clear they will probably not get time to share during the second part of the introspective unless there is spare time available after the other members of their circle have shared.

CHAPTER 57: Personal introspective

Answering the questions

Begin the session by handing out a personal introspective card and a pen if needed to each attendee. If attendees are already seated in their small circles, have them temporarily turn their chairs to face you. Then spend a few minutes explaining the first part of the personal introspective—answering the five questions on the card. Here's what I might say:

> *"Welcome, everyone, to your personal introspective! By now you've had many different learning experiences at this conference. The purpose of this session is to give you an opportunity to explore changes you may want to make in your life and work after the conference is over. This is an opportunity for you: a session to dive into, to experience fully. It will work best if you don't think too much; instead, respond from your gut!*
>
> *You start your personal introspective by answering for yourself the five questions on the card you've just been given. Let's go through these five questions in detail.*
>
> *Number One: What do I want to have happen? Think about what you want to change in your life in the future. These changes could be in any aspect of your life. They could be something mundane, they could be something major. What are your desires, your dreams? What have you just started that you want to keep on doing? What do you want to give up? What are you inspired to do in a different way? What are you inspired to do that you haven't done before?*
>
> *These are exciting questions. Think about your answers and write them down!*
>
> *Number Two: What is the current situation? Time for a reality check. This is a fairly easy question to answer. Before you can go somewhere, you need to know where you are now. So take a minute or two to summarize the current situation, the starting point for the changes you want to have happen. Be as specific as necessary.*
>
> *Number Three: What are you willing to do? This question is about action. To make happen what you want to have happen, you need to do stuff. So, what are you willing to do? What are the steps? Write them all down!*
>
> *Number Four: How will you know when it happens? This is an important question, and probably the hardest to answer. Its purpose is to check that you're setting goals, actions, and outcomes that can be measured in a way that's meaningful to you. If your goals, actions, and outcomes are measurable, you can manage the process of getting where you want to go, gauge your progress toward achieving your goals, and you will know when you've succeeded. If you don't have measurable goals, actions, and outcomes, you're going to be frustrated carrying out what you decide here today. So, use this question to review your earlier answers and, if necessary, work on how you can reframe them so they are measurable.*
>
> *To further illustrate the difference between vague and measurable answers to this question, take a look at the examples shown here. [Display your customized examples, like those shown in Table 57.1.]*

TABLE 57.1 • *Goals/Actions—Vague versus Measurable*

VAGUE GOAL OR ACTION	MEASURABLE GOAL OR ACTION
"I'll be more positive."	"The ratio of positive to negative comments in my daily journal will double in the next 6 months."
"I will get over my fear of public speaking."	"I will join my local Toastmasters club at next month's meeting."
"I'm going to learn more about X."	"I will subscribe to the *X* journal and attend the *X* conference in July."
"I will treat my direct reports better."	"Starting today, I will implement weekly one-on-ones with all my direct reports, and give them my undivided attention during the meetings."

Number Five: Where and how will I get support? During this conference you may have discovered resources that can support the changes you want to make. These resources may be reference materials, they may be other conferences, local or online communities you can join, or people you've met here. While they're fresh in your mind, write down the resources you'll use for support as your answer to this question.

I can't overemphasize the importance of identifying specific, measurable answers to these questions. Ending up with concrete, measurable goals, actions, and outcomes is key to benefiting from this introspective.

Any questions about these five questions?"

Pause for questions.

When any questions have been answered, continue like this:

"I'm going to give you [5 to 10] minutes to answer these questions for yourself. Remember, there are no wrong answers to these questions. Don't think too much, get those answers down! Go!"

Give attendees the time you have just stated to answer the questions. If necessary, ask people who have finished to refrain from talking while others are still writing. I watch for signs that the majority of people are done, then gently announce that a minute or two remains for those still writing. If a significant number of attendees are using computers to record their responses, you may need to ask for a show of hands to determine who is now surfing the internet, and who is still writing down answers.

At this point, if participants are not yet in small circles, have them move their chairs to form the small circles described in the previous section.

CHAPTER 57: Personal introspective

Time to share

How you introduce the sharing portion of the personal introspective will depend to some degree on your conference topic. You likely don't need to talk much about safety if your conference topic is highly technical and the peer sessions have not been about "people issues." I prefer to play it safe and emphasize that people don't have to share with the group. I might say something like this:

"I hope this exercise has been useful for you. Now it's time for the second part of the personal introspective. In this part you'll each be given an opportunity for sharing what came up for you during this exercise. I want to emphasize that your answers are private, and you can choose whether or not to share. You may not want to share anything. That's OK! You may not want to share everything. That's OK too.

Having said that, I encourage you to talk about whatever you feel you can. Many people find that it can be very helpful to share their answers. We have enough time to give each of you [the average sharing time you calculated]; *you'll hear a warning sound when you have 30 seconds left* [demonstrate] *and this ending sound* [demonstrate] *when your time is up. Please end promptly when you hear the ending chime, as otherwise you will reduce the following person's time to share. If someone doesn't use their entire time, discuss or ask questions about what has already been shared, but be ready to start with the next person in your group as soon as you're asked to do so.*

Don't interrupt while people are sharing. If there's time before the next person, you're welcome to ask questions or comment, as appropriate. Do not continue with the next person's sharing until you hear the "time's-up" sound.

The first person to share chooses which way the sharing passes around the circle, to his or her left or right. After each sharing is over, sharing passes in the same direction to the next person in your circle.

Any questions? [Pause]

OK, who wants to go first in each group? Please raise your hand."

Wait until someone has raised his hand in every circle. Say:

"Remember, don't switch to another person's sharing until you hear the 'time's-up' sound. First person in each group . . . begin!"

Start your timer. When the first person's time is up, ask him to choose which direction to share around the circle, and then repeat the personal sharing time for the next set of group members.

If you notice that groups are staying silent because the current person sharing has finished, remind them that they can ask questions or comment on what's been said so far.

If there's time left over when the sharing is complete, you can:

- Ask whether there is anything that people would like to share with the whole group. Have people put their hand up if they have something to say. Because the group atmosphere usually has become quite intimate and intense during this session, it's not unusual for people to make general comments about the session and their experience of it. Let this all happen as it will, and facilitate any whole group sharing that follows.
- Give groups some more time to share among themselves. Point out that some who passed over the sharing opportunity may now want to speak, while people may want to add to what they said or comment on what they heard.

Before closing the exercise, say:

"Keep your personal introspective card to remind yourself about what you've decided to change today. Before we close I'd like to emphasize that the private portion of the personal introspective, your answers to the five questions on the card, can be reviewed and expanded on at any time, and you should do this as soon as possible, especially if you wish you'd had more time to prepare your answers.

Finally, if there are resources here in this room—people you identified who can help you make these changes—find them now before the conference is over, check in with them, and make appointments to get the assistance you identified, want, and need."

When small group sharing has largely run its course, or time is up, thank attendees for their contributions and bring the session to an end.

CHAPTER 58
Group spective

Description

For many years I have included a personal introspective, described in the previous chapter, and a *group spective* as closing sessions at my conferences. The personal introspective and the group spective encourage attendees to take stock, reflect on where they started, the path traveled, and the journey yet to come. The personal introspective enables attendees to make this assessment personally, while the group spective, the final session of a conference, provides a time and place to make this assessment of the past, present, and potential future collectively.

The word *spective* is my own invention: a word that attempts to encompass the scope of two human activities. The first is a *retrospective*: activity that looks back on what has happened. The second is a prospective: a word taken from Chaucer's *Squires Tale* that describes a glass or mirror that allows one to see objects or events not immediately present. Seeking a term that combined looking back *and* looking forward, I decided to discard both prefixes and simply call this closing session a *spective*, reflecting the Latin root *spicere*, to look at or see.

Of the participation techniques described in this book, the group spective has the most fluid format. It may evolve into a general discussion, decisions about future meetings, a push to alter the conference format or schedule, a time when bold initiatives are proposed and/or adopted, a critique of the conference status quo, a place where ideas for action are formulated and explored, or any of a hundred different combinations of these and other themes.

As a result, facilitating a group spective is challenging. Many of the participation techniques covered in this book may be included in a group spective, so prior experience and familiarity with them is a definite plus.

When?

Use a group spective for the final session of a conference. If you want or need to add a post-spective social, don't include additional formal conference content, such as a keynote, as it will add a discordant end to the event.

Resources

The resources needed for a group spective are based on the individual participation techniques that will be used. As those techniques are often not determined until the session is underway, I like to be prepared for a range of possibilities. For example, I might have large cards or sticky notes, flip chart paper, pens, markers, tape, and colored dots available so that we can run Plus/Delta, impromptu affinity grouping, and/or dot voting.

You'll also usually need to arrange for one or more scribes to capture ideas and themes on whiteboards, flip charts, or a Google Doc. A camera for photographing manual scribe notes is a time-saver.

Decide on the basic techniques you plan to use, and refer to the relevant chapters in this book to ensure you have the resources you need to implement them.

Depending on the techniques you use, you'll need a room setup that can handle your entire conference group with seating initially set in curved theater style, circular, fishbowl, etcetera, as appropriate. If you are using affinity grouping, you'll need a suitable wall or whiteboard to capture and organize ideas. Plan ahead on how to have participants switch to small group seating if needed.

Unless the conference is very small, it's a good idea to have sound reinforcement with a microphone for the facilitator and at least one handheld microphone, as well as computer video projection available.

How?

Group spectives are closing conference sessions that provide time for attendees to collectively take stock, reflecting on where they started, the path traveled, and the journey yet to come.

More than any other session, running a group spective requires the ability to adapt to the unexpected, stay flexible, regroup, and go with the direction of the group's energy as it develops.

Engineering and facilitating a group spective that stays open to what emerges is a challenge. I recommend reading *Project Retrospectives: A Handbook For Team Reviews*,[185] which, although covering a somewhat different kind of spective, contains much relevant and useful material, and in greater detail than I can give here. Particularly relevant is Chapter 9, in which Kerth describes skills, lessons learned, and various facilitation procedures to help a spective facilitator improve her art. What follows are my thoughts on and adaptations of his work that are relevant for a group spective.

Preparing for a group spective

If this is the first time your conference has been held, start with an activity that allows attendees to discover and express their responses to the conference experience. I am a fan of beginning with the Plus/Delta assessment technique described earlier. For a small group, a facilitated informal discussion may be sufficient. Or you may decide to use a go-around (whereby you start with one person in the circle and proceed around the circle) with a list of questions that sparks comments and ideas. For a larger group, a fourth alternative is to use affinity grouping to discover topics and ideas for later discussion. If you are planning to have informal discussion during the spective, decide on an appropriate set of questions in advance and create copies to distribute to participants.

For a repeated conference, consider using a more targeted group spective. There may be clear questions that the group should spend time on: whether to spend money on a conference technology update, feedback on an initiative that was started as a result of last year's conference, incorporating the group as a nonprofit, and so on. Under these circumstances, I like to use a focused discussion. Even when there are known issues to cover, time should be set aside in every group spective so that new ideas and perspectives have an opportunity to emerge.

If the conference is designed to foster and support action outcomes, consider starting with an action Plus/Delta followed by a facilitated discussion of the issues revealed. Alternatively, a Pro Action Café can be used.

Adding to the challenge of a group spective is the fact that the session is scheduled at the end of a conference, when a facilitator's energy level may be low. Perhaps the most important advice I can give on preparation is to ensure ample sleep the night before, and some quiet time before the session starts for rest, collecting your thoughts, and preparing for the continual intensity of listening and focus that effective spective facilitation requires.

Facilitating a group spective

To effectively facilitate a group spective, bear in mind Kerth's first lesson (slightly paraphrased from the previously referred-to *Project Retrospectives: A Handbook For Team Reviews*):

> *"Manage current topic, flow of ideas, and quality by making sure that everyone knows what is being talked about, and that all are talking about the same thing, by channeling the flow of ideas to keep people focused and to keep abreast of people's moods, and by maintaining a high standard for the quality of the discussion."*

To channel the flow of a river of ideas you need to build facilitative banks. If the banks are too high, the flow's path will only reflect your ideas, not those of the group, while if they are too low, the discussion will dissipate without traveling anywhere significant. Effectively facilitating a group discussion requires maintaining a judicious balance of control over the conversation. Here are some guiding points for facilitators:

- Make continual decisions, based on how the interplay between group members develops;
- Strive for clarity by summarizing discussion when conversations seem to be drifting or disconnected;
- Gently dissuade irrelevant diversions from the broad courses that the discussion takes; and
- Help the group reach closure when appropriate or possible.

Satisfying these multiple needs, as the group discussion goes through the phases of generating themes, exploring and clarifying them, and then turning them into plans and future actions, is extremely challenging. A good facilitator maintains focused listening to the group conversation, allowing careful attention and appropriate responses to the dynamics of attendee interactions.

As Kerth points out, books will only get you part of the way to developing skill at this work. Studying with teachers, and taking advantage of opportunities to improve your interpersonal skills will bring you further along the path. Above all, practice facilitation with sufficient courage to trust your intuition, try new approaches, and remain comfortable with the failures that inevitably occur to bring you ever closer toward the goal of being a skilled facilitator.

Conclusion

Don't agonize about which approach(es) to choose. What's ultimately important is that you provide a place and time for people to reflect, share, discuss, and perhaps decide on future projects and activities.

If you've been using participative techniques throughout your event, you'll likely find that the conference has already prepared the way for an atmosphere in which attendees are open to this work. Any combination of these techniques helps create a coherent and valuable transition from the formal end of the conference to individual and collective future actions, events, and connections that occur long after everyone has left the conference.

APPENDIX 1
Minimum Room Dimensions for Roundtable and Closing Sessions

NUMBER OF CHAIRS

	30	35	40	45	50	55	60	65	70	75	80	85	90	95	100
24	34	37	41	44	47	50	53	56	60	63	66	69	72	76	79
26	36	39	43	46	50	53	57	60	64	67	70	74	77	81	84
28	38	41	45	49	53	56	60	64	67	71	75	79	82	86	90
30	40	44	48	51	55	59	63	67	71	75	79	83	87	91	95
32	41	46	50	54	58	63	67	71	75	80	84	88	92	97	101
34	43	48	52	57	61	66	70	75	79	84	88	93	97	102	106
36	45	50	55	59	64	69	74	78	83	88	93	97	102	107	112
38	47	52	57	62	67	72	77	82	87	92	97	102	107	112	117
40	49	54	59	64	70	75	80	86	91	96	102	107	112	118	123
42	50	56	62	67	73	78	84	89	95	101	106	112	117	123	128
44	52	58	64	70	76	81	87	93	99	105	111	116	122	128	134
46	54	60	66	72	78	84	91	97	103	109	115	121	127	133	139
48	56	62	69	75	81	88	94	100	107	113	119	126	132	139	145

SEAT WIDTH (INCHES)

Dimensions given are based on using a circle of chairs with four gaps with 6 feet between the circle and the walls of the room on all sides.

Example: If the seat width of your chairs is 28 inches, and you are expecting 45 attendees, you will need a room that is at least 49-feet square.

APPENDIX 2
Personal Introspective Question Card

Personal introspective questions

What do I want to have happen?

What is the current situation?

What am I willing to do?

How will I know when it happens?

Where and how will I get support?

Notes

[1] *Scott Berkun*, Confessions of a Public Speaker, O'Reilly, 2009.

[2] *Jeannie Courtney*, www.linkedin.com/pub/jeannie-courtney/a/210/a32.

[3] *Martin Buber*, I and Thou, Touchstone, 1971.

[4] *David Weinberger*, www.hyperorg.com/blogger/2013/07/28/the-history-of-the-history-of-technology/.

[5] *Kevin Kelly*, What Technology Wants, Viking Adult, 2010.

[6] Wikipedia, https://en.wikipedia.org/wiki/Technology.

[7] *Alan Watts*, The Book on the Taboo Against Knowing Who You Are, numerous editions, first published 1966.

[8] The very word *lecture* beautifully illustrates this model. The word is derived from the Latin *lectūra*, which means—to read! The first books were so rare that a group who wished to study a book's content would have someone read the book aloud while the others copied down what they heard.

[9] Wikipedia, https://en.wikipedia.org/wiki/Mathematics_education.

[10] For a good overview, see *Tom Loveless*, The Curriculum Wars, Hoover Institution, www.hoover.org/research/curriculum-wars.

[11] *Michael M. Lombardo and Robert W. Eichinger*, The Career Architect Development Planner, Lominger, 1996.

[12] Center for Workforce Development, The Teaching Firm: Where Productive Work and Learning Converge, Education Development Center, www.edc.org/sites/edc.org/files/pdfs/teaching_firm.pdf.

[13] Derived from *John Cleveland and Peter Plastrik*, Learning, Learning Organizations, and TQM, Total Quality Management: Implications for Higher Education, Prescott Publishing, 1995; *Shanna Ratner*, Emerging Issues in Learning Communities, Yellow Wood Associates, 1997; and *Lee Rainie*, www.slideshare.net/PewInternet/how-teens-do-research-act-college-planners-pdf, 2014.

[14] See *Kelly Kajewski and Valerie Madsen*'s Demystifying 70:20:10 for an overview, deakinprime.com/media/47821/002978_dpw_70-20-10wp_v01_fa.pdf.

[15] *Ivan Illich*, Deschooling Society, Harper & Row, 1971.

[16] *John Holt*, Growing Without Schooling Magazine, No. 40, 1984.

[17] *Kate Fillion* interview in Maclean's, November 2011, www.macleans.ca/general/whats-wrong-with-the-way-we-teach-and-how-a-year-out-of-university-changed-her-sons-life.

[18] *Jerry Weinberg*, Experiential Learning: Beginning, Leanpub, 2012.

[19] *Charles Bonwell and James Eison*, Active Learning: Creating Excitement in the Classroom AEHE-ERIC Higher Education Report No. 1. 1991, files.eric.ed.gov/fulltext/ED336049.pdf.

[20] *Jeff Hurt*, From M&Ms To Supernatural Learning: Attributes Of Effective Learning Strategies, jeffhurtblog.com/2012/07/24/from-mms-supernatural-learning-attributes-of-effective-learning-strategies/.

[21] *Malcolm Shepherd Knowles*, The Modern Practice of Adult Education: From Pedagogy to Andragogy, Cambridge Book Company, 1980.

[22] *John Medina*, Brain Rules, Pear Press, 2009.

[23] *Benedict Carey*, How We Learn, Random House, 2014; *Julie Dirksen*, Design For How People Learn, New Riders, 2012; *John Medina*, Brain Rules, Pear Press, 2009.

Notes

[24] *Michael Polanyi*, The Tacit Dimension, Doubleday, 1966.

[25] *Henry James*, The Principles of Psychology Vol. 1, Dover Publications Reprint, 1950.

[26] *Hermann Ebbinghaus*, Memory: A Contribution to Experimental Psychology, psychclassics.yorku.ca/Ebbinghaus/index.htm.

[27] Ibid, Chapter 7.

[28] *John Dunlosky*, Strengthening the Student Toolbox: Study Strategies to Boost Learning, American Educator, Vol. 37, #3, pp. 12–21, www.aft.org/pdfs/americaneducator/fall2013/Dunlosky.pdf.

[29] *Edwina E. Abbott*, "On the Analysis of the Factor of Recall in the Learning Process," Psychological Monographs 11 (1909): 159–177.

[30] *Daniel T. Willingham*, Allocating Student Study Time: 'Massed' versus 'Distributed' Practice, www.aft.org/periodical/american-educator/summer-2002/ask-cognitive-scientist.

[31] *Quintilian*, Institutio Oratoria, Book XI, Chapter 2, penelope.uchicago.edu/Thayer/E/Roman/Texts/Quintilian/Institutio_Oratoria/11B*.html.

[32] *Deborah Halber*, Sleep helps build long-term memories, MIT News, newsoffice.mit.edu/2009/memories-0624.

[33] *Philip Boswood Ballard*, Obliviscence and Reminiscence, Cambridge University Press, 1913.

[34] *Daniel Godden and Alan Baddeley*, Context-dependent Memory in Two Natural Environments: on land and under water, British J. of Psych 66 (1975).

[35] *Matthew Hugh Erdelyi*, The ups and downs of memory, American Psychologist, Vol. 65(7), Oct 2010.

[36] *Sparrow*, The Sun Magazine, thesunmagazine.org/issues/461/imaginary_friends.

[37] *Simon Chu and John Downes*, Odour-evoked Autobiographical Memories: Psychological Investigations of Proustian Phenomena, Chem. Senses, 2000, chemse.oxfordjournals.org/content/25/1/111.full.

[38] *John Medina*, Brain Rules, Pear Press, 2009.

[39] *C. Bushdid, M. O. Magnasco, L. B. Vosshall, A. Keller*, Humans Can Discriminate More than 1 Trillion Olfactory Stimuli, Science, Vol. 343, 21 March 2014.

[40] *Dan Kois* quoted by Emily Bazelon, Our Best and Worst Summer Romances, Slate, 2013, www.slate.com/articles/life/culturebox/2013/08/slate_s_best_and_worst_summer_romances.html.

[41] LEGO® SERIOUS PLAY®, www.seriousplay.com.

[42] *Adrian Segar*, Conferences That Work Supplement, www.conferencesthatwork.com/index.php/free-downloads/.

[43] *Ruth Clark and Richard Mayer*, e-Learning and the Science of Instruction, Wiley, 2011.

[44] *Adrian Segar*, "Walking to work: loving my treadmill desk," www.conferencesthatwork.com/index.php/personal-effectiveness/2012/08/walking-to-work-loving-my-treadmill-desk/ and "My treadmill desk: some follow-up observations," www.conferencesthatwork.com/index.php/personal-effectiveness/2012/10/my-treadmill-desk-some-follow-up-observations/.

[45] *Marily Oppezzo and Daniel L. Schwartz*, Give Your Ideas Some Legs: The Positive Effect of Walking on Creative Thinking, Journal of Experimental Psychology: Learning, Memory, and Cognition, Online First Publication, April 21, 2014, www.apa.org/pubs/journals/releases/xlm-a0036577.pdf.

[46] *John Ratey*, Spark! The Revolutionary New Science of Exercise and the Brain, Little Brown and Company, 2008.

[47] Ibid, page 35.

[48] Ibid, page 41.

[49] *B.A. Sibley and J.L. Etnier*, The relationship between physical activity and cognition in children: a meta-analysis, Pediatric Exercise Science, https://peandhealth.wikispaces.com/file/view/Sibley+and+Etnier+2003.pdf, 2003.

[50] *Henriette van Praag*, Exercise and the brain: something to chew on, Trends in Neuroscience, www.ncbi.nlm.nih.gov/pmc/articles/PMC2680508/, 2009.

[51] *Jonah Berger*, Contagious, Simon & Schuster, 2012.

52 *Victoria Rideout, Ulla Foehr, and Donald Roberts*, Generation M2: Media in the Lives of 8- to 18-Year-Olds, kaiserfamilyfoundation.files.wordpress.com/2013/04/8010.pdf.

[53] *Carl Marci*, A (biometric) day in the life: Engaging across media, innerscoperesearch.com/news_old/time_warner-whitepaper-2013.pdf.

[54] *Larry Rosen, Mark Carrier, and Nancy Cheever*, Facebook and texting made me do it: Media-induced task-switching while studying, Computers in Human Behavior, www.csudh.edu/psych/Facebook_and_Texting_Made_Me_Do_It-Media-Induced_Task-Switching_While_Studying-Computers_in_Human_Behavior-2013-Rosen_Carrier_Cheever.pdf.

[55] *Larry D. Rosen*, Rewired: Understanding the iGeneration and the Way They Learn, Palgrave Macmillan, 2010.

[56] *Nico Bunzeck and Emrah Dfzel*, Absolute Coding of Stimulus Novelty in the Human Substantia Nigra/VTA, Neuron, 2006.

[57] *Uri Hasson et al.*, Speaker–listener neural coupling underlies successful communication, Proceedings of the National Academy of Sciences, 2010, www.ncbi.nlm.nih.gov/pmc/articles/PMC2922522/.

[58] *Shekhar Kapur*, TED talk, www.ted.com/talks/shekhar_kapur_we_are_the_stories_we_tell_ourselves.

[59] *Ruth Weiss*, Emotion and Learning, Training & Development, November 2000.

[60] *Jonathan Haidt*, The Righteous Mind: Why Good People Are Divided by Politics and Religion, Pantheon Books, 2012.

[61] *Daniel Kahneman*, Thinking, Fast and Slow, Farrar, Straus and Giroux, 2013.

[62] *Geoffrey Cohen and Gregory Walton*, A Question of Belonging: Race, Social Fit, and Achievement, web.stanford.edu/~gwalton/home/Research_files/Walton%20&%20Cohen-A%20Question%20of%20Belonging.pdf.

[63] *Jay Cross*, Overcoming bipolar thinking, www.informl.com/2010/12/24/overcoming-bipolar-thinking/.

[64] *Matthew Lieberman*, Social: Why Our Brains Are Wired To Connect, Crown, 2013.

[65] *Malcolm Gladwell*, Outliers, Little, Brown, 2008.

[66] *Robert Kelley*, How to be a Star at Work, Crown Business, 1999.

[67] *Harold Jarche*, Social learning for business, jarche.com/2011/01/social-learning-for-business/.

[68] *Jay Cross*, Social Learning Gets Real, 2009, www.internettime.com/2009/11/social-learning-gets-real/.

[69] *Jonathan Haidt*, The Righteous Mind: Why Good People Are Divided by Politics and Religion, Pantheon Books, 2012.

[70] *Scott Freeman et al.*, Active learning increases student performance in science, engineering, and mathematics, Proceedings of the National Academy of Sciences of the United States of America, May 12, 2014, www.pnas.org/content/111/23/8410.full.

[71] *Eric Mazur*, news.sciencemag.org/education/2014/05/lectures-arent-just-boring-theyre-ineffective-too-study-finds.

[72] *Robert Putnam*, Bowling Alone, Simon & Schuster, 2000.

[73] *James S. House*, Psychosomatic Medicine 63:273–274, 2001.

[74] *Jonah Berger*, Contagious, Simon & Schuster, 2013.

[75] *Jonah Berger*, Arousal Increases Social Transmission of Information, Psychological Science, July 2011.

[76] *Andrew Knight and Markus Baer*, Get Up, Stand Up: The Effects of a Non-Sedentary Workspace on Information Elaboration and Group Performance, Social Psychological and Personality Science, June 2014.

[77] *Howard Givner*, howardgivner.com/articles/the-un-conference-participant-driven-agenda-mashup-networking-relationship-building-on-steroids.

[78] *David Weinberger*, MOOCs as networks, www.hyperorg.com/blogger/2012/11/16/2b2k-moocs-as-networks/.

[79] *Mike McCurry*, Is Confidential Content the Best Approach for an EventCamp Conference?, www.michaelmccurry.net/2010/11/13/is-confidential-content-the-best-approach-for-an-eventcamp-conference/.

[80] *Eric Lukazewski*, ibid.

[81] Wikipedia, https://en.wikipedia.org/wiki/Net_Promoter Scoring.

[82] *Etienne Wenger*, ewenger.com/theory/.

[83] *Jono Bacon*, www.artofcommunityonline.org/.

[84] Ibid.

[85] *Bill Toliver*, www.speakers.ca/speakers/bill-toliver/.

[86] *Adrian Segar*, Anatomy of a name badge, www.conferencesthatwork.com/index.php/event-design/2010/10/anatomy-of-a-name-badge/.

[87] Seattle Times, blog.seattletimes.nwsource.com/festivalblog/2008_03.html.

[88] *Adrian Segar*, Chapter 13 of Conferences That Work: Creating Events That People Love, Booklocker, 2009.

[89] *Jennifer Veitch*, The Physiological and Psychological Effects of Windows, Daylight, and View at Home, nparc.cisti-icist.nrc-cnrc.gc.ca/npsi/ctrl?action=shwart&index=an&req=20375039&lang=en.

[90] *Morton Walker*, The Power of Color, Avery, 1990.

[91] *M. Boltz, M. Schulkind, and S. Kantra*, Effects of background music on the remembering of filmed events, Memory & Cognition, 1991.

[92] *Ravi Mehta, Rui (Juliet) Zhu, and Amar Cheema*, Is Noise Always Bad? Exploring the Effects of Ambient Noise on Creative Cognition, Journal of Consumer Research, 2012.

[93] *Ferris Jabr*, Let's Get Physical: The Psychology of Effective Workout Music, Scientific American, 2013.

[94] Sid Lee, sidlee.com.

[95] *Paul O. Radde*, Seating Matters, Thriving Publications, 2009.

[96] *Rui (Juliet) Zhu and Jennifer J. Argo*, Exploring the Impact of Various Shaped Seating Arrangements on Persuasion, Journal of Consumer Research: August 2013, www.jcr-admin.org/files/pressreleases/061713155841_ZhuRelease.pdf.

[97] *Robert Lucas*, The Big Book of Flip Charts, McGraw-Hill, 1999.

[98] e.g., 3M Scotch 9415PC Removable Repositionable Tape (Double-Sided), www.amazon.com/3M-Removable-Repositionable-9415PC-Translucent/dp/B000V4PDW0.

[99] e.g., 3M Repositionable Clear Spray Adhesive, www.amazon.com/3M-75-Repositionable-Adhesive-10-25-Ounce/dp/B000BKQD82.

[100] 6″ × 8″ Post-it® Brand Super Sticky Meeting Notes, www.amazon.com/Post—Sticky-Notes—Assorted-Inches-45-Sheet/dp/B000CD0MHQ.

[101] Scotch® Mounting Squares for Fabric Walls, www.amazon.com/Scotch-Mounting-Squares-Fabric-Walls/dp/B00006IF77.

[102] Officemate Cubicle Clips, www.amazon.com/Officemate-Cubicle-Assorted-Colors-30178/dp/B002MCZA3Q.

[103] Static Easel Pad Sheets, www.amazon.com/National-Brand-Write-Static-Sheets/dp/B0000E2RGH.

Notes

[104] IdeaPaint, www.ideapaint.com.

[105] The Event App Bible, www.eventmanagerblog.com/event-app-bible-2015.

[106] Red Sweater Software, www.red-sweater.com/flextime/.

[107] iTunes: How to convert a song to a different file format, support.apple.com/en-us/HT204310.

[108] *Peggy Holman, Tom Devane, and Steven Cady*, The Change Handbook, Berrett-Koehler, 2007.

[109] *Jeffery A. Lackney*, report excerpt from the brain-based workshop track of the CEFPI Midwest Regional Conference, www.designshare.com/Research/BrainBasedLearn98.htm.

[110] *Laura Grace Weldon*, www.educationrevolution.org/blog/fun-theory/.

[111] For an example, read the "Graduate student story" on pages 62–64 of my first book: "Conferences That Work."

[112] *Virginia Satir*, Making Contact, Celestial Arts, 1976; *Donald C. Gause and Gerald M. Weinberg*, Exploring Requirements: Quality Before Design, Dorset House, 1989; *Norman L. Kerth*, Project Retrospectives, Dorset House, 2001.

[113] *Steve Denning*, Q&A With The Authors of A New Culture of Learning, Forbes Magazine, March 20, 2011, blogs.forbes.com/stevedenning/2011/03/20/qa-about-a-new-culture-of-learning/.

[114] *Bernie DeKoven*, www.deepfun.com/fun/2012/10/the-need-to-play/.

[115] *John Cleese*, www.avclub.com/article/john-cleese-14197.

[116] Catalyst Ranch, www.catalystranchmeetings.com/.

[117] One resource for play areas is Office Playground, www.officeplayground.com.

[118] *Bernie DeKoven*, www.deepfun.com.

[119] *Bernie DeKoven*, Play, Laughter, Health And Happiness, www.deepfun.com/play-laughter-health-and-happiness/.

[120] My favorites are: *S. Kaner, M. Doyle, L. Lind and C. Toldi*, Facilitator's Guide to Participatory Decision-Making, Jossey-Bass, 2007; *Roger Schwarz*, The Skilled Facilitator: A Comprehensive Resource for Consultants, Facilitators, Managers, Trainers, and Coaches, Jossey-Bass, 2002; and *I. Bens and J. MacCausland*, Facilitation at a Glance!: Your Pocket Guide to Facilitation, goalqpc, 2012.

[121] *Adrian Segar*, Conferences That Work: Creating Events That People Love, Booklocker, 2009.

[122] Video clip from "Ferris Bueller's Day Off," www.youtube.com/watch?v=uhiCFdWeQfA.

[123] *Dorothy Strachan*, Making Questions Work, Jossey-Bass, 2007.

[124] *Eric de Groot and Mike van der Vijver*, Into the Heart of Meetings, MindMeeting BV, 2013.

[125] *Adrian Segar*, Anatomy of a name badge, www.conferencesthatwork.com/index.php/event-design/2010/10/anatomy-of-a-name-badge/.

[126] Hat tip to *Viv McWaters*.

[127] How to create a "My Map" in Google Maps, www.youtube.com/watch?v=TftFnot5uXw.

[128] European Meetings & Events Conference 2011, www.mpiweb.org/events/emec2011/home.

[129] Images from the first Solution Room experiment, www.flickr.com/photos/tnoc/sets/72157625939645495/.

[130] Video of the first Solution Room experiment, www.youtube.com/watch?v=4USEzXpRGB4.

[131] Testimonials for the first Solution Room experiment, www.youtube.com/watch?v=ktBU3B7SAho.

[132] Creative Commons images for The Solution Room: jungle image, www.flickr.com/photos/localsurfer/200885757/sizes/o/ and campfire image, www.flickr.com/photos/jenorton/5647856557/sizes/o/.

[133] *Donald Bligh*, What's The Use of Lectures, Jossey-Bass, 2000.

[134] Ibid.

[135] *R. Brian Stanfield (Editor)*, The Art of Focused Conversation: 100 Ways to Access Group Wisdom in the Workplace, New Society Publishers, 2000.

[136] *Harrison Owen*, Open Space Technology: A User's Guide, Berrett-Koehler Publishers, 1997.

[137] Art of Hosting harvesting techniques: www.artofhosting.org/thepractice/artofharvesting/, and chriscorrigan.com/parkinglot/?p=3713.

[138] *Margaret Wheatley*, Preface for The World Café: Shaping Our Futures Through Conversations That Matter, www.margaretwheatley.com/articles/prefacetoworldcafe.html.

[139] *Juanita Brown and David Isaacs*, The World Café: Shaping Our Futures Through Conversations That Matter, Berrett-Koehler Publishers, 2005.

[140] *Margaret Wheatley*, Preface for The World Café: Shaping Our Futures Through Conversations That Matter, www.margaretwheatley.com/articles/prefacetoworldcafe.html.

[141] See www.co-intelligence.org/P-cafeQs.html; also *Juanita Brown and David Isaacs*, The World Café: Shaping Our Futures Through Conversations That Matter, Berrett-Koehler Publishers, 2005.

[142] The World Café, www.theworldcafe.com.

[143] #eventprofs Feb. 7, 2012, chat on interactive conferences with *Viv McWaters*, storify.com/asegar/eventprofs-feb-7-2012-chat-on-interactive-confere.

[144] *Chris Corrigan*, Not to fight with one another, chriscorrigan.com/parkinglot/?p=3607.

[145] *Keith Sawyer*, Group Genius: The Creative Power of Collaboration, Basic Books, 2007.

[146] *R. Brian Stanfield*, The Workshop Book, New Society Publishers, 2002.

[147] International Society on Multiple Criteria Decision Making, www.mcdmsociety.org.

[148] *Harry L. Dangel and Charles Xiaoxue Wang*, SRS in Higher Education: Moving Beyond Linear Teaching and Surface Learning, Society of International Chinese in Educational Technology Journal, www.sicet.org/journals/jetde/jetde08/paper08.pdf.

[149] Facebook comment by *Jeff Hurt*, www.facebook.com/groups/169544466419300/370229279684150/.

[150] Alternative ways to use hands to vote: See en.wikipedia.org/wiki/Consensus_decision-making#Hand_signals, and seedsforchange.org.uk/free/handsig.pdf.

[151] *Esther Derby*, Self-facilitation Skills for Teams © 2004–2005, www.estherderby.com/2010/07/self-facilitation-skills-for-teams.html.

[152] Idea Rating Sheets, www.idearatingsheets.org/.

[153] Dot voting rules of thumb, www.albany.edu/cpr/gf/resources/Voting_with_dots.html.

[154] *Sivasailam Thiagarajan*, www.thiagi.com/pfp/IE4H/march2008.html#Framegame.

[155] Pecha Kucha Nights: www.pecha-kucha.org/night/#night-sub; Ignite Nights: igniteshow.com/.

[156] Pecha Kucha: pecha-kucha.org; Ignite: igniteshow.com/howto.

[157] The Pecha Kucha graphic badge can be downloaded from gallery.mailchimp.com/65380664563589752890700f/images/pk_badge.jpg.

[158] Pecha Kucha and Ignite templates and instructions, www.box.net/shared/kc81sthvt76bg82vmi7v.

[159] *Louis B. Barnes, C. Roland Christensen, and Abby J. Hansen*, Teaching and the Case Method, Harvard Business Review Press, 1981.

[160] *J. Boehrer and M. Linsky*, "Teaching with Cases: Learning to Question." In M. D. Svinicki (editor), The Changing Face of College Teaching. New Directions for Teaching and Learning, No. 42, Jossey-Bass, 1990.

[161] See, for example, sciencecases.lib.buffalo.edu/cs/.

[162] *Gerald M. Weinberg*, Experiential Learning 3: Simulation, Leanpub, 2012.

[163] Ibid.

[164] Case Studies-Teaching Excellence & Educational Innovation-Carnegie Mellon University, www.cmu.edu/teaching/designteach/teach/instructionalstrategies/casestudies.html.

[165] Ibid.

[166] *Louis B. Barnes, C. Roland Christensen, and Abby J. Hansen*, Teaching and the Case Method, 3rd edition. Boston, MA: Harvard Business School Press, 1994.

[167] *Clyde Freeman Herreid*, www.actionbioscience.org/education/herreid.html.

[168] The William Davidson Institute at the University of Michigan, www.globalens.com/DocFiles/PDF/cases/Preview/GL1429140P.pdf.

[169] Case Studies-Teaching Excellence & Educational Innovation-Carnegie Mellon University, www.cmu.edu/teaching/designteach/teach/instructionalstrategies/casestudies.html.

[170] Case Collection, National Center for Case Study Teaching in Science, sciencecases.lib.buffalo.edu/cs/collection/.

[171] *Brian P. Coppola*, Progress in Practice: Teaching and Learning with Case Studies, The Chemical Educator, Vol. 1, No. 4, Springer-Verlag, 1996, www-personal.umich.edu/~bcoppola/publications/17.%2014cop897.pdf.

[172] Writing Case Studies: A Manual, International Records Management Trust adapted by Saskatoon Public Schools Online Learning Center, olc.spsd.sk.ca/DE/PD/instr/strats/casestd/casestds.pdf.

[173] Ethical Dilemmas, Cases, and Case Studies, USC Levan Institute: Online Ethics Resource Center, dornsife.usc.edu/dilemmas-and-case-studies/.

[174] Center For Medical Simulation, harvardmedsim.org.

[175] Society for Modeling & Simulation International, scs.org.

[176] *John Taylor and Rex Walford*, Simulation in the classroom, Penguin Books, 1972.

[177] *Jerry Weinberg*, Experiential Learning 3: Simulation, Leanpub, 2012.

[178] *(Martha) Jane Dunkel Chilcott*, Effective Use of Simulations in the Classroom, www.clexchange.org/ftp/documents/Implementation/IM1996-01EffectiveUseOfSims.pdf.

[179] *Sivasailam Thiagi Thiagarajan and Raja Thiagarajan*, Barnga: A Simulation Game on Cultural Clashes (25th Anniversary Edition), Intercultural Press, 2011.

[180] *Dennis Meadows*, Harvest, www.thiagi.com/pfp/IE4H/january2005.html#SimulationGame.

[181] *Linda Booth Sweeney and Dennis Meadows*, The Systems Thinking Playbook, Sustainability Institute, 2008.

[182] *Chris Corrigan*, Practice Notes: Cafés for taking a conference to action, chriscorrigan.com/parkinglot/?p=3718.

[183] Plus/Delta Google Doc template, bit.ly/POPplusdelta.

[184] Sharing Google Docs, support.google.com/docs/bin/answer.py?hl=en&answer=180199.

[185] *Norman Kerth*, Project Retrospectives: A Handbook For Team Reviews, Dorset House, 2001.

Pass it on!

Both this book and my first book
Conferences That Work: Creating Events That People Love
(which shows you how to design and execute remarkable conferences)
can be purchased as an ebook or signed paperback from me at
tiny.cc/pofp
All direct purchases include a free consultation!

I'd love your help, in *any* of the following four ways.

First, if you liked this book please share the above link.

Second, I'd greatly appreciate a review on Amazon.com at *tiny.cc/popreview*.

Third, let others know about this book on your blog or favorite online services. (Want to interview me? Just get in touch!)

Finally, please recommend this book to anyone who might find it useful!

Check out my website *www.conferencesthatwork.com* where I blog mightily on all kinds of interesting topics. It's also the place where digital updates to this book will be posted for you to download for free at *tiny.cc/popupdate*. Use this link any time for the latest update, or email me and I'll let you know when new updates become available.

Thanks!

Adrian Segar
adrian@segar.com

Printed in Poland
by Amazon Fulfillment
Poland Sp. z o.o., Wrocław